What People a

TAROT—Unlocking the Arcana

"One of the first books from a whole new generation of young tarot readers, and an outstanding book it is. In a casual, conversational style Angelo quickly does away with old myths and attitudes that stand in the way of a fresh appreciation of the cards."

—Mary Greer
Grandmaster of the American Tarot Association

"Angelo Nasios's book *Tarot—Unlocking the Arcana*, is a welcome addition to the world of Tarot. With every chapter, he demonstrates a thorough understanding of the Tarot and a masterful ability to teach the reader how to comfortably and competently work with the symbols of this venerable art. Especially helpful is his chapter on sample readings where he demystifies the process of interpreting and communicating the messages of the Tarot. Whether you are a beginner or an experienced practitioner, you will find Angelo's book to be an indispensable ally on your Tarot journey."

—Sheilaa Hite
Master in Karmic Balancing, Healing & Relationships

"In 2008, Angelo Nasios established himself as a rising star in the Tarot universe for his clear and insightful YouTube videos about Tarot divination. Now, in his first book, Angelo takes us on his personal journey through learning the Tarot, understanding its symbols, and speaking its language. His approach is straightforward, clearly explained, and enjoyable. Drawing on his heritage as a Greek American who is enthralled by philosophy and world religions, Angelo offers a fresh perspective that will be welcomed by newbies and experienced readers alike. Highly recommended!"

—Anthony Louis
Author of *Tarot Plain and Simple*

ANGELO NASIOS

TAROT
Unlocking the Arcana

Schiffer Publishing Ltd®

4880 Lower Valley Road · Atglen, PA 19310

Published by Schiffer Publishing, Ltd.
4880 Lower Valley Road
Atglen, PA 19310
Phone: (610) 593-1777;
Fax: (610) 593-2002
E-mail: Info@schifferbooks.com

For our complete selection of fine books
on this and related subjects, please visit our
website at www.schifferbooks.com. You may
also write for a free catalog.

This book may be purchased from the
publisher. Please try your bookstore first.

We are always looking for people to write
books on new and related subjects. If you
have an idea for a book, please contact us at
proposals@schifferbooks.com.

Schiffer Publishing's titles are available at
special discounts for bulk purchases for sales
promotions or premiums. Special editions,
including personalized covers, corporate
imprints, and excerpts can be created in
large quantities for special needs. For more
information, contact the publisher.

Other Schiffer Books on Related Subjects:

Tarot, Rituals, & You: The Power of Tarot Combined with the Power of Ritual,
Bonnie Cehovet, ISBN: 978-0-7643-4318-6

The Celtic Cross Tarot Spread: Cutting to the Chase, Shannon MacLeod
Illustrations by Beth Seilonen, ISBN: 978-0-7643-4588-3

The Tarot Playbook: 78 Novel Ways to Connect with Your Cards,
Lynda Cowles, ISBN: 978-0-7643-3988-2

The Tarot Game, Jude Alexander, ISBN: 978-0-7643-3448-1

For my father

Acknowledgments

This book has been a work in progress for many years. Through the years, there have been many people who have encouraged me and supported my dreams. To Sarah, my first guide and mentor, thank you for holding up the Hermit's lantern for me. To Megan Lang, thank you for your hard labor editing all my grammatical errors, run-on sentences, unfinished thoughts, and more. To my Tarot "mothers" Donnaleigh deLaRose and Theresa Reed, thank you for your constant encouragement. Barbara Moore, you helped me to "find my voice" that allowed me to refine this book.

CONTENTS

Preface 07

Introduction 09

Section One: INTRODUCTION TO THE TAROT 13

Section Two: GETTING STARTED 25

Section Three: ATTRIBUTIONS—
ASTROLOGY, ELEMENTS, QABALAH, AND MORE 41

Section Four: TAROT HISTORY, RELIGION,
AND PHILOSOPHY 53

Section Five: SPREADS 71

Section Six: SAMPLE READINGS 93

Section Seven: TAROT EXPANDED 105

Section Eight: THE MINOR ARCANA 109

Section Nine: THE ROYAL FAMILIES—COURT CARDS 157

Section Ten: THE MAJOR ARCANA 183

BIBLIOGRAPHY 239

PREFACE

It was late spring 2002 when Tarot entered into my life. I was thirteen and magically curious. I grew up watching shows like *Buffy the Vampire Slayer*, *Charmed*, *Sabrina the Teenage Witch,* along with the classics, *Bewitched* and *I Dream of Jeannie*. I wanted to explore the supernatural to see what it was really all about. I fell into Wicca but abandoned it once I found the Tarot.

When I found the Tarot, I automatically knew this was what I had been searching for. This was my tool for magick. My intentions were not very noble—I *was* thirteen after all; I wanted to be like Harry Potter and I thought I'd found my wand. I thought to myself, *I will learn the Tarot and predict the future!* That would be so cool! Little did I know that the purchase of a single deck of cards would profoundly change my life from that moment onward.

I am fortunate to have picked up the Tarot at a young age and right around the rapid growth of the Internet. With the web at my fingertips, I was able to explore the Tarot privately without the condemnation of family. I practiced in secret for the better part of ten years, until I finally laid the cards out for all to know, and I have never been happier.

I began to share my passion for Tarot on YouTube in 2008, noticing that there was little Tarot activity there. Whatever videos I could find were often about card meanings or recorded readings. There were few people offering commentary, advice, techniques, spreads, reviews, and general ramblings. I set out to offer just that: a channel where all I did was talk about Tarot. In addition to reading books, I thought that offering videos would be a valuable supplement for others learning Tarot. Books are wonderful in that they present material with a defined structure. Some people are visual learners, however; videos are perfect for these types of learners.

My first video was "How to Shuffle a Deck of Tarot Cards." I did not show my face, I was nervous, but boy did that change! I did political readings, like who would win the presidential election in 2008. Alas, they did predict Obama would win. I produced videos on history, how to read reversals, ethics, and offered my insights on questions from viewers. Should you and how do you cleanse a deck? I made deck and book reviews and recommended videos. I presented and demonstrated spreads and sample readings. I also chronicled my progress when writing this very book. *Tarot: Unlocking the Arcana* has been a labor of love. The goal of this book was to record what I'd learned thus far in my journey, and what I present in these pages is almost everything I've learned and would want to teach to others.

Tarot is an amazing system that, over time, has evolved. It has not always been presented or taught, as it is today, with the pseudo-psychological and layers of esoteric baggage. Pick up any old book on Tarot or fortunetelling from 100 years ago or more and you would hardly understand how some of the meanings applied to the cards could ever make sense. This is because we have been so deeply influenced by the Hermetic Order of the Golden Dawn and their teachings of what Tarot "is." The point I am trying to make is that whenever you learn Tarot from someone else, you are often receiving knowledge that stems from the Golden Dawn. I know that to be the case with me. A lot of the information that is in this book is Golden Dawn based even without my knowing it because the influence is so deeply rooted in Tarot literature. When you read my book and see statements, such as "The Hermit is astrologically associated with Virgo," know that this statement is based on the teachings of the Golden Dawn. The example statement is true in the Golden Dawn system but is not a universal truth. Different systems exist, but for my own reasons, mostly for consistency, I lean toward their interpretations—not because I believe it to be the "Absolute Truth of Tarot" but out of uniformity for how I have been taught. Anytime someone tells you "this is that or that is this," take it with a grain of salt; it is based on one system or another and is not the "end all, be all."

When reading this book, I want you to picture you and me sitting in a coffee shop (granted I don't drink coffee) on big couches with overly obnoxious pillows and exploring the Tarot through deep conversation. "Angelo, tell me about The Wheel of Fortune," you might say. I would tell you everything I see in that card, from the mythological, philosophical, psychological, numerological, and anything else I can extract to delve into the mysteries. The cards are doors to rooms of wisdom, and together we will unlock the Arcana.

INTRODUCTION

There is an air of mystery around Tarot cards: images filled with esoteric symbols, hidden philosophies to be uncovered, and speculative myths regarding their origins, told and retold over time. The Tarot conjures to mind many different things for people. For some, it is a novelty—the sort of thing you would do for entertainment or to satisfy your curiosity. For others, the Tarot is a sacred spiritual practice that requires a lifetime of dedicated study and practice.

With these different perceptions, you may not be sure what Tarot really is. You've picked up this book for a reason. You may be a curious "newbie" to Tarot, wanting to learn more about the cards and see what they can offer you. You might be a longtime reader and looking to continue your Tarot studies. Either way, I invite you to come and explore the Tarot with me. For the newbie, I will explain what Tarot is all about and you will walk away with a better understanding. Together, we will explore what Tarot can offer you. For the longtime reader, I am confident that you will leave with a new perspective of the Tarot that will deepen your connection with the cards.

In *Tarot: Unlocking the Arcana*, I break the esoteric shell and reveal the Tarot, its symbols, meanings, and uses. Tarot is a symbolic language. A symbol is an image, which represents an idea/concept, that connects to a deeper meaning or cosmic truth.

We live in a world saturated with symbols. Symbols appear in our daily lives without us noticing: the coffee cup you drink from in the morning could be a symbol of the divine feminine as the vessel that carries life (some cannot live without their morning caffeine fix). Symbols are in media of all kinds: books, movies, TV shows, music videos, and so on. Music videos are always placing occult and religious symbols someplace, hidden or in the open. Look at Kesha's "Die Young" and videos from Lady Gaga. Symbols can be anything—an animal, certain colors, and/or shapes—though not everything has symbolic meaning; it all depends on its placement and context, so pay attention.

Learning Tarot is about learning to understand the symbols you see, how to spot them, and how to speak their language. To understand the cards and symbols, you will be exploring the many levels in which a card can be unlocked. You can unlock the Tarot with astrology, numerology, mythology, philosophy, Qabalah, psychology, and more. Each is a key to viewing the images and symbols for what they represent.

The symbols within the Tarot represent archetypal qualities (universally recognizable) that speak to our collective unconscious. The images in the cards are not the archetypes themselves—they point to the archetype. The collective unconscious, as defined by Carl Jung, is the shared unconscious mind that all people inherit at birth. The collective unconscious contains two main aspects: archetypes and instincts. For the purposes of our work with Tarot, the archetypes are our main focus. The archetypes are patterns and images collected deep within the unconscious that are tightly woven into our being. The Tarot, specifically the Major Arcana, embodies these archetypal patterns and images. For example, The Sun and The Moon cards embody astrological images, whereas Death and Judgment embody religious or spiritual significance.

The symbols in the Tarot are timeless and classic. Changing cultural attitudes may modify their associations or meanings. However, one thing is sure: the symbols themselves don't change and their core concept typically stays consistent. For a symbol to acquire an entirely new meaning, the old meaning/association would have to be completely broken and rebuilt, which is a difficult task.

Tarot presents within the cards the spectrum of emotions, feelings, actions, thoughts, fears, dreams, desires, skills, weaknesses, etc. For example, the swastika would be recognized as a symbol associated with the atrocities that occurred aft the hands of the Nazis in World War II. However, the swastika was originally a sacred symbol in Hinduism and Buddhism. It would be very hard for people to disassociate the swastika with the Nazis and go back to the original meaning and usages. Tarot reflects the psyche of a person and allows us to explore ourselves through the symbols. This may sound very difficult at first glance, but it is easier than it sounds. Simply, the Tarot is a mirror to our souls. At first, the mirror may be dark and hazy, but with enough practice, you will see with clarity.

Clarity is the ultimate goal of the Tarot. When you use Tarot long enough for guidance and reflective work, then your mental processes becomes clearer. It has been my observation that most people (not all, but a large majority) seem to be unaware of the reasons why they act the way they do or feel the way they feel in situations. People seem not to use enough critical thinking (from my observations); they tend to react instinctively and impulsively—we are all guilty of this, even the most logical of us. After using the Tarot over a long period of time, you will develop a habit of asking questions. This is because Tarot relies on questions; you have to ask questions to use the Tarot. Over time, you will naturally ask these questions as things happen to you in your daily life. For example, at work, instead of getting mad at your boss for something, you may stop and ask yourself, "Why am I getting mad?" This will allow you to either come to a conclusion on your own, or you could pull out your cards and ask them.

The book is broken down into the following parts:

Section One: Introduction to the Tarot

An introduction to some Tarot fundamentals. Firstly, a definition of Tarot will be explored: what Tarot is and what it is not. Myths and misconceptions are explored and debunked. You will learn theories as to how Tarot works: is it magick or the mind?

Section Two: Getting Started

Keeping a Tarot journal, asking the right questions, and exploring some basic concepts to each of the cards, as well as how to deal with reversals.

Section Three: Attributions—Astrology, Elements, Qabalah, and More

Explore the esoteric connections inside the cards. Astrology, elements, qabalah, and numerology will be covered.

Section Four: Tarot History, Religion, and Philosophy

Learn essential Tarot history pertaining to its origins. Important religious and philosophical issues will be investigated. Many of the monotheistic religions ban the practice of divination. You will learn about these prohibitions and be taught a good defense against those who cite them.

Section Five: Spreads

Some unique and specially made spreads that will utilize the cards for self-discovery and guidance.

Section Six: Sample Readings

Samples of ways you can practice Tarot: Super Bowl predictions, media events, and more.

Section Seven: Tarot Expanded

Engage in community conversations regarding some controversial topics, such as certification and taboos.

Section Eight: The Minor Arcana

Learn the meanings and symbolism of the Minor Arcana.

Section Nine: The Royal Families—Court Cards

Learn the personalities of the court cards using psychology, astrology, and qabalah.

Section Ten: The Major Arcana

Unlock the mysteries of the archetypes, the Major Arcana.

INTRODUCTION TO THE TAROT

What is Tarot?

First we need to ask, what makes a Tarot deck? Tarot traditionally has seventy-eight cards. Older decks did not have a predefined number of cards; however, the standard now is seventy-eight with some variants, depending on the deck and artistic freedom. The deck is split into two main groups. The first group is the Major j, which is Latin for "greater secrets." The Majors consist of twenty-two cards, numbered from zero to twenty-one and are titled with names such as The Fool, The Moon, The Sun, The Wheel of Fortune, etc. The Major Arcana often represents highly important spiritual influences in our lives represented by archetypal images. At other times, on a mundane level, the Majors represent the internal psychological force and external influences present in our lives that pull or push us, or another, one way.

The remaining fifty-six cards make up the second group, the Minor Arcana, meaning the "lesser secrets." The Minor Arcana consists of four sub-groups known as the suits. The standard names for the suits are Wands, Cups, Swords, and Pentacles. Some decks use different titles for their suits (again, artistic variances). You may see Wands replaced with Rods or Staffs. Cups can appear as Chalices and Pentacles as Coins, while Swords typically stay swords. Each suit consists of fourteen cards—called the pips—ace through ten, and the court cards, consisting of the Page, Knight, Queen, and King. Some decks use different titles for the court cards, such as in the *Thoth Tarot*, which uses Princess, Prince, Knight, and Queen. The Minor Arcana normally represent mundane events and energies that we experience in our daily lives, forces that you have more control over. Court cards represent people, character traits, behaviors, actions, and motives.

Tarot's Purpose

Tarot is a tool with many purposes. I teach two distinct paths for using the Tarot: the first is the internal path and second the external path.

The internal path is used as an effective tool for self-understanding and transformation. With the cards, you explore your life, the events that happen to you, the feelings you experience, and everything in between. Tarot has a profound way of offering insight to our problems. In the internal view, Tarot acts like a mirror that reflects our soul or unconscious to our conscious self. We see a metaphorical reflection of our lives through the images of the cards. With practice, you will be able to understand the symbols and the meanings of the cards, which will allow you to probe into the mysteries of your subconscious and the processes of your conscious. I use Tarot mainly for this type of internal work.

With an external path, Tarot steps outside of time to explore that which we call past, present, and the future we are creating. The external view looks at the larger picture of our interactions in the world. Cause and effect become clear. We come to understand how our actions affect everything else. Predictive readings (fortunetelling) are a main aspect to external Tarot.

At the core of both paths, Tarot is a tool for empowerment. Tarot allows you to see where you are weak and how to make improvements. It allows you to know what you are blind to and how to become enlightened. Tarot urges you to focus on the present over everything else. As the Buddha said, "Do not dwell in the past, do not dream of the future, concentrate the mind on the present moment." The present is all we have. To create the future we want, we need to focus on the present and Tarot allows us to fulfill this.

Myths and Misconceptions

In coming to understand Tarot, you will need to understand what Tarot is not. Here are a few myths and misconceptions surrounding the Tarot.

Tarot is evil/Devil stuff.

I've heard this coming out my mother's mouth when I bought my first deck and she found me reading them when I was thirteen. I was so excited when I'd gotten home with my brand new *Rider Waite Smith Deck*. I opened the box and started to look at the cards and read the little white book that came with it, seeing instructions for the Celtic Cross spread. I laid out the cards on my bedroom floor. Then, I heard my mother coming up the stairs and I knew she was going to open my door. She did and asked me what "those cards" were. When I told her that they were Tarot cards, she told me that they were "Devil stuff," took them from me, and tossed them into a dumpster outside. When she left, I went out to retrieve my cards—which I nicknamed the "dumpster deck." From then on, until just recently, my entire involvement with Tarot was a secretive affair.

Understand this clearly: Tarot is not evil or of the Devil. You may hear this (mostly from Christian fundamentalists or other generally religious people).

Jews won't say it is from the Devil, because they do not have a Devil in their faith, but they will say it is forbidden by their religion. For Muslims, divination is also forbidden.

The "Devil stuff" is a strong prejudice that some people have about Tarot. This idea comes from the Old Testament of the Bible. You will learn about scripture, religion, and divination later on in the book. However, right now, I can simply say this is untrue.

Tarot invites demons into your home/life.

The idea that Tarot cards can invite a negative spirit or demon is absolutely false. Some would say Tarot is like a Ouija board, which is used to communicate with spirits. Ouija boards have the ability to invite a negative spirit (but not always) because most of the time people use the board with the intent on communicating with any spirit. It is equivalent to opening your front door and screaming outside, "Anyone there? Come on in!" This is an **open system** of communication—open to anything. Tarot does not connect with spirits wandering around and does not act as a portal like Ouija boards do. Tarot connects to your higher self/unconscious or divinity. Because Tarot works with these inner processes, this makes it a **closed system**. Even when we open the Tarot up to beyond our inner self, Tarot connects to the universe as a whole or to divinity. This is a **limited open system,** open to only one source, which is a positive one.

Tarot speaks half-truths. Tarot is always right.

Some will say the Tarot can be misleading, telling you half-truths to gain your trust, only to sell you a larger lie to harm you. This belief goes hand-in-hand with the idea that Tarot is evil and that you are communing with evil spirits. Some say that evil spirits want to run amuck in your life and cause trouble. So they tell half-truths through the Tarot. This is not true, as I've stated before, with the closed system of communication. On the other hand, many readers will say that the Tarot never lies. It will always tell you the truth. The trick is this: can you understand the answers provided? Tarot is a symbolic language that is interpreted by the reader. The problem lies with the reader and their ability to understand what the cards are saying. Better readers will be able to get the message, while less astute readers may miss the mark. Readers are human. We make errors and it has nothing to do with spirits or the devil. I also believe that not every question has an answer; therefore, the Tarot may not always provide you with an answer. If the cards make no sense, abandon the reading and ask the questions at another time. Remember that readers can be wrong (gasp!).

Tarot is magic.

Some believe that the cards hold within them magical powers that enable them to work. I do not hold this belief. It is my opinion that the cards are just that—cards. They are paper with pictures printed on them. The Tarot is only a tool. The real magic comes from within the reader who uses the Tarot to connect with themselves and divinity. The reader powers the Tarot; the cards do not power themselves.

Tarot is anti-religion.

Tarot has no religion; it is blind to religion. You can be any faith or no faith and still use the Tarot. Atheists can read Tarot, because God or divinity does not need to be a prerequisite for reading the cards. Tarot is universal and anyone can use it. Tarot does not convert you to a new faith, but it may open you to a new spiritual understanding of the universe, as it did with me. This led me down a path of spiritual study and growth beyond my birth religion.

Tarot is only used for fortunetelling.

Fortunetelling is an extremely common association with Tarot. The Tarot was not always used for fortunetelling, as you will later find out in section two. However, things evolve and change over time. The purposes have changed greatly over the years. Today, you can have a Tarot deck, use it, and never participate in fortunetelling. Some use Tarot for meditation, a creative writing tool, a magical aid in spell casting, or anything your mind allows. The use as a tool for introspection has been increasing. Using Tarot for introspection allows you to self-evaluate your thoughts and feelings.

Card meanings are static.

Yes and no. Each card has certain core meanings or themes to them that seem to stay consistent. However, with each reading, the meanings change based on the context of the situation. Your intuition is used to guide you in determining what each card means for every reading. We need to also keep in mind that meanings do actually change over long periods of time. As society changes and the views and opinions of people change, the meanings of cards can also change. If we could bring a Tarot reader from 100 years ago together with a contemporary reader, you will see differences of interpretations; however, I oddly think they both would provide accurate and relevant readings regardless.

Are There Any Concrete Rules?

I would like to stress something, and I tell this to anyone and everyone who is learning to read Tarot: there are NO rules or laws in Tarot reading. There are, however, suggested ways of reading that are effective or useful. Tarot is not a science. It is an art. In science, there are laws, such as Newton's laws of motion or universal gravitation. While such laws are objective, impersonal, and concrete (to our current knowledge), Tarot is subjective, personal, and abstract. How you shuffle, pick cards, lay the cards, store, and protect your deck is all up to you. The way you read is up to you. There is no "correct" way, only your way.

Here is a list of ten myths that most people believe or have heard:

1. You must receive a deck as a gift.

If this were true, then there would be no readers at all. How would the first person get a Tarot deck if it must be gifted? What came first, the Tarot deck or the Tarot reader? Can we say chicken or the egg anyone? While gifting decks is wonderful and creates a positive memory for the receiver, it is not required.

2. The origins of Tarot are a mystery/unknown.

Not so mysterious as once thought. See section four on Tarot history.

3. Never let anyone touch your deck.

If you don't like germs, then don't let anyone touch them. Otherwise it is fine. Just make sure their hands are clean, as we don't want to dirty our pretty cards.

4. You have to use a specific shuffle ritual for the cards to work.

Wrong. Cut them how you wish. Whatever you like is fine. Just don't damage them in the process.

5. The cards must be wrapped in a silk cloth.

It is a nice way to wrap up your cards to keep them clean, but it is not a must. You can put them in a tote bag or keep them in the box they came in.

6. You must perform cleansings rituals regularly.

If you're into that thing, then sure, why not, but it is not needed. It's one of those preference things. The rituals can vary and include incense, sage, crystals, magic incantations, or prayer.

7. You must keep your cards under your pillow at night to connect with them.

I tried this one and it did not help with anything. Plus, I did not like the feeling of the deck underneath the pillow (ouch!).

8. You need to be psychic to read Tarot.

I am not a psychic; therefore, you don't need to be either. It does not *hurt* to be psychic. We all have some level of intuitive abilities that seem to aid us in our readings. Some readers have strong psychic abilities and use the Tarot alongside their abilities. However, many people simply read the card's symbols, which is enough to do a reading.

9. You should not read for yourself.

Really? We can't? I did not get the memo. I am still alive, so you can do it, too! It can be hard to read for yourself, though. Trying to be objective and unbiased can be difficult, which may be the reason people say you should not read for yourself. Here is a tip: try not to be so invested in one outcome when doing a reading for yourself. If you are too invested in a certain outcome, you will be biased and try to make the cards fit to your expectations and or ignore the cards when they tell you something opposite of what you want (cognitive dissonance).

10. You cannot do more than one reading at a time.

It can be unwise to keep reading the same issue over and over in a short time period. This will only lead to confusion. If you are going to re-read, then alter the question to gain a different perspective.

How Tarot Works

Now that you understand what Tarot is and is not, let's continue with understanding more about how Tarot works. You may have asked yourself:

- How does Tarot work?
- How is it able to make profound statements about our lives?
- It seems that it is able to reflect the past, present, and even predict the future with accuracy.
- What powers the cards to do the things it does?

No one truly knows how Tarot works. This issue falls under Tarot philosophy (section four) and anyone's theory is as good as the next. There are two types of basic ideas on how Tarot works. Tarot is believed to either work by **supernatural** or **natural** means. The one thing that most readers do agree upon is that the Tarot cards do not hold any power within them inherently causing them to do what they do. Readers either see themselves as the source of power (connecting to their higher self) or they are a medium that channels the power from another source (Higher Power/Divinity) or both. With this said, to understand how Tarot works, we must ask where or what we are connecting to when we are reading. What are we, as the readers, doing to gain the knowledge that we seem to be getting from the cards?

Supernatural

Tarot is a form of divination and the act of any type of divination is supernatural in nature by definition. Divination is a form of communication with the divine or higher power/awareness. If Tarot works in this way, then what gives it a connection with this divine or higher source? What source is the Tarot connecting with? Here are some theories.

Direct to the Divine

This is the "old school" ancient belief that you are communicating with God or gods directly and that their will is told to you through the tool used. In ancient cultures, lots were drawn to determine the will of God(s). *Lots* is a form of divination that can be found in the Old Testament of the Bible, but was also used across the ancient world. If this is true, then when you conduct a reading with Tarot, then you are communicating with God directly. This may seem a bit odd or heretical. In our western Christian-based worldview, we are raised to think communicating with God is a one-way street. We are to pray and hope God listens and does something for us. Divination is a two-way style of communicating. In divination, God has the ability to respond back to you. We are also raised to think that we are not worthy for God to speak to us. God only spoke to the prophets or saints—people who were important. This is not true. It is our right from birth to communicate with God, the Divine or higher source.

The Akashic Records

The Akashic Records is said to be a nonphysical realm in which all events are recorded. It holds all knowledge across the universe from the start to the "end." This belief removes the idea of a God(s) as the source and replaces it with what we view as an impersonal entity. When a reading is preformed, the reader is connecting with this record. By accessing this source of knowledge, the cards give insight and information. Because this record contains your personal imprint with all your actions, thoughts, emotions, your past, and present, you are gaining advice that is personal to your own soul. Access to this source can be done without Tarot. Tarot is just one way to gain access.

Energy/Forces

This theory is based on a more down to earth idea that says we are connecting with the "energies" of the issue or people involved. We are not connecting to anything that is considered "Divine" or "Higher," but forms of individual energies. It is a little vague, since we cannot say what the "energy" is exactly, because we do not use it in the same term as a scientist would use energy. The way energy is used in a spiritual term is that it is that thing which unites body with mind and the individual with the cosmos. The concept of *chi* in the East is a comparable term.

Synchronicity

This term was coined by psychiatrist Carl Jung. Synchronicity explains meaningful coincidences. Two separate events relate to each other but are not the cause of one or the other. Jung believed in the collective unconscious and felt that events do not occur by chance. This brings the belief that everything in life happens for some reason, that events are not "random," and that there are meanings to the random things that happen. Applied to Tarot, the cards that come up, which seem to be random and happen by coincidence, actually have meaning to the issue in question.

Natural

On the other side of this issue, we have those who find that Tarot is not something mystical, magical, or supernatural. Tarot, for some, works naturally. This move to a natural view removes any interactions with the divine or higher source of knowledge. The common view is that Tarot is a spiritual practice and that it would be odd to find an atheist who reads Tarot, but if you are looking at Tarot in a natural view, then it is not odd. People who hold a natural view do not need to accept a supernatural explanation. When encountering new clients who know nothing about Tarot, I will explain the natural explanations for how Tarot works first, as it is more accepting by those who may be more skeptical of the supernatural explanation.

Apophenia

This natural view is the skeptical reasoning and understanding to Carl Jung's view of synchronicity. Klaus Conrad coined the term in the 1950s. Apophenia is the experience of seeing patterns or meaning in something that is random, meaningless, and unrelated. The human mind tries to find meaning and patterns in things that are random. Synchronicity is not real and is an example of how we find and give meaning to events that are meaningless. In this mindset, Tarot is then seen as completely random and the reader finds meaning in the cards according to the situation. It does not matter which cards come up, as any card can be applied to any issue. This view may seem negative or make Tarot look bad, but on the contrary, it does not. Why would it? It does not say Tarot is not useful. It just explains a possible way it works or how we use it. It does not "prove" Tarot to be false. It only removes the supernatural aspect—and that's fine. You don't have to accept the notion that Tarot is supernaturally connected to give validity to its usefulness.

Psychological/subconscious

A great alternative to the spiritual explanation is a psychological explanation. There are a series of projective psychological tests that Tarot could be said to fall under. A projective test allows a person to respond to ambiguous stimuli, which reveals the unconscious emotions, motivations, and internal conflicts. One of these tests is the very popular Rorschach test (inkblot test) that most of the public is aware of. The other test is called the Thematic Apperception Test. While many readers compare Tarot to a Rorschach test, a better comparison would be to the Thematic Apperception Test because this test uses scenic photos of people, which are interpreted by the patient by explaining what they see happening before, during, and after in the image. In short, they are creating a story. The story is fueled by the subconscious. For example, an image could have the drawing of an adult male approaching a young girl crying. One may say the child hurt herself and the man is the father coming to comfort her. Another could say that the girl is lost and the man is a stranger either coming to help or not. This process is a major part of Tarot: the creating of stories based on the images in the cards. Each card holds within it its own story to be told and when placed together with other cards, creates a more in-depth story. The story process does not need to involve any supernatural connections. Some would argue that this story creation process involves intuition, but then we could then say intuition is simply a spiritual word for creative imagination. This method is highly important when reading the cards for self-improvement and introspection. Your unconscious will manifest through the cards like that of the Thematic Apperception Test cards.

It is not certain what powers the Tarot possesses or how it works, whether it is by supernatural or natural means. It is my opinion and my experience that Tarot works utilizing both supernatural and natural means. Do not get too hung up on the technicalities of how it works. With enough use, you will understand that it simply works.

Selecting Your Deck

It is now time to find yourself a deck, if you have not done so already. Remember that you don't need someone to give you a deck as a gift and please don't steal one! That's just myth and stealing is not nice.

Picking your first deck is a great moment. You should know that there are hundreds (or more) of decks to choose from; it can be hard to pick just one. I suggest getting two. The first deck should be the *Rider Waite-Smith* (or variations known as clones), as it is the most used and recognizable deck in the world. However, there are many who have mixed feelings about the images, as some do not connect with them. An important thing to note is that most decks are based on the Rider-Waite-Smith tradition and most books use the Rider-Waite-Smith for their material, so when you learn the meanings in the *Rider Waite Smith*, you will find it easier to use other decks. Themes stay consistent for the most part with symbols staying similar, but you will see additions and changes based on the artist's tastes and vision. You should look at the deck online and see if you like it. If you do not like the regular version, there are other decks out that are recolored to make the deck look different and, many times, better. The *Universal Waite* and the *Radiant Rider Waite* are two very nice examples of the recoloring of the deck. When describing cards, I will be referring to the *Rider Waite Smith Deck*. It will help you if you have this deck to refer to as you read the book.

If you want to go a different path than the *Rider Waite-Smith Deck* and its clones, there are other great beginner decks. The *Morgan-Greer Tarot, Robin Wood Tarot, Hanson-Roberts Tarot, The Gilded Tarot,* and *Silver Era Tarot* are a few decks that are recommended to new readers. These are not the only decks to choose from, but are a good starting place to begin your search. You can also do a web search for "beginner Tarot decks" that will help guide you in the right direction.

The second deck you purchase is a deck that you find personally appealing. You will need to do your research on this as well. Go online and browse the decks online. Look for sample card images. This secondary deck should speak to you and appeal to your tastes, preferences, and style. Want a feminine deck? *The Gaian Tarot* may be good for you. Want something a little on the shadowy side? Look at the *Deviant Moon Tarot*. Are you into steampunk? There is the *Steampunk Tarot* that will be perfect for you. Like witches and wizards? Look up the *Wizards Tarot* or *Witches Tarot*. Do you love Greek Mythology? Check out the *Mythic Tarot*. There are endless themed decks for almost any interest.

A lot of decks may look pretty and nice, but make sure you feel a connection with it. If you cannot get a connection with the cards, then you may want to skip that deck and find something else, or work with the deck to establish a connection. Some decks are not good for new readers simply because they may have complex images or stray from "traditional" symbolism and meaning that is specific to that deck only.

It is also useful to have two decks to start with because you can use one deck as your study deck and the other as your reading deck. The *Rider Waite Smith* could be the study deck and your second personal choice can be your reading deck or vice versa. Being able to read with multiple decks also allows you to use different decks for varying tasks, clients, and situations. A good example of this is my preference to use the *Mythic Tarot* for a more psychological reading. I default to the *Rider Waite Smith* for the majority of my readings unless I am breaking in a new deck. There are readers who only use one deck and kudos to them. Others like variety every once in a while.

GETTING STARTED

Practice Makes Perfect

To become an effective reader, you need to use your cards. You can spend your whole life reading books on Tarot theory, but without any real practice and experience, you won't learn much. Tarot is all about experience. Each reading you do will make you connect with your deck and understand how cards interact with each other. Patterns arise, connections are made between the cards, and you will become better at understanding them.

Keeping a Journal

Keeping a Tarot journal is a great way to keep track of your readings and anything you want to write down that you learn. You can create this journal in a physical book, which is beneficial in contrast to typing, because when you write things out by hand, your brain remembers it better. You can keep your journal on your computer using a word processor if you like. You can also then print out what you've typed later and put it in a binder. You can keep your journal online as a blog where you can share your readings and thoughts on Tarot, and others can learn along with you. You can also learn from others as they post comments. The journal can be a creative project to unleash your creativity. If you are good at arts and crafts, you can use those skills into journal making. This will make journaling a fun and magical activity.

Daily Readings

One of the easiest ways to start practicing is to conduct daily readings either at the start or end of your day. Daily readings normally look at what you could expect to experience throughout the day. You can also use daily readings to ask for guidance for the day. The cards can advise you with actions that should or should not be taken. For example, if I asked the cards, "What actions should I take today?" and got the Four of Swords, this would suggest that I should consider taking time to rest and unplug from the world a little—take a nap, for example. If I were to ask, "What actions should I not take today?" and got the Five of Wands, this might say that I should not get into arguments and start conflicts with people.

Daily readings can help you shape your day to the way you would like it to be. One day, back in high school, I pulled the Five of Wands for my daily reading. I saw that as a possible fight, so I made sure to stay out of trouble. While in gym, there was a situation where a fight could have happened, but I made sure I kept quiet and no fight occurred. That is Tarot at work at an everyday level. Now I do daily readings when I get into the office before the day starts.

You can conduct your daily reading at night, too, as a way to sum up the events of the day. If I conduct a night reading, I might ask questions like, "What lessons did I learn or should have learned today?" You can test Tarot and ask, "What happened to me today?" and see if Tarot reflects back the events of the day or gives you a new perspective on the events that transpired. You can ask questions to better understand certain events that took place. Your boss was rude to you today, so you might ask the Tarot, "Why is my boss being rude to me?" or, "What can I do to make [someone] treat me kinder?" It is easier to understand past events. Remember that hindsight is 20/20. The more you use the Tarot and make associations between the cards and the events that happen in your life, the more you can they apply them to future events.

Fair warning, I do not suggest you ask, "What will happen to me today?" because you will most likely freak out if you pull the Tower, Death, 10 of Swords, or 9 of Swords. You can ruin your day by doing this. Unless you are the type of person who would not be bothered by that kind of message and, instead, look forward to see how things would play out, then by all means do it. If you are someone sensitive and highly invested in the cards, then you may take it too much to heart.

Make sure to write down your daily readings in your journal. You can also use a calendar, writing down each card that you pulled for each day. As the month comes to a close, you can review the month and see which cards are repeating, what influences are manifesting, and at what times of the month. I do this at work and have noticed, at one point, that a majority of the Court Cards were coming up in my daily readings. This represents advice on how to behave and act.

Setting the Mood

Setting the mood for your reading, contradictory to what you may think, does not require you to have New Age, hypnotic music playing in the background. Nor do you need dim lights or a hundred candles burning (because *that* is a fire hazard after all). The essentials to setting the mood for conducive readings are a quiet room (or room that you find peaceful; some do like noise), your cards, and a clean reading surface. Everything else—music, candles, or incense—is optional and serves the reader more than the reading itself. These items are tools that set the mood in a way that may relax you and allow you to connect to the sacred realm, which is what ritual helps achieve. There are candles that are magically made with herbs and oils that can be used when reading Tarot. These candles are created with the primary focus on intuition and psychic abilities. Individual readers determine their effectiveness.

Wording Your Questions

You come to the Tarot because you have a question and need answers. To get a clear answer, you need a clear question to ask. The number one rule to remember is that vague questions will get you vague answers. There are two kinds of questions: **closed-ended questions** and **open-ended questions**. Closed-ended questions result in short answers. Here's an example: "Will so-and-so call me?" The answer is yes or no. An open-ended question allows for meaningful answers. For example: "Tell me about my relationship with so-and-so." These kinds of questions allow for conversation and a meaningful reading.

When asking Tarot a question, stick to the open-ended questions. If you have a closed-ended question, you would be better off with a Lenormand deck (consisting of thirty-six cards and named for Mademoiselle Marie Anne Lenormand, a French fortuneteller from the nineteenth century). There are ways to answer a Yes/No question using Tarot though. Questions worded with "how, what, would, and why" are ideal when asking Tarot a question. These kinds of question allow you to explore the issue and decide what you feel you should do. Questions worded with "will, should, and when" are more limiting to your free will, as these questions are asking the cards to tell you what to do or what is going to happen.

Questions about other people should be asked with caution. Many people come to me asking to know about someone else's motivations/feelings/thoughts, etc. This is a very difficult issue, because no matter how skilled the reader, without the other person present, the reading will always be speculative. I think you can pull a card or two on the matter, but the real focus needs to be redirected to you and your relation to the issue. It will always be beneficial to focus on what you can do or what you can learn. Yes, knowing the "why" is satisfying, but so too is eating a quart of ice cream—both yield no positive benefit.

Preparation and Protection

When preparing for a reading, you should clear your mind of random thoughts (to the best of your ability). Focus on the reading. There are some rituals readers may do before a reading. A Tarot ritual is a behavior/practice a reader uses to get into "reading mode." Some readers may smudge their reading area with sage. Some also may meditate before a reading or say a little prayer of protection. Some may simply take a deep breath and a moment to clear their minds. Do what you like. No one method is better than the other.

Rituals are meant to be something personal that you feel a meaningful connection with. They are also powerful psychological tools. The real purpose of ritual is to allow you to be put in a different mindset. To separate the mundane from the sacred, Tarot is seen by many readers as a spiritual act and the reading area becomes a sacred area. The ritual allows for a distinction to be created. Your mind goes from normal thinking and into a sacred mindset. Final words on ritual: do not let ritual rule you or dictate the reading. You do not always have to conduct a ritual act before a reading.

My approach to ritual is simple: I try not to get hung up with it. I change it up every once in a while. I sometimes include incense, candles... I often do an invocation of a deity and ask for their guidance. I sometimes use music in my readings. I find meditative music that focuses on theta brain waves useful. Theta waves border between the conscious and unconscious mind, which is a wave you want to promote while reading.

Some readers take protective measures before a reading to ward off negative influences that may hinder the reading. One example of this is "casting a circle." There are different ways to cast a circle. I do not cast a circle, so I will not be providing specific information on this subject. I will let you research the matter if you feel you want to try circle casting. A simple web search for "Golden Dawn circle casting" is all you need to begin your search. I simply calm my mind and invoke a deity while shuffling the cards to guide me and provide clarity in the reading. I like to keep things simple and circle casting does not fit into my personal simplistic philosophy.

Activating the Question

You have already selected a question to ask; before you shuffle the cards, you can consider "activating" the question. Activating the question is more of a ritualistic idea that I have come to through my own practice and study of magick. (You do not have to follow me on this, but this *is* something I do.) I think it is not enough to think of the question in your head because the question remains internal and private to yourself. To activate the question it needs to be released into the universe by way of the four elements.

You *think* the question (Air), *speak* the question into existence (Fire), and *write* the question on paper (Water and Earth). If you use a pen, the ink represents Water and the paper is Earth. The way I see this process, you are conceptualizing the question and manifesting it into reality (birthing the question to life). This makes the question a thing, and releasing the question to the universe allows it to be answered by whatever it is you connect with (God, Goddess, Spirit, and Higher Self). After the question is "activated" you can shuffle.

Shuffling

Shuffling is very important. You will want to shuffle your deck thoroughly when you ask your question. A good shuffle allows the cards to mix well and, in my experience, results in effective readings. I look at it as the cards settling in the way they are meant to be for the reading. While you shuffle the deck, use that time to focus on the question either by saying it out loud or silently in your mind.

The duration of the shuffle can be as long as you feel appropriate. When should you stop shuffling? There are two ways to go about this. The first is intuitively and the second is ritualistically. In the first option, you may get a feeling that says to stop shuffling. You may simply *feel* the cards are ready. This method is wholly intuitive and comes from within. With ritual, you may set up a pattern of how many shuffles and cuts you perform before laying the cards.

I combine both methods. When reading for others, I will take the deck, shuffle it a few times, and then I cut the deck and do a bridge shuffle. I repeat this process about three times. At the end of the last bridge shuffle, I use my intuition to then tell me when to stop. Try both. See what you like and go with what works for you.

Cutting the Deck and Laying the Cards

After you shuffled your deck, you will now have to lay out cards. You can select cards intuitively or ritualistically.

If you are inclined towards using intuition, split the deck into three piles, right to left. The first pile is placed to the left of the main pile and the second pile is cut once more. Now pick one pile from the three from which you want to use for your reading. You can place your hand over each pile and see if you sense any sort of sensation from them. Some may feel heat, cold, a tingly sensation or, again, a simple gut feeling. The pile you select will be the pile you read from, dealing the cards one after the other.

Ritualistic selection of the cards entails again cutting the deck into three piles as instructed above. This time you will use all three piles. The way this is done is that you pull the top card of each pile beginning with the first pile on the left (the last pile you cut). You pull the left pile as "Card One" of your spread, the middle pile would be your "Card Two," and the right pile would be the "Card Three" in your spread. If you are working with a larger spread, you repeat this process (Card Four would be pulled from the left pile, Card Five from the middle, and Card Six from the right pile) until all the cards you need are pulled.

Special note: If you are only selecting one card from the deck, for example, for your daily reading or you simply want to ask a question and pull two cards, you can select the card by pulling the top card from the deck after shuffling.

For intuitive selection, fan/spread the deck across the table and select one card from the entire deck.

You may also select a number one through ten and select a card by dealing cards until you get to the number you picked. For example, if I picked the number four (the day of the month I was born) then I would deal cards until I got to the fourth card in the deck and that would be my card. For daily readings, you could use the numerical value of the day. For example the twentieth of the month, count until you come to the twentieth card.

The Spread

I have already introduced the word "spread" during cutting and picking your cards. A spread is the layout in which the cards are placed to perform a reading. This section will only introduce one spread for demonstration; a more in-depth exploration will take place later in the book. For right now, I will give a simple spread for instruction:

PAST   PRESENT   FUTURE

In the prior example, I mentioned a simple three-card spread. Beginners often learn three-card spreads first, as opposed to large spreads using more cards, to avoid anxiety or feeling overwhelmed by the complexity. Three-card spreads are great because they are simple and right to the point.

The spread shown is called a Past, Present, and Future spread. The left card represents the past, the middle card represents the present, and the right card represents the future.

Using what you have learned so far, formulate a question to ask the Tarot, which this spread will answer. In your journal or on a computer, write down which cards you drew, including any observations and possible meanings you may feel from the cards. Right now, you do not need to be "right." Just go with your reactions to the cards. Later, at the end of the book, you can use the book's meanings to see if more insights can be gained or if your initial thoughts were aligned with the book.

Overview of the Minor Arcana

The Minor Arcana is grouped into four suits. Each suit rules over a domain of influence. These domains are based on the suit's elemental association, which you will learn in the next chapter. The domains are:

Wands: Domain of aspirations, the spirit.
Cups: Domain of emotions, the heart.
Swords: Domain of the thoughts, the mind.
Pentacles: Domain of the material world, the earth.

The Wands

Ace: New adventure, risk, inspiration.
Two: Vision and starting point of change. Choices.
Three: First action, expansion, development.
Four: First success and results. Foundations established.
Five: Confrontation, struggle, strife, ambition.
Six: Recognition, pride, accomplishment. Rewards.
Seven: Defending your beliefs or opinions. Standing your ground against opposition.
Eight: News, change, movement. Focused and directed energy.
Nine: Perseverance, creating a barrier, self-protecting.
Ten: Burdens, responsibilities, endeavors coming to a close.
Page of Wands: enthusiasm, risk taker, invitations.
Knight of Wands: Excitement, adventure, spontaneity.
Queen of Wands: Attraction, energetic, influential.
King of Wands: Power, leadership, innovative.

The Cups

Ace: Emotional expression and new love.
Two: Connection, union, synthesis, reflection.
Three: Celebration, pleasure, happiness, friendship, community.
Four: Withdrawal, dissatisfaction, refusal.
Five: Loss, sadness, regret.
Six: The past, nostalgia, generosity, safety.
Seven: Options, choices, illusions, dreams.
Eight: Moving on, searching, unfulfilled.
Nine: Wish come true, satisfaction, external happiness.
Ten: Family, internal happiness.

Page of Cups: Surprises, sensitive, empathy, imagination.
Knight of Cups: Idealism, compassion, following the heart.
Queen of Cups: Comforter, insightful, understanding.
King of Cups: Transformative, spiritual guide, mentorship.

The Swords

Ace: New intellectual insight, righteousness, truth.
Two: Procrastination, dilemma, blocked.
Three: Sorrow, hard choices, sadness.
Four: Rest, recovery, healing.
Five: Defeat, unethical, slyness.
Six: Movement, change, assistance.
Seven: Stealth, trickery, undercover, inventive.
Eight: Confusion, restriction, repression.
Nine: Anxiety, worry, panic, distressed.
Ten: End, release.
Page of Swords: Curiosity, experimentation, investigation.
Knight of Swords: Intelligent, debater, fast action.
Queen of Swords: Clever, cunning, fair.
King of Swords: Authority, law, rule, ethics.

The Pentacles

Ace: New goals, new opportunities.
Two: Balance, weighing options, flux.
Three: Work, creation, growth.
Four: Stagnation, hoarding, material security.
Five: Struggle, loss, hardship, spiritual emptiness.
Six: Loan, assistance, generosity, reciprocation.
Seven: Investment, review, reconsider, patience.
Eight: Skills, learning, repetition, practical knowledge.
Nine: Autonomy, self-sufficient, material gains.
Ten: Inheritance, legacy and lasting foundations.
Page of Pentacles: Study, internship, financial opportunities.
Knight of Pentacles: Steadiness, productive, focused on goals.
Queen of Pentacles: Generosity, hospitality, economics.
King of Pentacles: Enterprise, wealth, management.

Overview of The Major Arcana

Here is a quick introduction to the Major Arcana card meanings. (For a deeper analysis of each card, read section ten on The Major Arcana.) I suggest that you examine each of the cards yourself and read the descriptions that follow. In your journal, write your thoughts about each of the cards. Then, when you read the meanings here, write in your journal where you see these meanings within the card. What in the card represents the meanings? For example, The Fool is a risk taker. What in the card signifies him as such? Maybe it is because he is walking too close to the edge of the cliff without knowing. Do this with all the cards at your own pace.

0 The Fool

The Fool represents pure spirit, unassociated with the material. He represents beginnings, optimism, innocence, and a childlike, carefree attitude. The Fool is a risk taker.

I The Magician

Since The Fool represented the number zero, The Magician is the first true card in the Major Arcana. He is the first action, the first cause that sets things into motion. He represents action, confidence, skill, and talent. He is a source of manifestation and is also someone who creates and builds.

II The High Priestess

The counter balance to The Magician is The High Priestess. Where he is active, she is passive. The High Priestess is associated with intuition, the unconscious mind, psychic forces, silence, observation, and recording. She holds occult and esoteric knowledge.

III The Empress

The Empress embodies the great earth Goddesses of many cultures; she is a source of creative endeavors, birth (of all sorts of things), and abundance in many aspects in life. The Empress is the authority or power over the vegetative cycle, thus she also represents fertility and growth. She has a motherly nature, offering support and nurturing others.

IV The Emperor

The counterpoint to The Empress is The Emperor, the father figure. He represents authority of any kind, your actual father, the police, the military, and the government—basically, anything that has power over you. The Emperor represents stability, order, and organization.

V The Hierophant

While The Emperor was the earthly authority, The Hierophant is the spiritual authority. He holds within him exoteric (outer) knowledge and order. He is opposite The High Priestess who holds esoteric (inner) knowledge. The Hierophant deals with rules, dogma, the established order, and the way of things. He represents groups, societies, and organizations of all sorts, any assembly of people who unite together and calm a common identity amongst each other.

VI The Lovers

The Lovers focuses on the individual who must determine their own values outside the society or group they are in. The Lovers represents choices between desires, issues about unions, and relationships. The Lovers are a symbolic representation of sexual awakening.

VII The Chariot

The Chariot represents movement, taking action, and being determined in goals. It embodies pure willpower and the conquering of the desires and oppositions that were encountered in The Lovers.

VIII Strength

Strength can represent psychical strength, but mostly symbolizes inner strengths like patience, courage, and compassion. The Chariot conquered through force, whereas Strength conquers with gentleness. Strength is not always about who has the biggest stick; it's who has the strongest foundations.

IX The Hermit

The Hermit represents withdrawal, solitude, and introspection. He is a deeper thinker; a philosopher. He acts as a guide or teacher to others. He looks within himself for answers through thoughtful contemplation. He is seeking meaning and purpose to something, be it his life or just a dilemma. He rejects the outside world, the material, and develops his inner world and spirituality.

X The Wheel of Fortune

The Wheel of Fortune represents Fortuna, fate, and fortune. It is a force beyond our control and power to understand. This is why it comes right after The Hermit. It is random and blind to whom it affects. It represents cycles of change, ups and downs, highs and lows. One moment you are the King and the next you are a peasant. The Wheel of Fortune indicates a changing point.

XI Justice

Justice represents an opposite aspect to the Wheel of Fortune. While the Wheel was random in its dealing, Justice is not. It deals out reward or punishment because you deserve it due to past actions. Justice is linked with the concept of Karma for this reason. Also, justice represents responsibility, understanding cause and effect, and being honest. Justice can also represent legal matters.

XII The Hanged Man

The Hanged Man represents a time out. It represents needing to let go of the need to act and do something and to simply go with the flow of things. Let a higher power take care of it right now. Sacrifice is an important concept in this card, mostly self-sacrifice for another or giving something up to gain something greater.

XIII Death

Do not fear the Death card. It is actually a good card in many ways. For one, it doesn't represent actual bodily death, but a metaphorical death. Death represents change through the ending of something. It symbolizes the removal of what is no longer useful to us and holds us back. It is a transition card, between one stage to another.

XIV Temperance

Temperance means moderation. It is the golden mean, according to Aristotle and the middle way, which is taught in Buddhism. Temperance represents balance, harmony, cooperation, and synthesis between two opposites.

XV The Devil

The Devil does not represent nor is it associated with the Devil in Christian theology. It has taken the name Devil to express certain qualities. The Devil is associated with attachments, bondage, addiction, materialism, lust, and ignorance.

XVI The Tower

The Tower is a card of destruction and sudden unexpected change. The kind of destruction it brings can either be positive or negative. Not all destruction is bad. The Tower follows after The Devil, which represented ignorance. The Tower destroys this and brings a ground-shaking revelation. The Tower shows that our old ideas and beliefs are revealed to be false, weak, or to be doing us a disservice. This can be a painful experience, because it changes all that we believed in.

XVII The Star

The Star represents healing. She is naked to express her vulnerability and exposure, which was experienced in The Tower. It is a time to heal and recover from past wounds. The Star symbolizes hope and faith. There is a time now for peace and a moment's rest. The Star indicates that things are getting better from now on.

XVIII The Moon

The Moon is a mysterious card. It represents illusions, dreams, imagination, and how these things can play with our perceptions. The Moon indicates that not all is known. Only parts are revealed and the rest is filled in by your mind to get a complete picture. Also, The Moon can be a great source for creativity. On the other hand, The Moon can be irrational and instinctual.

XIX The Sun

The Sun is the counterbalance to The Moon. The Moon was irrational whereas The Sun is rational. The Sun's light is warm and safe; it provides vital life energy. Also, it symbolizes happiness and success.

XX Judgment

Judgment represents a renewal, becoming energized, and feeling brought back to life. It indicates that a change is at hand, one that is profound and with purpose. It shows that you are being called to something. It can also represent a decision (judgment) needing to be made. You are awakened to some new knowledge or insights—an epiphany.

XXI The World

The last card in the Major Arcana, The World signals completion, closure, endings, success, reaching your goals, feeling satisfied, fulfilled, and accomplished. On the same token, The World also symbolizes a new start or that a new cycle is going to start because you have reached the end of the current cycle.

Reversed Cards

A reversed card appears upside down. The use of reversals is completely up to you. For beginners, it is recommended that you do not use reversals and to focus on the normal upright meanings of the cards. Once you have created a firm foundation of understanding of the cards' upright meanings, then you can move on to reversals if you do decide to use them.

Reversals are a complicated subject, because many readers have different ideas about how to use them or if they should be used at all. One side views reversals as a good thing. Using reversals allows you to see more and understand the reading better, because you get to explore another dimension of the cards through reversals. The other thought is that you do not need reversals to get the whole picture, because upright cards hold within them both positive and negative aspects.

In the end, it all boils down to your preference. Below is a list of possible ways of interpreting a reversed card:

Opposite: A very simple way of reading a reversed card is to see it as a complete opposite to its upright meaning. Good becomes bad and bad becomes good.

Gaining: The energy of the card is either gaining importance or influence. The energy is related to the future or energy coming into the situation.

Fading: The energy of the card is fading in importance or in influence. The energy is more related to the past or recent events leaving the situation.

Fanatical/Extreme: The card is seen in an extreme view that takes the energy of the card and pushes it to its limits. This impacts the card negatively through exhaustion.

Weak/Lessened: The card is seen as weak and its energy is lessened. This makes the card show a lessened degree of its meaning.

Blocked/Resisted: The normal energy is blocked, repressed, and rejected.
Absent/Missing: The energy of the card is missing from the issue. This could provide an area of insight as to what needs to be added in order to improve the issue.

Karmic/Past life: The card is representing energies that are related to a past life or karmic debt. This can be an opportunity for a karmic lesson.

As you see, there are many ways to read a reversed card. The ones I have picked are the methods I use or have been useful and relevant to reading reversals. Next, we will look at an example of a reading with a reversed card and apply some of these methods.

Example of Reading with Reversals

Let's put these methods of reading reversals into action with examples.

Scenario: Julia comes seeking advice on her relationship with Timothy. Julia has been with Tim for two years now and, up until now, things have been fine. She tells you that recently he has been acting odd. She wants to know where the relationship stands right now. We pull one card for the issue. We will then show each method with a different card. Julia asks, "What is the present state of the relationship?"

Example of opposite or fading

If the Ace of Cups, I would see this either opposite or fading. Normally, the Ace of Cups is about love and affection. The water pouring out of the Cups show love as a never-ending fountain. Reversed, it shows that the love fountain has run out of water. In other words, love is absent. If it were fading, it would show that his love for Julia is also fading.

Example of gaining

In the upright position, the Tower would signal that currently a major shift in the relationship is taking place. The Tower is about changes that happen quickly. Remember that Julia had said that Tim had recently changed. This card shows that this change was abrupt. Since the card is reversed, we must decide which method we should use. Right away, I would go with "gaining" since this issue is one that is new. Change is occurring and gaining influence over the matter. The energy is not at its full potential, so there is time to address the main issue with Tim. Something may have happened to him that has shocked him in some way and has changed his attitude, which would be the reason he is acting odd.

Example of fanatical/extreme

The Sun is an extreme example that would show that the relationship is taking up a lot of energy and attention. You can see that the upright card shows a strong sense of vitality and energy. The reversed method of extreme makes it so strong that it can cause a burnout effect of the people in it. The relationship may be experiencing a hyped sense of happiness or an overly inflated sense of optimism while ignoring signs of trouble.

Example of weak or lessened

The 9 of Swords upright shows worries and anxiety. She is having trouble sleeping and experiencing nightmares. Fear is shown here; maybe Julia worries about the relationship. Maybe Tim is cheating? This is often a common reason to worry in a relationship, but not the only thing. In the reversed method of weak or lessened, it shows that the worries are not that big and maybe her fears have no foundations. She has no real reasons to have anxiety over his changed behavior. It might be normal and she is sweating over nothing.

Example of blocked/resisted

Upright, Temperance in relationships speaks of cooperation and well-balanced communications between the two in the relationship. The two lovers mix well with one another like the liquids being poured in and out of the cups in the card. The reversed method of blocked or resisted shows that this energy is blocked. Communication has stopped. They are not talking like they used to. They are not mixing with one another anymore. Balance is out of order. If communication was resisted, someone is making communication with the other difficult.

Example of absent/missing

Upright, the Ace of Wands shows similar energy to The Sun. The Ace of Wands shows a spark of fire, life, energy, passion, excitement, and growth. In the reversed method of absent or missing, it shows that the energy is missing from the relationship. They do not have that spark, passion, or any new growth. This absent energy has caused the change in the relationship.

Example of karmic/past life

Upright, the Six of Pentacles is about generosity and helping someone out or asking for help. In the reversed method of Karmic or Past life, it may show that a lesson was to be learned here. In a past life, someone helped the other greatly and a debt was owed to him or her. It was never repaid and, in this life, it finally was repaid and the two can move on.

ATTRIBUTIONS:
Astrology, Elements, Qabalah, and More

In the previous chapter, you were introduced to an overview of the Tarot cards' basic meanings. You may wonder, how do these meanings come about? What or why does any given card have the meanings it has? It is partly based on the image at face value. But, in addition to the image, the cards are built upon a blueprint of attributions. Attributions are associations between the cards with different esoteric systems, which give them an inner foundation of meaning beyond their external image. To understand the attributions allows you to understand the cards in a deeper way. To start, we will look at the elements, which are the first set of attributions to learn.

The Elements

The four minor suits of the Tarot can be grouped into four basic elements. These are referred to as the classical elements. They can be found in Greece, Babylonia, India, China, and Japan. It was pre-Socratic philosopher Empedocles who spoke about these elements and called them the "roots" for which all things are created from or are comprised of. The four suits of Tarot are then associated with the four elements as followed.

ELEMENT	SUIT
Fire	Wands
Aire	Swords
Water	Cups
Earth	Pentacles

There are some differing views on which element goes with which suit. This tradition was established by The Hermetic Order of the Golden Dawn and is the standard framework the majority of Tarot decks are based upon. Some argue that

Fire is Swords and Air is Wands. However, there is some reasoning behind the elemental associations.

Swords are connected to Air because air deals with the realm of the mind. If you look at the suit of the Swords, they deal with these types of issues within the actual images. The Wands, on the other hand, deal with issues of Fire, such as competition, pressure, endurance, and strife, which can be seen in the images. As for the other two suits, Water goes with Cups because they deal with issues such as love, intuition, dreams, sadness, and happiness. Earth goes to Pentacles because they deal with the physical realm of money, work, craft, skills, and learning.

There is also a fifth element in the mix that Aristotle added called Aether. The four elements were seen as earthy elements and Aether was a heavenly element. The fifth element is the quintessence, the prime principle of the cosmos. Hindus called this fifth element Akash, which is where we get the word Akashic, as in the Akashic Records. Aether is also referred to as the void, sky, or space. No matter its name, it represents what is beyond the everyday, higher nature, and the heavenly world. This element is associated with the Major Arcana, which deals with archetypal symbols, universal themes, and beyond everyday dealings. It all fits so wonderfully, doesn't it? The element attribution is my favorite, because it fits so perfectly to the Tarot suits. Understanding elements is the ground for understanding the cards.

Understanding the Elements

The elements are grouped into two pairs: *positive* (+) and *negative* (-). However, do not look at this as moral *good* and *bad*. These terms are better understood as *yin* and *yang* of Chinese philosophy: yin is the "negative" force and yang is the "positive" force. Yin represents *receptivity* and *the feminine,* while yang represents *activity* and *the masculine.* They are polarities of how energy expresses itself. Creation is based on this principle.

Yang (Active) Elements

Fire—Wands

The first yang element is Fire. This element corresponds with the suit of Wands. The principle of Fire is *identity.* Fire is associated with the life force (chi) of the world and is the source that moves all things into motion. It represents change, courage, optimism, pride, and enthusiasm. In ancient Greek philosophy, it was believed that the soul was made of the element Fire, for fire rises up to the sky, which is where the soul originated from and returns to after death. Fire is a force for creation as well as destruction. This association with soul and fire is why many ancient cultures cremated the dead. It is a means to release the soul from the body and allow it to reach the gods.

Wands deal with the Self, pride, determinism, ambitions, actions, and consciousness. Wands express our personal/career goals and creative projects. As you look at the Wands, you will see a general story dealing with envisioning an idea and the process in obtaining that vision in reality.

Air—Swords

The second of the yang element is Air, which corresponds with the suit of Swords. Air itself is seen as the breath of God. In many mythologies and in the Abrahamic religions, God breathed life into mankind. The Latin word *inspirare,* from which we get the word "inspiration," means to inhale or breathe in. Breath in antiquity was seen as the substance that mixed with the air and exchanged intelligence with others. So in this worldview, inspiration was breathing in the knowledge of others. The Hebrew word *ruh* means "breath as well as spirit. We see a close connection between our breath and that of the Spirit or God. Along with Fire, Air is also an alternate element for which the soul is made of as proclaimed by the philosopher Anaximenes.

It is important to note the close connection between Air and Fire, both of which we see as a close connection with spirit and the higher realm. Air feeds fire, which makes it stronger. You cannot have fire without air. Both these elements are Yang, masculine, and you can remember this because both the suit of Wands and Swords can be seen as phallic symbols. (Look at the Ace of Wands and Ace of Swords; you should see the phallic reference.)

Air deals with the realm of mental activity: intellect, ideas, thoughts, and communication. Swords have common themes with Wands, as they both share a desire to make change, take action, and assert their power. However, Swords rely on their minds more so than brute strength of the Wands. When looking at the Swords, you will see a general theme of conflict and drama.

Yin (Receptive) Elements

Water—Cups

Water is the first of the yin (receptive) elements and corresponds with the suit of Cups. It has no shape itself. Water is dependent on its surrounding environment to gain shape. Across cultures, in many mythologies and religions, the world was created out of an abyss. This void is often associated with water. Genesis 1:2 says that, "And the Spirit of God moved upon the face of the waters." Again, we are going back to Spirit and the notion of breath/air. The story we see in Genesis reflects an older tradition from the Middle East. Other cultures share the same theme: Greek, Egyptian, Japanese, and Native American traditions. It was the philosopher Thales of Miletus who claimed that water was the element of which all things are composed. Water can be a force for creation as well as destruction, much like any of the other elements. Many cultures have a destruction myth by flood—the most famous of which is the flood in the Genesis. Flood myths serve the role of cleansing and purification.

Water is associated with the heart, feelings, emotions, creativity, the unconscious mind, and intuition. Cups deal with love and relationships (romantic or platonic) as they seek meaning and understanding. They offer compassion and sympathy. Cups are sensitive and empathetic to others. Also, Cups deal with how we perceive our feelings and our feelings toward other people and things. When you look at the Cups, you see a general theme: relationships, connections, and various emotions from happiness to sorrow.

Earth—Pentacles

The last of the yin elements is Earth, which corresponds with the suit of Pentacles. Looking across cultures, the large majority of the names of the earth are feminine. This includes Gaia from Greece, Shakti from India, and Erda from the Norse. The notion that Earth is feminine makes earth a symbolic womb from which all things material are born. Earth is symbolic of all things that are physical and tangible. Earth is the lowest, most dense and concrete, of the elements.

Water and Earth are yin (passive) because they are dense and fall down to earth. While Air and Fire rise up Water and Earth do not. They are heavy and attract to each other. Earth cannot grow without Water to provide it nutriment.

Earth corresponds with the five senses: sight, touch, taste, smell, and sound. Pentacles deal with our money, careers, material possessions, resources, home life, and real estate. Pentacles are practical in their dealings; they look at what will be efficient. It is in the Pentacles where we find manifestation of all things that the other suits were trying to achieve. It provides stability and security. When you look at the Pentacles, you will see a general theme dealing with money, work, labor, hardship, and rewards.

Numerology and The Tree of Life

After the elements, we look at the numbers through numerology. Numerology is the study of numbers and their interaction or relation to our lives and the cosmos. What do numbers have to do with our lives? Numerology goes back to Pythagoras, the Greek mathematician and mystic who said that, through numbers, we could understand the cosmos. All things can be explained by mathematical theorems. In a modern view, this is true, because physics is represented in mathematical equations. Pythagoras also viewed numbers as real things that exist in our world.

The numerology used in Tarot is different than the numerology used by the Pythagoreans. In Tarot, we look at the common theme of a number in the Minor Arcana. When we look, for example, at all the fives in the Minor Arcana, which is the essence of the five? To answer this, we look at The Tree of Life to see the pattern all the suits follow.

Qabalah is Jewish mysticism influenced by Greek Platonic philosophy, which was merged with Tarot. Tarot fits very nicely within The Tree of Life, which is a representation of the process in which God created the world. This creation was through successive emanation of God through different stages (a concept borrowed from Neo-Platonism). What follows is a list of the emanations. The first emanation is Kether and moves down to the tenth, Malkuth.

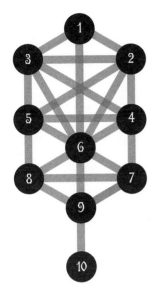

1. Kether: Creation—seed, beginnings
2. Chockmah: First swirling—uncertainty
3. Binah: First forming—initial progress
4. Chesed: Expansion—initial results
5. Geburah: Contraction—restrictions
6. Tipharah: Balance—harmonizing
7. Netzach: Cycles—energy and force
8. Hod: Focus—unity
9. Yesod: Foundation—results
10. Malkuth: Completion—endings and fusion

Going back to our example, the fives: what do all fives represent? According to this system, it is "contraction/restriction." So let us explore all the fives and see how this applies.

Five of Wands: I see contraction and restriction here in that all the individuals here are battling each other, thus restricting any development or teamwork. If they worked together, there would be no restriction.

Five of Cups: I see contraction and restriction here in the person clinging on to what is lost. There is no movement or progress.

Five of Swords: I see contraction and restriction here in that allies or friends are lost. Nothing is really gained or won here. Your efforts work against you.

Five of Pentacles: I see contraction and restriction here in the poverty of these two figures. They have lost so much and are held back because of it.

Now in your journal go though each of the minor arcana and see how each of the cards manifest themselves in this system. Take time to examine each set of cards and note your ideas and observations like those that I did above with the fives.

General Numerology

Besides the Tree of Life we can use classic numerology in combinations with Tarot—even though it is not the main factor influencing the development of the cards, it is still useful.

One: The number one is the beginning point and creation. One is associated with Aries.

Two: The number two is about relationship and connection for when you have two you can create a line between two points. Two symbolizes duality, balance, and also separation, the splitting apart of one into two. Two is associated with Libra.

Three: Three is a number associated with all sorts of trinities across cultures. It is a number of spirit and the first sign of manifestation. It is also a number of knowledge and understanding. Three is associated with Leo.

Four: The number four represents the material world, the psychical and what is stability and order. Four is associated with Taurus.

Five: This is the middle number within the minor arcana. It is here where we see a changing point. Five is rebellious and unexpected. The fives depict challenge, but also a time to learn. Five is associated with Gemini.

Six: The number six represents balance of opposites. It is a number of love and generosity. Six is concerned with community and service. Six is also protective. Six is associated with Cancer.

Seven: The number seven is a number of withdrawal, contemplation, and intelligence. Seven is associated with Pisces.

Eight: Eight represents infinity and expansion. It shows mastery of something and the ability to solve problems. Eight is associated with Capricorn.

Nine: This is the number of completion, conclusions, and limits. Nine is associated with Scorpio.

Ten: Ten shows cycles and the transition between them. Ten reduces down to one, which leads us back to Ace. So we have this connection of death and rebirth. Tens show the essence of the suit. Pentacles and Cups show the joys, while the Swords and Wands show woes.

Astrology

Astrology proves itself to be one of the most important systems for understanding the cards. While the associations may not be direct in older decks, newer decks sometimes make the astrological connections apparent by including the glyphs directly into the art.

The way astrology is used in Tarot is by paring the zodiac signs with the cards. We use the zodiac signs and the planets that rule the signs and assign them to a card. Thus, each sign will have two cards: one for the sign and the other for a planet.

ZODIAC SIGN	RULING PLANET	MAJOR ARCANA
Aries	Mars	Emperor/Tower
Taurus	Venus	Hierophant/Empress
Gemini	Mercury	Lovers/Magician
Cancer	Moon	Chariot/High Priestess
Leo	Sun	Strength/Sun
Virgo	Mercury	Hermit/Magician
Libra	Venus	Justice/Empress
Scorpio	Pluto	Death/Judgment
Sagittarius	Jupiter	Temperance/Wheel of Fortune
Capricorn	Saturn	Devil/World
Aquarius	Uranus	Star/Fool
Pieces	Neptune	Moon/Hanged Man

Astrology and Tarot

Astrology is a very ancient art, much older than Tarot. Tarot is a fairly recent development in comparison. While Tarot arose in fifteenth century Italy, astrology reaches much further back in human history. In the second millennium BCE, the Babylonians developed the first organized system of astrology.

It spread from Babylonia into Greece and it was the Greeks who named the constellations and expanded astrology to what we know it to be today.

Even before the influx of Babylonian astrology into Greek culture, there was an existing belief by the ancient Greeks of celestial influences. Plato believed that the movements of the stars showed the rational design of the cosmos. The Stoics believed there existed sympathy between the movement of the stars and events on earth. It was in the Hellenistic world (most notably Alexandria, Egypt) where astrology as we would recognize it developed.

Astrology is the combination of two Greek words, *aster* "star" and *logos* "reason," thus astrology is the reasoning of the stars. The stars give us reason to the mundane and profound events that occur in our lives. Astrology has been viewed as a scientific form of divination since the times of the Greeks and Romans. This is because astrology was based on careful observations of the stars, which relied on mathematical calculations. Astrology could be learned by anyone. Tarot, on the other hand, has been often described as an art of divination mainly because it is open to subjective, intuitive interpretations. Tarot and astrology represent two different disciplines based on two different principles.

Astrology finds itself right at home inside the Tarot. Tarot decks have depicted, and still do to this day, celestial bodies like the sun, moon, and stars. It was in 1785 that Jean-Baptiste Alliette created a comprehensive list of correspondences between Tarot and astrology. Later in the nineteenth and early twentieth century, the Hermetic Order of the Golden Dawn set forth to create a unified system by weaving together different systems into the Tarot. Astrology was one of these systems.

This stitching together of systems is apparent with the designing of decks. As mentioned, the influence of the zodiac can be embodied in the images of the cards. The Major Arcana is the ideal place to find the associations with the zodiac. Each of the cards from the Minor Arcana can also be placed on the wheel of the zodiac, giving each card a time of the year.

In this section, I will give a brief description of the planets and zodiac signs and the connection between these and the Major Arcana. (I will not be focusing on the Minor Arcana and the astrological connections; for an extensive examination on that matter read *Tarot and Astrology: Enhance Your Readings with the Wisdom of the Zodiac* by Corrine Kenner.)

Astrological Keywords, Signs, and Planets

Aries: Pioneering, assertive, impulsive, leading, independent, eager, headstrong. Impatient, careless, argumentative, arrogant, overzealous.

Mars: Masculinity, force, anger, effort, conquest, sex, war, passion.

Taurus: Earthly, stability, material, productive, practical, dependable. Possessive, controlling, lazy, stubborn, conservative.

Venus: Femininity, attraction, beauty, love, indulgence, rhythm.

Gemini: Intelligent, communicative, curious, dualistic, sociable, adaptable, alert. Abstract, spacey, unstable, restless, gossipy, fickle.

Mercury: Thinking, thoughts, reason, wit, learning, travel, commerce, flexibility. Trickery, slyness, emotionless, confusion.

Cancer: Feeling, emotional, gentle, sympathetic, nurturing, receptive, protective, shy, moody, touchy, clinging.

The Moon: Unconscious, emotional changes, habits, reactions.

Leo: Confidence, courage, charisma, big-hearted, giving, proud, dramatic, regal, vain, selfish, arrogant, snobbish, egocentric, flashy.

The Sun: Power, life force, importance, consciousness, ego, identity.

Virgo: Efficient, analytical, hardworking, dedicated, perfectionist, picky, petty, skeptical, worrisome, intolerant.

Virgo is ruled by Mercury, see keywords for Mercury.

Libra: Sharing, cooperative, fair, just, diplomatic, balanced, refined, indecisive, passive, superficial, imbalanced, and indifferent.

Libra is ruled by Venus, see keywords for Venus.

Scorpio: Transformation, death & rebirth, rejuvenation, secretive, penetrating, depth, investigative, jealous, destructive, extreme, possessive, deceptive, repressed.

Pluto: Regeneration, break down, break through, elimination, release, catharsis, cleansing, metamorphosis, hidden force.

Sagittarius: Thoughtful, thinking, learning, understanding, open minded, idealistic, jovial, self-righteous, demanding, dogmatic, scattered, excessive, and apathetic.

Jupiter: Growth, expansion, luck, abundance, moral, ethics, trust, faith.

Capricorn: Material, worldly, orderly, systematic, responsible, achieving, compulsive, materialistic, fearful, pessimistic, calculating.

Saturn: Limitation, form, order, structure, discipline, obstacles, seriousness, caution.

Aquarius: Progressive, revolution, change, independent, altruistic, rebellious, aloof, deviant, eccentric, erratic, detached, antisocial.

Uranus: Rebel, liberator, reform, discovery, originality, genius.

Pisces: Dreamy, intuitive, artistic, empathetic, imaginative, sensitive, compassionate, slow, phobic, gullible, unreal, impractical, chaotic, procrastinating.

Neptune: Oneness, wholeness, unity, visions, real of forms, visionary, healing.

Astrology in the Major Arcana

The archetypal images of the Major Arcana embody the qualities of the zodiac signs and planets.

Aries and Mars are associated with **The Emperor** and **The Tower**.
The connection can be seen by their fiery nature. The Emperor embodies the qualities of leadership and assertiveness from Aries. The Tower is a sudden blast and the release of energy that is directly related to Mars.

Taurus and Venus are associated with **The Hierophant** and **The Empress**.
The connection can be seen by The Hierophant's dogmatic and traditional ways, which come from Taurus. The Empress expresses Venusian qualities like beauty and attraction.

Gemini and Mercury are associated with **The Lovers** and **The Magician**.
The Lovers embody the Gemini qualities of duality and communication. The Magician expresses Mercurial qualities like skill, reason, and wit, as well as trickery.

Cancer and the Moon are associated with **The Chariot** and **High Priestess**.
The connection between Cancer and The Chariot has been an odd association. However, Corrine Kenner explains the relationship in *Tarot and Astrology: Enhance Your Readings with the Wisdom of the Zodiac*. Corrine says that Cancer manifests in The Chariot's strong sense to protect (one's family, for example). The High Priestess is linked with the Moon and expresses qualities like intuition and the unconscious.

Leo and the Sun are associated with **Strength** and **The Sun**.
Strength represents qualities like courage and caring. The Sun well represents the Sun and expresses it in qualities like life force, energy, and consciousness.

Virgo is associated with **The Hermit**.
This is expressed in The Hermit's analytic nature. The Hermit is disciplined, unselfish, and can be skeptical.

Libra is associated with **Justice**.
The connection between these two is visual as both are easily identified with the scales. Justice embodies the qualities of Libra's qualities of balance, fairness, and diplomacy.

Scorpio and Pluto are associated with **Death** and **Judgment**.
In Death, we have endings, which are related to Scorpio. Death also embodies Scorpio qualities like transformation, depth, and permeation for Death is inescapable. Judgment embodies qualities of Pluto, which are regeneration, release, and metamorphosis.

Special Note: Some readers see Death as death and rebirth, however, with my astrological associations, I place rebirth with Judgment (Pluto) and leave Death with endings (Scorpio).

Sagittarius and Jupiter are associated with **Temperance**
and **The Wheel of Fortune.**
Temperance expresses Sagittarian qualities such as understanding and an optimistic nature. The Wheel of Fortune radiates Jupiter qualities like expansion, luck, and good fortune.

Capricorn and Saturn are associated with **The Devil** and **The World**.
We can see the influence of Capricorn (negatively) in The Devil, such as materialism, fear, and repression. As the last card, The World represents Saturn-like qualities such as boundaries and limits.

Aquarius and Uranus are associated with **The Star** and **The Fool**.
The Star is associated with Aquarius. Like Aquarius, The Star moves forward, not backward. The Star is hopeful and generous, which can be connected with Aquarius's altruistic nature. The Fool embodies Uranus clearly in qualities like rebellion, liberation, freedom loving, unorthodoxy, and uniqueness.

Pisces and Neptune are associated with **The Moon** and **The Hanged Man**.
The Moon embodies Pisces's qualities, such as imagination, dreams, illusions, and deception. The Hanged Man, which is associated with Neptune, is seen in qualities like sacrifice, surrender, and martyring.

SECTION FOUR

TAROT HISTORY, RELIGION, AND PHILOSOPHY

Crash Course in Tarot History

The history surrounding the Tarot has been, up to recent times, a controversial topic. People have given the Tarot a mysterious and mystic history to add an aura of magic to it. It is for this reason the occultists made up the story that Tarot originated in Ancient Egypt from the god Thoth. There was a Tarot reader/psychic on a very popular morning American talk show that read for one of the hosts. This reader purported that no one knows where Tarot came from, that gypsies carrying them around Europe was the earliest history. Old recycled notions like this have been in circulation for many years.

Tarot has a very rich history. The images are rooted deeply in mythology, theology, and symbols, but its origins can be documented throughout history. It is not as mysterious as once thought. Things do not appear out of nowhere, fully developed. Things are created and they evolve over time. We *are* able to research and find the roots of Tarot. Robert M. Place in his book *Tarot: History, Symbolism, and Divination* refutes the Ancient Egyptian theory simply because you need paper to make cards, and the Egyptians did not have paper! Paper was invented in China by Cai Lun, an official to the Imperial court during the Han Dynasty in 105 CE. Papermaking made its way into the Islamic world during battles between the Tang Dynasty and the Islamic people in 751 CE. Chinese papermakers were captured and forced to teach their captors the secret knowledge of papermaking. It is some 350 years later, during the Mamluk Dynasty that was ruling Egypt and Syria, we have the creation of the Mamluk deck. The Mamluk deck is the earliest to resemble the structure of a deck of cards as we know them today. The Mamluk deck has four suits: Cups, Coins, Swords, and Polo sticks. Over some period of time, the deck made its way into Europe through Italy and Spain in the fourteenth century. The Mamluk deck was adapted to make the *tarocchi* as it was called in Italy. Tarocchi was a sort of playing card game like our modern-day bridge. Tarocchi is still played in Europe today; you will find it in France and Italy, as well as some other European countries. In addition to playing games, the cards were also used for divination.

The Tarot takes an occult turn in 1781, when the French author Antoine Court de Gébelin published his works on Tarot. This is the man who started the mystical history of Tarot being created in Egypt and the like. In 1780s, Ettellia, a French occultist, modified the Tarot deck for the purpose of divination, which was called *The Ettellia Deck*. Etellia is known as the first professional Tarot reader. However, Gébelin and Ettellia's ideas of Tarot did not have their full effect until the 1800s. It was then that occultists like Eliphas Levi, Papus, Paul Christian, and Oswald Writh promoted occult associations to the Tarot. These views influenced the Hermetic Order of the Golden Dawn. Everyone's ideas blended together and, for a while, people forgot the truth to Tarot origins and the same old story was retold as fact.

REℒIGIOɼ

Divination and Religion

In the first section (Myths and Misconceptions), I touched on the subject of Tarot being seen as evil. In this section, I wish to delve deeper into the subject of Tarot and religion. It is from religion, specifically the Abrahamic faiths of Judaism, Christianity, and Islam, that we get the idea of Tarot being evil. Why am I talking about this in the first place? What purpose does it serve to mention and discuss this? For one, I have not seen the subject covered in other books, so for that reason I want to cover it. Second, I have a strong interest in studying and understanding religion, so I want to include the topic. Third, many readers who come from a religious background where Tarot is associated as evil need to understand where the idea comes from, the context and history of such ideas, and how to work through them if they still are devout in their faith. There can be a sense of guilt and shame that can develop if a reader feels their faith conflicts with their study and use of Tarot. I want to remove this guilt.

My main focus will be on Christianity, but what can be said about what Christians say can easily be applied to Jews and Muslims as well, with some slight difference. For example, Muslims cite the Quran for their objections towards divination, while Jews and Christians use the Torah/Old Testament. My goal here is for Christians who still identify as Christian to find a compatible scriptural support for their Tarot practice and faith.

Since Tarot is a divinatory system, let's start with its definition: divination comes from the Latin *divinare,* "to foresee, to be inspired by a god," which is related to "*divinus*"—divine. Simply, divination is the attempt to foretell (prophesy/predict) future events by ways of interpretation of omens, the reading of signs, or any form that attempts to commune with deity or transcendent reality. Divination does not always have to be concerned with predicting the future; it can be simple communication with the Divine.

There are many methods and tools often used in divination. Some methods or tools are Tarot cards, palmistry, astrology, scrying, spirit or talking boards, or dream interpretation. Divination can be found in practically every culture: the Greeks, Egyptians, Israelites, Sumerians, Romans, and Chinese—everyone had some form of it. Divination appears many times in the Bible; but in Deuteronomy, it is called an "abomination." This is what we are concerned about, the prohibition of divination and how we ought to understand and deal with it.

Here is a secret: what many people don't know is that divination was not originally used to foretell future events. Divination was used to reveal the will of the gods, which was more important than knowing the future. People of the ancient world wanted to make sure they were doing what their god(s) wanted them to do. The focus was on the present, not the future. They wanted to ensure they were in the favor of their god(s) in the present moment. They wanted insight, not foresight.

Divination is an "abomination" to the God of Israel. This is a very bold statement for Tarot readers who find this teaching a confliction between their faith and love of Tarot. The word "abomination," *to'ebah* in Hebrew means something that is offensive to God. The word *to'ebah* is also a relative term, dependent on human perception. For example, something can be offensive to the Israelites but not offensive to an Egyptian, and can be okay. The Israelites don't care what other nations do. They are focused on themselves and their relationship with their God, not about other people and their gods.

To understand why divination is offensive in context, we will need to compare Israelite religion with the religions of their neighbors, the pagans. We are comparing monotheism on one side and polytheism on the other. Paganism or polytheism, the belief and worship of many gods and goddesses, postulate a different worldview from that of the monotheistic worldview.

The common theme of pagan religion is the idea of a realm that preexists the gods and creation. This is a realm that is beyond the gods, a realm that the gods are subject to. In pagan cosmogonies (creation myths), the common motif is that of an eternal abyss often made of water. In classical Greek myth, in the beginning was Chaos, the abyss. Out of this abyss came the first three immortal beings: Gaea (Earth), Tartarus (deepest dark region of the underworld), and Eros (love). Gaea gave birth to Oranos (Sky), Ourea (Mountains), and Pontus (sea). Her union with Oranos gave life to the Titans, who subsequently gave rise to the Olympians. This theme runs throughout all pagan mythology. In Egypt, the sun god Ra emerged from his father, the watery abyss, then spoke into creation the world (similar to God in the Bible speaking creation into existence). Babylonian creation myth states, in the beginning, there was Apsu, the sky god, and Tiamat, the chaos Goddess. From their union came all of creation. This theme is not limited to these cultures and can be found across the world.

This worldview of creation postulates that there exists a Transcendent-Divine Realm. This is the source of creation, the cosmic womb where everything sprung into existence. This includes gods, humans, and nature. All three are made from the same source and, thus, are related to each other and blend together. For example, nature was seen as divine, filled with nymphs and spirits. Gods could walk on Earth and mate with humans. These unions resulted in demi-gods like Hercules. Humans also could one day become divine after death or during life. There was fluidity between human and divine nature; there was no absolute separateness, other than death or immortality.

The gods in pagan tradition are limited and not absolute in their power and knowledge. They are superior to humans but still have flaws. They possess qualities as attributes but not as essentials. Example: Athena is Goddess of Wisdom. She has wisdom as an attribute but not as an absolute essential to her nature. She is wise but not all knowing. The gods are also capricious, and other gods can outdo one another. Their word is not final. Even Zeus, king of the gods, sometimes is forced to compromise with others. For example, when Hades took Persephone, her mother, Demeter, made the Earth bare from her mourning. The others gods, terrified that the humans would no longer give offerings to them, pleaded with Zeus to do something. Zeus had to compromise with Demeter and Hades. Since Persephone had eaten food (six pomegranate seeds) in the underworld, she had to stay six months of the year in the underworld. The other six she could return to her mother.

In a Transcendent-Divine Realm worldview nature, material objects are viewed as having power fused inside them, as they are connected to the realm. This allows magic to be possible, because magic is the manipulation of the sympathetic relationship between the object and the Transcendent-Divine Realm. The object allows you to circumvent the gods and to go directly to the source. Divination is a magical practice. Divination is directed towards this realm as another way to bypass the gods and go directly to the source for knowledge. Gods can be a medium for which you can connect to the realm or to understand the will of the gods. Oracles were said to speak the word of a god; for example, the Oracle of Delphi spoke for Apollo. Magic and divination both are related and interconnected because, to the Greeks, they are ways to attain salvation (escape) from the capricious nature of the gods and of the influences of negative spirits or forces.

Now that we have a clear and detailed understanding of the pagan worldview, which hypothesis is on a realm, which all creation comes from, we have on the other side the monotheistic view. The monotheistic worldview can be seen as a revolution from the religious norm of the ancient world. Across the Hebrew Scriptures, we see the idea develop of the one God who is unlimited, timeless, and everlasting, who is not created by a pre-existent entity. God is the source of all being. God is a Creator, never the created. God is Absolute and Supreme. In the first verse of Genesis, chapter one, we see God create Heaven and Earth from the watery abyss. This is similar to the myths we have examined in the pagan view; however, the difference is that God is the creator of these things. God does not come from them. This worldview removes the Transcendent-Divine Realm.

With the removal of the Transcendent-Divine Realm, we lose the foundations for everything in the pagan worldview. God is unlimited; He transcends nature and is not a personification of it. Material objects hold no power of themselves. Magic is now gone; it is useless and futile. In this worldview, there is no bypass around God to a Realm above Him that you can tap into. There is only God and God alone. Divination as well does not work because we do not have a Realm to bypass God to tap into to foretell future events. Doing such is ungodly. Divination does occur in the Bible but is used to make inquiries of God and, if God wills it, He will answer your question. You are not able to force God to provide an answer.

Going back to "offensive things," we can now understand why divination was seen as an offensive thing because, to the Israelites, divination was a wasted and mistaken idea. Israelites are not to practice divination, because it simply does not work in their worldview, so why practice something that does not work? It is not that it is evil. It is just not valid. The pagans use divination. In their worldview, it is accepted.

Divination was practiced in ancient Israel; we know this just by reading the Jewish scriptures. A few examples of this include the prophet Elija, who directed King Joash to throw two arrows through the window in order to find out whether the king would be victorious or not (2 Kings 13:14–19). God used omens to signal Gideon's victory over the Midianites. If the fleece of the sheep was wet and the ground was dry, it was a sign of ensuing success (Judges 6:36–40). Joseph was well known for his dream interpretation, which he credits God for allowing him to do (Genesis 40:8). Through the use of the Urim and Thumim, you could be given a yes or no answer to questions. The thing that made Hebrew diviners different from other cultures is that the position of diviner was a professional one as opposed to "freelance" mantic soothsayers. In other words, in Israel, the diviner was on the bankroll of the Temple and they did not like free agents. There was a monopoly on divination, it would appear. It would make sense then to ban other forms of divination unauthorized by the authorities.

Now let us take a look at Deuteronomy chapter 18. This is where you find the direct prohibition on divination. We have three versions: Hebrew, Greek, and English. Translating between different languages is difficult; there will be mistranslations, errors, which thus, lead to false understandings. For instance, the Bible as we read it in English is not a proper translation from the original language. The Torah (written in Hebrew) was then translated into Greek starting in the third century BCE and was completed in the first century BCE. It is from the Greek version, known as the Septuagint, that we get our English translation, not the original Hebrew. Because of the translations between languages, the context and meaning that the original text was trying to express is lost. I am going to break down Deuteronomy chapter 18 lines 10–11, comparing them between the Hebrew, Greek, and English to see how things became mixed up.

Hebrew

מֶסֶק שֶׁאָב וּתְבוּ־וְנֶב רִיבָעַמ דָב אַצַּמִי־אָל
וְהֶשְׁכְמוּ שֶׁחַנְמוּ וָנוֹעָמ סִיָּמְסַק
־לָא שֶׁרְדוּ יֹנַעְדְיָו בּוֹא לֶאֹשׁוּ רֶבָה רֻבֵּחוּ
סִיתֵּמַה

Translation into English

There shall not be found among you someone who passes his son or daughter through the fire, one who practices enchantment, a soothsayer or a diviner or a sorcerer or one who casts spells or who asks of a ghost or of a spirit of an acquaintance or inquires of the dead.

Greek

οὐχ εὑρεθήσεται ἐν σοὶ περικαθαίρων τὸν υἱὸν αὐτοῦ ἢ τὴν θυγατέρα αὐτοῦ ἐν πυρί μαντευόμενος μαντείαν κληδονιζόμενος καὶ οἰωνιζόμενος φαρμακός ἐπαείδων ἐπαοιδήν ἐγγαστρίμυθος καὶ τερατοσκόπος ἐπερωτῶν τοὺς νεκρούς

Translation into English

There shall not be found in you one purging his son or daughter in fire, or one using oracles for divination, or one prognosticating and foretelling, an administer of potions, one charming an enchantment, one who delivers oracles, and an observer of signs asking of the dead.

King James Version (KJV)

There shall not be found among you any one that maketh his son or his daughter to pass through the fire, or that useth divination, or an observer of times, or an enchanter, or a witch or a charmer, or a consulter with familiar spirits, or a wizard, or a necromancer.

When comparing the three English versions it looks like they are projecting a similar story. However, things are added in the Greek and King James versions that are not in the Hebrew version. This is probably due to current methods of the time that were similar to those things mentioned in the Hebrew version. For example, in the Greek version they use the word "oracle." The King James Version adds necromancer to the list. There is something important to note: King James lacks an important aspect that the Hebrew and Greek versions did have, which is context. The context of what the words meant did not carry over with the King James Version. The Hebrew use words, which imply harmful practices, such as casting spells (spoken words or tying knots) to injure people, as well as contacting spirits not of God.

The Greek version carries this over as well when it says, "farmakos" (Gk. φαρμακός) as being specifically about harmful potions. In the KJV, the context is lost and it seems any form of such acts is restricted. This, however, is opposite. With the case for divination, foretelling, and so forth, they do not mention whether or not it is for good or bad. We can assume that they might be referring to the use of such techniques in negative ways that are not allowed, as it would stick with the overall theme of harming others. I believe that they refer to the harmful usages, because the priests of the temple did practice divination, so it gives implications the good usages are okay.

Christianity

So far, we have focused on Judaism, the Torah, and the context between monotheism and polytheism. Now we will switch gears and move towards Christianity, focusing on divination and introduction of divine revelation and prophecy.

"Is it okay for a Christian to read Tarot?" This is a question asked by many readers who wonder if reading Tarot conflicts with their faith. For a long time, I was worried about this myself. I did research, read scriptures, read scholarly works, and came to my own conclusion. Though I do not associate myself to be a Christian, I feel more at home with platonic philosophy and Greek Polytheism. I am an eclectic spiritualist to say the least. However, for the Christian reading Tarot, as well as being a Christian, I find this to be a compatible endeavor. I will be using the New Testament as my source for reasoning this.

Taking a step back to what we have already learned, many rules about divination are in the Old Testament, mainly in the two books of Deuteronomy and Leviticus. However, the application and interpretation of these rules changed with the inclusion of the New Testament scriptures. There is something very important that most—if not all—Christians are not aware of: the laws in Deuteronomy are for the Israelites and them only. These laws do not apply to anyone else, which also means Christians. Looking back into scripture it says,

When you enter the land which the Lord your God gives you. . .

Deut 18:19

God is speaking to the Israelites, that when they enter the Promised Land, there would be certain rules. These rules don't apply to modern Christians and most people, for we are not the people who the land was promised to. This rule and all rules in the Old Testament apply to the Israelites. It is as simple as that. Christians do not follow all the Mosaic rules and laws of the old covenant (over 600 of them) in the Old Testament, because a new covenant was formed through Jesus Christ. The nullification of the Old Testament covenant is stated in Hebrews 8:13:

In that he says, "A new covenant," he has made the first old. But that which is becoming old and grows aged is near to vanishing away.

The Apostle Paul preached that people became right with God not by following the Law but by belief in Jesus. Galatians 2:16 says:

Knowing that a man is not justified by the works of the law, but by the faith of Jesus Christ, even we have believed in Jesus Christ, that we might be justified by the faith of Christ, and not by the works of the law: for by the works of the law shall no flesh be justified.

In a nutshell, the laws in the Old Testament are null and void to the Christians. If Christians had to follow the rules in the Old Testament, then Christians would not be able to eat pork, and would have to follow all the rules Jews follow. However, Christians do not; therefore, divination laws are voided as well.

Christians find their spiritual teachings from the New Testament. It is in the New Testament where we will find new rules and guidelines to the faith. With regards to divination, we must look at the Gifts of the Holy Spirit to understand how divination fits into the New Testament. A spiritual gift is any ability that is empowered by the Holy Spirit, be it natural or supernatural. There are many spiritual gifts. The main seven are: prophecy, teaching, miracles, healing, tongues and interpretation, word of wisdom, and distinguishing between spirits. The one specific spiritual gift we want to focus on is prophecy. In the Old Testament, prophecy was restricted only to the prophets, who spoke the word of God. However, there is mention to a time when prophecy would be available to everyone. Moses said:

> Would that all the Lord's people were prophets, that the Lord would put his spirit upon them!
>
> Num. 11:29

In the book of Joel, God prophesied through Joel:

> And it shall come to pass afterward, that I will pour out my spirit upon all flesh; your sons and your daughters shall prophesy, your old men shall dream dreams, your young men shall see visions. Even upon the menservants and maidservants in those days, I will pour out my spirit.
>
> Joel 2:28–29

Collectively, this refers to a time when God will pour his spirit onto mankind and they will be able to prophesize, have dreams, and see visions. It is through Jesus that he brings the Holy Spirit to his people by the new covenant. The followers of Jesus are baptized with the Holy Spirit and are given these Spiritual Gifts. As a baptized Christian, you may be gifted in one of these abilities.

In the New Testament, the words prophet and prophecy do not carry the same meaning as in the Old Testament. In the Old Testament, the prophets held Divine authority to speak the word of God. What the prophets said was the word of God. In the New Testament, Jesus does not use the word "prophet" to describe those who would speak the Word of God. He used a new term "apostle." The apostles now have divine authority to write and speak the word of God.

The understanding of the word prophecy also had changed, because the context of the word in Greek did not imply necessarily the ability to predict the future or reveal God's word. Prophecy had changed to a term used to describe something that has been revealed to you by external forces. It can also imply supernatural knowledge or sometimes predictions of the future. The most interesting thing, however, is that predictions are not always 100% correct. Prophecy in the church is understood to be the act of God causing a revelation in the mind of a person, what a person then speaks becomes a prophecy—it is not the word of God but the reporting of the revelation in their own words. Saint Paul valued the gift of prophecy so much that he told the Corinthians:

Follow the way of love and eagerly desire gifts of the Spirit, especially prophecy.

1 Cor. 14:1

Saint Paul also said,

So, my brethren, earnestly desire to prophesy.

1 Cor. 14:4

It seems that the act of prophesying is valued, important, and should be desired. How does this apply to reading Tarot? And how does Tarot fit into the New Testament idea of prophecy? We understand that when God gives us revelation, we report what has been revealed as prophecy. Our words are not God's word; it is how we understand the revelation and report it to be. This applies to Tarot. If one does readings that are reflective in nature (seeking wisdom, insight, guidance), then we are essentially seeking revelation. The cards prompt us to reflect and thus we gain revelation (by God, if you will).

What about predictive readings? We can also apply the New Testament understanding of prophecy to predictive readings. In the New Testament, it is very clear that only God knows the future. Prophecy is no exception. In the New Testament, prophecy is fallible when it comes to predictions. Predictions may come true or they may not. They may occur a little differently than what was predicted. Some will say that evil spirits give these false predictions. There is no indication that this is the cause of incorrect predictions. The reason for incorrect predictions is because humans give prophecy in human words based on our limited human understanding of the revelation.

Predictions in Tarot are no different. You have predictions that come true and others that don't. It is all in the reader's ability to accurately report what is being revealed in the reading. Clearly, we see based on New Testament scripture that Tarot is compatible with the Christian faith. I hope that this clears up any fears you may have had regarding this issue. Now you can still be a good Christian and read the Tarot!

Islam

The last of the three Abrahamic religions is Islam. What does Islam say about divination? Nothing different. Like the Bible, the Quran is against divination. Knowledge of the unknown and future is for Allah only. The Prophet Mohammed says that diviners are in the hellfire. However, what makes divination so sinful is the idea that the person who practices divination believes they hold within themselves some supernatural power separate from God. This is the sin in the Islamic view.

I want to express my personal views here, because I used to wonder if Tarot was a bad thing. I view Tarot as a tool, which I use to connect to the higher source. I do not have any supernatural powers. My ability to read the cards is a skill learned and crafted over years of study and practice. Tarot is a form of prophecy, a type of revealed knowledge by the Divine source, and nothing else. In context of the Abrahamic religions and seeing how I use Tarot, there is no conflict of interest. Neither should you find any conflict, either.

Other Religions and Philosophies

Exiting from the monotheistic tradition and expanding our religious and spiritual scope, we will see that divination is not a taboo and damned to the fires of hell. The main reason is that the theology and philosophies are different.

Hellenismos

(Ancient Greek Polytheism)

We explored much of the pagan worldview of the Transcendent-Divine Realm. Here we will add to it, focusing on the Greeks. The Greeks worshipped many Gods, Goddess, demigods, nature spirits, and the like. The Greeks did not have a Bible, Torah, or Quran, nor did they have a word for religion. They did have a few collections of works that were considered to be sacred and inspired by the divine. Hesiod's *Theogony, Works and Day*, Homer's *Iliad and Odyssey*, and Pindar's *Odes* were among the sacred texts of the Greeks. These texts did not list a series of dos and do nots. It did not list any thou shall nots either. The texts spoke of the origins of the universe, birth of the gods, and interactions between the gods and man. It is in the interactions between them where we get lessons and morals of the time. To the Greeks, hubris was the one thing the gods hated the most. Hubris is extreme arrogance and oftentimes the act of challenging the gods.

As with the lack for a word for religion, they lacked the idea of sin as we understand it. Sin to an ancient Greek was not living up to your potential, cheating yourself out of what you could be, but above all, not being true to who you are. This is very different when comparing to what sin is in the Abrahamic religions. The Greek gods were also more personal than the God of the monotheists. God in the monotheistic view is often personified as a heavenly father up in the clouds: one who is zealous and quick to anger and will wipe out the human race with a flood, and threatened Moses that he wanted to kill everyone all over again. The gods of Greece could be just as bad, but they would interfere with you just for the sake of interfering with you, regardless of what you did.

The gods acted like humans. They had human emotions and desires. Because the gods were unpredictable, the people wanted to know their will and desire. Ancient tablets and lead scrolls have been found with questions inscribed on them—questions that people asked the oracles. The questions are almost always posed to be answered with a "yes" or "no" reply. These tablets or scrolls recorded the name of the person and their question. Geris asked wither it would be best for him to take a wife. Heracleidas asked whether he and his wife would produce any offspring. Lysanias asked if the child his wife was pregnant with was his. Cleotas asked if it would be profitable for him to keep sheep.

An oracle was a virgin woman chosen by the priests of the temple to commune with a specific God. The Oracle of Delphi is the most famous of the oracles. She spoke with the god Apollo, who among many things, was the god of prophecy. Oracles spoke with the gods directly, but there were only a handful of them in the Greek world. Because of the scarcity of oracles, another category of diviners called mantis (μάντεις) or "seers" served the people when an oracle was not an option. Unlike the oracles, the seers did not speak to the gods directly, but interpreted omens sent by the gods. Think of Runes or even Tarot cards as a modern-day example. A man or woman could have been a mantis and, according to myth, you were born a mantis, but one can also learn a particular form of divination.

Divination was a part of the culture; they saw it as natural. Communing with the gods was normal and almost expected of the people. However, people did not go to the oracle asking about the future. They were more concerned with the present and making sure they were paying the right tribute to their god(s). It was actually ill-advised to ask for specific predictions of the future. It was proper to ask a question that would align you with your destiny. Example, when the Lydian King Croesus asked the oracle whether he should fight King Cyrus of Persia or negotiate with Cyrus for terms of peace. The Oracle told Croesus that if he went to war, he would destroy a great kingdom. Croesus went to war thinking he would be destroying King Cyrus, but alas in the irony of a Greek comedy, Croesus destroys his own kingdom.

The gods themselves even used divination. After the Olympians overthrew the Titans, Zeus himself drew lots with his brothers Poseidon and Hades to see who would rule what part of the world. This is a great example of the idea of the Transcendent-Divine Realm, which is above and beyond the gods. They needed to go to the source to know what to do next. They also needed to consult with Fate. Fate was outside of their control; no god could control fate. Fate ruled all and if you think about it, it would be unfitting for the gods to ban something they themselves had no control over.

Kabbalah

Kabbalah (Qabalah) is the Jewish mystical tradition founded in sixteenth-century Spain that relates to the understanding of the relationship between the creator (God) and his creation (people). The main scripture used in Kabbalah is the Zohar (The Book of Splendor). The Zohar is a collection of books that include commentary on the metaphysical understanding of the Torah, as well as scriptural interpretations, material on theosophy, and theology, among other spiritual topics. A Kabbalist reads the Bible with a different view than most people, as most people read the Bible literally. A Kabbalist reads the Bible looking for metaphysical understanding and trying to find deeper knowledge than what is shown on the surface. The "true" meaning is not apparent at the surface according to the Kabbalists. Dealing with the laws of Deuteronomy and divination, the view in Kabbalah is basically the view I proposed through my analysis of the translations and context I spoke of earlier. The Kabbalist believes that evil use of divination is prohibited.

One of the main principles in Kabbalistic teachings is that God has one purpose, which is to give. The universe is made so that the God would be able to share with someone. Thus divination is a way for which God can share with us his knowledge.

In astrology this is very important. The Kabbalist believes that when a soul incarnates on earth, they pick the date, time, and place to be born into the world. The soul picks the personality traits, challenges, and strengths to be given. This view is opposite of traditional Western astrology, which believes that we are born randomly and the planets govern our personality and behavior. You are more of a victim to the planets, but in the Kabbalistic astrology, you picked when to be born and are in control.

Eastern Philosophy

Why is it that when we escape the views of Abrahamic religious views about divination, we find belief systems that accept the practice of divination? The development of Eastern thought is different than what we find in the Abrahamic religions. When talking about religions of the east, I will use the term philosophies, because religion is not an accurate description. They are not as dogmatic as Western religions.

The four big eastern philosophies are Hinduism, Buddhism, Taoism, and Confucianism. They developed more openly and freely than the East. When I look at Eastern traditions, what I notice is that there is a sense that Divinity is more abstract in contrast to the God of the Bible, who seems to be more concrete. In the Eastern traditions, they are more focused on the bigger picture, the thing they call the oneness, the total reality, and the thing that transcends all things. In the West, we try to define the world and seek the Truth. In the East, they do not try to define the truth, but to live in harmony with the world.

The Eastern philosophies are not as dogmatic like the religions of the West that make laws restricting things like divination. Because there is little dogma in the East, you do not find any laws against divination.

Confucianism

The I Ching (*ee-jing*) was developed in China. The I Ching or Book of Changes is an oracle that was used for gaining advice on how to lead effectively and how to help society. The reason for this is because, in China, Confucianism was the main philosophical thought. In Confucianism, the focus is the stability and wholeness of society. Back to high school in world history, what they teach you about Confucianism is the importance for children to respect their elders. This is just a way for cultivating social stability. The use of divination is accepted because it is a way to bring guidance and finding advice that will help society become whole. Now this is a profound way of thinking—divination for the benefit of society. Too bad this idea did not cross the minds of people in the West. Instead of divination being seen as evil, the Eastern philosophies allow the use of divination because of the overall benefits it provides for the society and individual.

Hinduism

In Hinduism, there are no laws that prohibit the use of divination in any form or fashion. One of the main reasons is because Hinduism is not actually a religion in the traditional sense and the term Hinduism was created by the West as a way to describe all the religious beliefs in India and to try to merge them together. And, unlike the western religions of Christianity, Judaism, and Islam, that have a central holy book, such as the Bible, Torah, or Quran, the Hindus have many spiritual texts. The most popular is the Vedas. The Vedas is also among the oldest sacred texts known to mankind, which dates roughly to 1500 BCE to 1000 BCE.

Unlike in the western religions and culture that views divination in negative light and shuns participations in it, divination is accepted as a primary part of the Hindu culture. Astrology is the main form of divination used. In India, the type of astrology used is referred to as Vedic astrology and it is a major influence in Hindu life. When a couple is going to marry, their priest creates an electional chart to pick the right day for the wedding. Astrology is such a big part of the Indian culture that the University Grants Commission and the Ministry of Human Resource Deployment have decided to introduce Vedic astrology as a discipline of study in Indian universities. However, the matter did not go without protest. This decision upset the scientific community, considering it a step backwards. Clearly we can see that divination is an important part of the Hindu culture that is not seen as evil.

Buddhism

The Buddha did not hold fortunetelling in favor. The reason was the Buddha taught within his eightfold path (ways to end suffering) that people should make a living in a proper way. This is the fifth path in the eightfold path called "Right Livelihood." People should not engage in business/trade/occupations that harm other people directly or indirectly. Fortunetelling was seen as taking advantage of people, much like we see today with scam artists. However, this applies only for ill-intentioned readers. So fortunetelling with proper intentions is valid. The Dali Lama, the spiritual head of Buddhism, consults with the Nechung Oracle, the State Oracle of Tibet. We can see that divination is not rejected as long as it is used properly, in line with the Buddha's teachings.

Dr. Phil-osophy

There is a whole bucket of philosophical questions and issues that I want to explore in this section. I love philosophy. I love to study ideas and theories as to how and why the world works. From Neo-Platonism to Kabbalah, Gnosticism, Hermeticism, and everything in between—I love it all. I want to mainly focus on a few things in this section: the idea of what time is (past, present, and future) with a focus on the future. Can we change the future? Can we *really* predict the future? What about God? In the traditional role, God is omniscient in the religious views of Judaism, Christianity, and Islam. What are the explanations or the alternatives?

Predicting the future is the most common use or held belief by non-Tarot reading folk. In recent times, predicting the future has become a touchy subject in the Tarot community. This issue stems from an ethical standpoint. Is it ethical to predict the future? Does it provide any help or does it remove free will, thus hindering the client? The other standpoint is philosophical. What is time? Do we have free will? Can we change the future? How can we possibly change the future? These are heavy and deep issues that deal with theology and philosophy that are never easy, and you never really know the answer indefinitely. I will address many of the philosophical and theological issues dealing with predicting the future. As a Tarot reader, these are issues you should contemplate and form your own reading philosophy.

Two Types of Time

First, we must examine the concept of time. There are two types of time that are at the core of all cultures around the world. Time is either seen as linear or cyclical or, according to The Doctor from *Doctor Who*, time is "Wibbly-Wobbly Timey-Wimey." It's confusing and not easy to understand.

Linear time says that there was a beginning point (creation) and that we have been moving along in time ever since with events happening one right after another. Linear time theory also states that there will be an "end time," in which everything ends. Religions like those of the Abrahamic tradition claim a judgment day will come to end everything but to then reestablish God's Kingdom. It is not really an end of the world; it's more like a start to a better one. Scientists theorize that one day the cosmos will die, it will stop expanding (it has been expanding ever since the big bang), and will then constrict and contract back on its self. If you want to learn more, search "big freeze," "heat death," "big crunch." These are different theories of how the universe could end.

On the other hand, cyclical time says that time repeats itself over and over. It has no beginning or end like linear time theory. The saying "history repeats itself," for example, is a cyclical belief. You will find that cyclical time is the dominant view of time in ancient cultures, and is still the common belief in Eastern religions like Hinduism. Within these traditions, it is believed that the world goes through cycles of creation and destruction. In Hinduism, there are four ages or "Yugas" that lasts for 311 trillion and 40 billion years, which is the lifespan of Brahma, the creator of the universe. If we examine the symbolism of the Tarot, we see over and over again that Tarot sides with the cyclical theory. Cards like The Wheel of Fortune speak about cycles. The Moon symbolizes the lunar cycles. Death and Judgment speaks about death and rebirth and the cycle of life. The tens in the Minor Arcana normally symbolize a cycle change and are linked back to the Ace. Nothing has an ending in Tarot; it always cycles through phases and stages.

There are scientific theories that also support a cyclical style of creation and destruction through periods of expansion and cooling. There is not just one big bang. We could be just one in a continuous series of universes. Maybe Buddhism's theory has some weight to it.

Free Will

For Tarot practitioners, one of the most important philosophical issues to affect us is free will. Do we have it? Doe it exist? What does it entail and what does it implicate?

If you do Tarot for predictions and most spreads have a position for "outcome" you need to consider the role of free will and what you think free will is.

Can the future be known while still being able to have free will? Knowing the future must imply a deterministic view of life. Most readers who do give predictions in their readings usually emphasize the client's free will in influencing the final outcome. There is a common belief in the fluidity of the future as always being created and not fixed in stone. We must also ask, how do we define free will? Free will, in a basic definition, is a person's ability to make his or her own decision without being forced to make that decision by external forces. It also implies that a person is morally responsible for their actions, because they freely choose their actions.

There are three traditional positions regarding free will and determinism (no free will, all events are predetermined). Those who believe in free will and reject determinism are called *libertarians*. Those who deny free will and believe in determinism are called hard *determinists*. In the middle of both, we have *compatibilists*, who think it is a mistake to think that determinism has any significance on whether or not we have free will.

Going back to our ancient roots, we find the notion of Fate. According to the Greeks, Fate controls the major life events. Fatalistic events are bound to happen no matter what you do. This notion is best represented in Sophocles' play *Oedipus Rex*. An oracle tells King Laius that his son Oedipus is fated to kill him and marry his wife, the Queen Jocasta. The parents try to avoid this and have a servant take the child out into the wilderness to die. However, a shepherd finds the child and raises the baby Oedipus. Long story short, what the oracle said eventually comes to pass. Oedipus returns to his father's kingdom one day and kills him and ends up marrying his mother.

As the concept of Fate develops, Clotho, Lachesis, and Atropos personify it. In Greek mythology, the fates are viewed as above the gods and their influences. In the Greek worldview, Fate does not undermine our free will. Fate only impacts major life events; however, we freely choose the path that brings us to our final destination.

We also find the earliest form of determinism with two Greek philosophers in the fifth century BCE with Leucippus and Democritus. Leucippus in his *On the Mind* states that nothing happens at random, but everything for a reason and by necessity. All events have a cause; nothing occurs from nothing.

In the Hindu tradition, we have the notion of Karma, which is the power of actions to impose consequences or rewards in our future. Noble actions result in rewards in a future life, while adverse actions result in consequences in the future. Karma is different from Greek fate in that Karma does not depend on a god or gods to cause outcomes or to dispense reward and punishment. What is dispensed to you from Karma is always deserved and never arbitrary. Traditional views on Karma deny that Karma precludes free will. Karma does not determine every choice and action. Moral actions are not determined by Karma and good choices result in favor in the future.

In the Abrahamic religions, there are segments that believe in predestination. The Essenes, a Jewish sect, believed that fate governed all things. All things happen according to its determination. The Jabarites, an Islamic sect, also believed that God determines all things. By in large, the Abrahamic religions rejected predestination views on God. Humans have free choice. This is a prevalent belief in the Abrahamic faiths.

The one central concept in these traditions is that God is *omniscience*, all knowing. God knows all things, past, present, and future. Knowing this, it would be logical to say that God determines all things. However, the theologian St. Augustine stated that knowledge of the future does not mean our choices were forced. We still chose it. This was the same conclusion I came to when discussing this topic in my philosophy of religion class in college. Augustine uses the analogy that you can remember a past action. You cannot change that action, but it does not mean you did not act freely. The same is said of God. God knows everything as if it were a memory in his mind.

There are other views, one from a medieval theologian named Boethius. He stated that God was eternal and out of time. God being outside of time shows that God knows of a person's action as soon as it occurs and not before it occurs. Boethius says that God has no belief of time (yesterday, today, or tomorrow).

All things occur at once in front of God. This preserves free will according to Boethius. However, church fathers rejected this idea because, for one reason, it made God too transcendent and they believed God was still involved in the preservation of the world through continuous creation.

In Buddhism, we find the opposite of what we find in the Abrahamic faiths. Free will is impossible for the Buddhist. We think of free will coming from the Self. We make choices and decisions. However, to the Buddhist, the Self is an illusion. Thoughts and feelings are all that exists and they are momentary. This belief is in stark contrast to the idea of agent causation, that the agent (you) makes decisions, nothing else.

Does the future exist? Philosophically speaking from the Buddhist perspective, no, it does not. Time is an illusion of the mind. The only thing that really exists is the present. The present moment is the only thing we have that we know to be true. The past is simply a collection of memories and experiences and the future is simply our past projected into the future, but in an idealized form that we hope will be better than the past.

In the Tarot community, when the discussion of free will comes up, I get that there is a certain agreement among the majority. The majority believes that we do, in fact, have free will. The future is somewhat predictable, but it is changeable, for it is not set in stone. The future is fluid and dynamic, not static and determined. Many Tarot readers tend to favor spirituality rather than religious dogma and doctrines. Thus, they do not necessarily believe in an omniscient deity that knows the future. This notion works wonderfully outside of the monotheistic worldview.

But what about inside the monotheistic worldview? What if you believe that there is only one God, who knows the future and that the future cannot be changed? How can a Tarot reading allow someone to change his or her future? How can we help them shape their lives in contradiction to what the cards say will happen? I guess the simple answer is to view your interaction with the cards as a part of the divine plan.

My personal views on this are a little mixed. I do believe in Fate as my Greek ancestors believed. Some things are just meant to happen, such as profound moments in life. How we get to these events is up to us. In the end, we end up where we are meant to be. I also feel that things can be predicted because of human nature. People are creatures of habit and their actions can be predicted with enough data. In a way, Tarot is able to understand these patterns and predicts into the future, showing that if you act in the manner you normally do, then this result will occur. Where do I stand on deities knowing the future and what that means for our free will? If there is a God who knows the future, I do not believe it removes my free will, for knowledge of something does not mean it is forced on us as St. Augustine said. However, I tend to think that Divinity is not a thing that "knows" stuff like the future. So in the end, I personally try not to worry about this issue; however, it is still an issue you should think about to find where you stand on the matter.

SECTION FIVE

Spreads

Laying the Cards

Spreads are the backbone of a Tarot reading. It is the spread, which allows a reading to occur. A spread, also known as a layout, is like a map of assigned positions. These positions have certain meanings like "past," "future," "advice," and so on. The positions affect the meaning and interpretation of the card, which is inside the position. Simply put, the position defines the context in which the card is in and it helps you understand what the card is expressing.

You have already encountered one spread in this book in a previous chapter, the classic Past, Present, and Future spread. The first card indicated past influences, the middle card indicated current influences and the last card showed what may be in store for the future. There are countless spreads a reader can use. Many of these can be found online or in books. You can even create your own spreads and customize the ones you come across through your study.

In this section, I am going to provide a small collection of useful spreads. I will not attempt to present an extensive list of spreads, as there are countless other resources available for you. Instead, I want to give you quality over quantity. I feature a few spreads from other authors because they are useful, while others are of my creation, making them unique to this book.

The spreads tend to lean towards introspective purists. It is my belief that Tarot is an amazing tool of introspection and I want to give you spreads that make you think and explore your psyche, rather than simply give you fortune-telling style spreads. Just lay down the number of cards suggested and match the cards with the number definitions for a reading.

Daily Spreads

Pulling a daily card or cards are useful at getting a peek at the day ahead. Use these spreads to help plan your day. Get creative here, think up your own questions to ask the Tarot about the day ahead. The possibilities are numerous. Here are some questions you might ask:

- What guides me today?
- What should I try to learn today?
- How can I make the most out of today?
- What should I do?
- What shouldn't I do?

MY CALLING

This spread comes from a blog post I read by Agapi Stassinopoulos (http://unbindingtheheart.com/2013/08/5-essential-questions-to-lead-you-to-your-calling/) who wrote about finding one's calling in life. She came up with five questions to ask yourself in order to find your calling. These questions easily can become a Tarot spread.

1. What am I here to learn?
2. What am I here to teach?
3. What am I here to overcome?
4. What am I here to complete?
5. What am I here to express?

SPIRITUAL QUEST

I created this spread for a client who had a question about their spiritual quest.

1. Where am I spiritually at the moment?
2. Where should I be heading, spiritually?
3. What lesson am I here to learn?
4. How will I achieve this?

7 CARD HORSESHOE (CLASSIC)

1. **Past:** the recent past events that have influenced the present situation.
2. **Present:** the present situation being addressed, influences, things that are affecting the querent now.
3. **What is hidden:** the things/influences/events the querent cannot see or that which has been overlooked by the querent.
4. **Obstacles/Challenges:** what will block the querent in their path or present the most challenge for them; that which must be overcome before progress can be made.
5. **Surroundings:** that which surrounds the querent, e.g. environment, people, influences, that is useful and helpful to the querent.
6. **Advice:** best course of action to follow.
7. **Outcome:** what will happen if the advice in Card 6 is taken.

FACT OR FICTION

This spread is useful to understand what is illusionary and reality in relation to the question asked. Sometimes we have trouble telling what is not real with what is; use this spread to separate fact from fiction.

1. **Fiction, what the illusion is.** How you are misled, or what is false.
2. **Fact, the reality is this.** The truth of the matter.

THE SEVEN DEADLY SINS

Inspired by the seven deadly sins, this spread will open your eyes to things about yourself that you may not even have thought of. The Seven Deadly Sins were compiled by the fourth century Greek monk Evagrius Ponticus, who called them the "evil thoughts." He lists these "evil thoughts" as gluttony, fornication, avarice, hubris, envy, wrath, boasting, and dejection. In 590 AD, Pope Gregory revised the list into the one we know today, which are lust, gluttony, greed, sloth, wrath, envy, and pride.

1. **Pride**: The excessive belief in one's own abilities and this interferes with the individual's recognition of the grace of God. It has been called the sin from which all others arise. Pride is also known as Vanity.
2. **Envy**: The desire for others' traits, status, abilities, or situation.
3. **Gluttony**: The inordinate desire to consume more than that which one requires.
4. **Lust**: The excessive craving for the pleasures of the body.
5. **Anger**: The desire manifested in the individual who spurns love and opts instead for fury. It is also known as Wrath.
6. **Greed**: The desire for material wealth or gain, ignoring the realm of the spiritual. It is also called Avarice or Covetousness.
7. **Sloth**: The avoidance of physical or spiritual work.

The spread follows like this:

1. **Pride:** What in myself do I pride myself in? Why am I prideful?
2. **Envy:** What do I envy in others? Why do I envy others?
3. **Gluttony:** What do I desire excessively? Why do I desire this excessively?
4. **Lust:** What do I lust after? Why do I lust for the things I do?
5. **Anger:** What makes me angry? Why do I become angry?
6. **Greed:** What am I greedy for? Why do I become greedy?
7. **Sloth:** What spiritual work am I avoiding? Why do I avoid spiritual work?

THE SEVEN HEAVENLY VIRTUES

The seven heavenly virtues spread is a mix of the four cardinal virtues from Greek philosophy and the three theological virtues from Christianity. These seven virtues balance out the seven deadly sins. The virtues are as follows. They are listed in order matching with the sins above.

1. **Chastity**: purity, honesty, and embracing moral wholesomeness.
2. **Temperance**: Self-control/restraint. Moderation from excess. Prudence in judgments.
3. **Charity**: Generosity/sacrifice. Noble actions and love towards others.
4. **Diligence**: Productive work ethic, persistence, your efforts and convictions.
5. **Patience**: Enduring the unbearable through patience. Forgiving others and offer mercy.
6. **Kindness**: Compassion and friendship without prejudice, bias, or spite.
7. **Humility**: Modest behavior. Selflessness, thinking of yourself less and more about others. Faithfulness to your promises.

The spread for the virtues:

1. **Chastity:** What do I need to be more honest about or how do I be more honest?
2. **Temperance:** What needs moderation in my life or how can I practice moderation?
3. **Charity:** What do I need to be generous with or how can I spread love to others?
4. **Diligence:** What must I not give up on or how do I stay diligent?
5. **Patience:** What requires more patience or how do I endure the unbearable?
6. **Kindness:** What prejudice do I hold or how do I remove prejudice?
7. **Humility:** What ways can I be more modest or how do I put others before me?

PLATO'S SOUL SPREAD

In Platonic philosophy, there are three parts that constitute the soul: *Logos* (The Rational), the *Thymos* (The Spirited), and *Eros* (The Appetitive).

Logos represents our mind and reasoning (intellect, thinking). This part of the soul seeks truth and knowledge.

Thymos represents our emotion, spiritedness, and the masculine aspect. It is the part of the soul where you find temper and anger. This part of the soul seeks power, honor, and fame. It is our ambitious aspect.

Eros represents desire, our physical needs (appetitive), and is the feminine aspect. This part of the soul seeks to satisfy its present needs. Instant gratification is the most primitive and animalistic part of the soul.

To understand what your soul is feeling and the advice it has to give you regarding a particular situation, you can pull one card for each aspect of the soul.

1. **Logos**: The rational thing, the truth of the matter—what can be learned?
2. **Thymos**: The motivation behind everything—what do you seek to gain?
3. **Eros**: The self-gratification aspect—what do you desire right now, the thing that should be controlled or limited.

ANGELO'S THREE CARDS

For a simple and fast reading, simply pull three cards. The catch is that there are no positional meanings. Look at the cards and see what story is being created from them. Imagine that the cards are blurred into one another, creating one image. What story arises? This method requires you to see the cards as interacting with one another. Pay attention. Here are some things to look for and ask yourself.

- Are the cards facing in the same direction? Looking right can denote movement forward, looking to the future. Looking to the left shows thinking of the past.
- Look at the middle card. How important does it look? Sometimes the middle card can represent the significant energy while the outside cards support or hinder this middle card.
- Opposition or Agreement. Do the cards agree or disagree with one another? Is there an agreement between the card's meaning (do they share similar qualities) or are the cards at odds with one another? Why? How does the interplay manifest?
- Is there balance in the cards? Look at the outer cards and their relation to the middle card.
- Are there any parings appearing? Who is the odd man out? One card may appear out of place next to the other two cards. Why? How does this affect things?

ANGELO'S THREE CARDS EXPANDED

This is an expanded version of my three-card reading, which uses the three main cards without positional meanings and adds four cards on top.

1-2-3. **The dynamic of the situation.**
4. **Your feelings**: the subjective aspect, feelings, and emotions.
5. **Your mind**: the objective aspect, thoughts, and reason.
6. **Challenge**: what blocks you, and the problem.
7. **Advice:** how to overcome this.
8. **Outcome**.

WHEEL OF FORTUNE

This spread is another expanded version of my three-card spread. Pull three cards and place them in a row. The three cards have no positional meanings. The remaining cards are placed in the circle around the three cards with positional meanings. The spread is based off The Wheel of Fortune, which shows influences present, fading, missing, and rising.

1-2-3. **The dynamic of the situation.**
4. **High Influence:** What is most strong now and presently impacting the situation.
5. **Fading Influence:** What is weakening and losing influence over the situation.
6. **Absent Influence:** What is lacking and or what you need to remove.
7. **Rising Influence**: What is entering into the situation or what you need to add.

WEIGHING OPTIONS

Have you ever had to choose between two or more options? How do you decide? As children, we are often taught that a good way to solve this problem is making a list of pros and cons of both sides to come to a conclusion. This spread helps you foresee which options will be best by peeking at the long-term pros and cons that you may not know about in the present. For example, you have two job offers. Which one is best?

1. Pros of options one.
2. Pros of option two.
3. Cons of options one.
4. Cons of option two.
5. Long-term results option one.
6. Long-term results of option two.

PROBLEM SOLVING

Use this spread to help you solve problems.

1. The problem (as it really is).
2. What can be changed.
3. What cannot be changed.
4. Other options.
5. Guidance; next steps to take.

P.E.A.C.E

The following spread is an adaptation from a philosophical counseling technique from Lou Marinoff's book *Plato Not Prozac! Applying Eternal Wisdom to Everyday Problems*.

P.E.A.C.E, according to Marinoff, is a five-step process for dealing with problems in philosophical counseling. The acronym stands for the following: **P**roblem, **E**motion, **A**nalysis, **C**ontemplation, and **E**quilibrium.

Step One (Problem): In the first step, identify the problem at hand. Put into words and create a clear understanding of what the problem is.

Step Two (Emotion): This step examines your emotional reaction; what emotion(s) you are expressing and experiencing from the problem.

Step Three (Analysis): In this step, evaluate your options for solving the problem. In this stage, it is best to find a solution that will settle both the problem and your emotions.

Step Four (Contemplation): In this step, contemplate your philosophical position on the matter.

Step Five (Equilibrium): In the final step, take an appropriate and justifiable action.

Once I saw this process, I felt that it would make a good Tarot spread. The more I read about philosophical counseling, the more I feel a strong resonation between it and Tarot. Below is the spread based on this method:

1. **Identifying the problem:** If you know the problem already, select a card from the deck that represents it, or, if it is unknown, let Tarot reveal it to you.
2. **Expressing Emotion:** How is this problem making you feel? What emotion needs to be properly expressed and experienced?
3. **Analysis:** What are your options for finding a solution that addresses both the problem and your emotion?
4. **Contemplation:** Use this card to reflect and contemplate your personal philosophies, ethics, values, and beliefs. Where does this card align with these aspects? Maybe there is an alternative that you have not considered.
5. **Equilibrium:** This card reveals the appropriate and justifiable action to take.

THE CELTIC CROSS

The classic Celtic Cross spread is a treasured spread by many readers. It took me some time to find the usefulness of the Celtic Cross; it was when I read Joan Bunning's *Learning The Tarot* that I finally understood it. The backbone of how I teach the Celtic Cross is based on Joan's methodology.

This spread is divided into two sections: the *Cross* and *Staff*.

1. Traditionally called "that which covers you." This card represents the heart of the issue, is also a primary factor (dominate, major feature). It can be the present environment or is either internal (mental/emotional) or external (environmental, people, etc.). This card will often reveal what is going on at the moment as well as the issue at hand.

2. Traditionally called "that which is crossing you." This card represents the influence of factor, which either is an opposition, or reinforcement of the primary card. This second card can help or hinder the first card depending on the first card. Ask yourself if these two cards are similar or different and how so. The second card can also represent a secondary issue after the primary.

3. Traditionally called "that which is beneath you." This card represents what may be the root cause of the situation. This card explains why the situation is the way it is. Also, this card can reveal what motives or actions are going on in the unconscious.

4. This card reveals influences from the past that lead you to where you are now. This can be people, thoughts, actions, hopes, fears, events, etc. The past card can represent factors that have been resolved. The past card can also advise you about what you should release.

5. Traditionally called "what could come into being," this card can represent other options or possibilities for the future. This card represents your goals regarding the issue. This card can also represent your mind, what you are thinking and focused on. This card represents the conscious mind and what you are aware of.

6. This card represents influences that will be important in the future. This can be people, thoughts, actions, hopes, fears, events, etc. The future card can represent things which have been left open and unresolved, as well as things which should be embraced.

7. Traditionally called, "you as you see yourself," this card represents how you see yourself in relation to the issue, self-image, your sense of self, and you as you present yourself to others.

8. Traditionally called, "how others see you," this card represents other people's views or an outsider's view on the situation other than your own. It shows another point of view. This card can also reveal the environment you are surrounded by.

9. Traditionally called, "hopes and fears," this card represents that which you hope for or are fearful of happening. This can be ideal dreams or inner demons. This card can also represent advice.
10. Outcome; the end result of the situation.

New Love

A helpful spread when starting a new relationship.

1. What you bring to the relationship.
2. What the other person is bringing to the relationship.
3. Will you be happy in this relationship?
4. Will the other person be happy in this relationship?
5. What supports the relationship?
6. What hinders the relationship?
7. Will the relationship last or is there a long-term outcome?

Dream Interpretation

The following spread comes from *Tarot & Dream Interpretation* by Julie Gillentine. This is a three-card spread called the Levels of the Mind.

1. **Subconscious message:** this is the foundation of the reading. This may represent the meaning of the dream.
2. **Conscious awareness:** this indicates what you may be aware of, what may block or help you.
3. **Super conscious guidance:** higher influences on a spiritual level.

The Relationship and Its Qualities

This spread is from *The Tarot Bible* by Sarah Barlett. This spread is to be used as a way to understand the relationship at the time of the reading. Sarah writes that this spread reveals the dynamics and mechanics of the relationship. She also recommends that you use the Major Arcana only for a deeper exploration of these factors. You can do this if you want or use the whole deck.

1. Its energy.
2. Its communication.
3. Its strength.
4. Its weakness.
5. Its reality.
6. Its passion.
7. Its key to the future.

The Looking Glass Spread

This is a spread designed to explore your psyche using the theme of a looking glass or mirror. It is a wonderful introspective spread.

1. Holding the glass (Foundation); what I have brought into this moment of my life.
2. Dark glass image (Dark Self); flaws I need to address.
3. Bright glass image (Bright Self); potential I need to use.
4. Breaking the glass (Obstacles); what do I hang on to that I need to shatter so I can move on?
5. Looking into the glass (Perception); how I see myself.
6. Looking out of the glass (Others); how I see others.
7. Mirror, mirror on the wall (Advice); the final piece of advice.

James Well's Zero to Twenty-One

Many thanks go to James Well for contributing this spread for my book. This spread is useful when examining your journey through a particular situation or goal that you have. It requires only the Major Arcana cards; separate the Majors from the rest of the deck and follow these steps:

1. Articulate what you want to explore. One of these questions may be helpful to you:

   - What does my journey though [name situation] look like?
   - What does my journey to [name goal] look like?

2. Mix the twenty-two Major Arcana cards while reflecting on your question.
3. Without disturbing the order of the cards, turn the pack over so you can see the images face up. Look for the Fool (0) and The World (XXI) cards.
4. Lay out The Fool and The World cards and all the cards that are between them in a row in the order in which you found them. Place The Fool to the left of the row and The World to the right, at the end.
5. Allow the sequence of cards from left to the right to suggest a story to you. You might even begin with, "Once upon a time…"
6. Summarize the story: "This is a story about…" Then apply the summary to your situation or goal.
7. Allow each card in the row to be steps in, or strategy for, the journey. The order of the cards from left to right in the sequence indicate the steps and/or experiences.
8. Summarize the reading: "What I understand the cards to be saying is…"

If The Fool and The World turn up immediately beside another, the experience is brief, but intense. The beginning and ending might even be simultaneous. The more cards that show up between The Fool and The World, the more steps are to be taken, requiring more time and less intensity.

Sample Readings

News/Media Readings

Practice makes perfect, as people always say. Practicing Tarot readings can be fun. This is because Tarot is flexible to your style, how you want to read, and in what ways you choose to accomplish it. Normally, people practice Tarot by either reading for themselves or for other people. These two methods are great, but for some people, they can't read for others because they keep their Tarot interests hidden. Many people hide their love for Tarot because of the fear that people will react critically if they knew. There are also only so many times you can read for yourself without becoming bored and there is only so much you can read on other people you know. On the other hand, there are plenty of other ways to practice Tarot. For instance, you can do readings on events in the news or media as a way to practice. Why is this a good method? Because as events play out in the media, you can follow along and see how your reading pans out. You can make predictions and see if they come true and, if not, you can possibly see how you misinterpreted things. It is a good way to learn without having to involve other people. You can say what you want in the reading, which allows you to test your intuitive abilities.

I will show you examples of readings I have done in the past that were about events in the news, so you can see how accurate they can be, but more importantly, how you can learn from any mistakes in interpretations you may make.

Super Bowl Predictions

One of my favorite things to do is predictive readings of sporting events like the Super Bowl. I am not a football fan, but I like making predictions on the big game. The following are my predictions from 2007 through 2013 for the Super Bowl. Every year the spread I chose was not exactly the same, so please forgive the inconsistency.

2007—Colts vs. Bears

In this prediction I pulled two cards for each team. I pulled one card for "Who has a better chance at winning" and one card for "Who will win?" The following are my original readings.

Who has a better chance at winning?
Colts: Nine of Swords Reversed.

> This looked good. When reversed, this card would say troubles, anxiety, and worries will be lifted and calmness will be restored. So during the Super Bowl, we might have seen the Colts in a bad spot and everyone would think that they would lose, but all that would change later on. Their hope and faith would give them a good upper hand. But would it be enough to win?

Who will win?
Colts: Ace of Swords.

> This looked to be a good card. I would say this card would be yes, but let's look into the card. This card speaks about analyzing and cutting through the mist and confusion. Thinking clearly and acting with reason. This is good when playing a sport. The clearer your mind, the better the decisions you make.

Who has better chance at winning?
Bears: Knight of Pentacles reversed.

> I would say that the Bears would not have things too well-planned out. They may have tried rushing things, all the while not really working well together as a team. Thus, this was not a good thing.

Who will win?
Bears: Six of Swords.

> This looked like they were defeated and accepting it and just learning from their mistakes for improving themselves in the future. This card indicated "Low point"—sadness and the "Blues."

My prediction from this reading was that the Colts would win. Mainly because I felt that the Ace of Swords was a sign of victory and that you could clearly see that the Six of Swords for the Bears was not good. By comparing both cards, looking at what you should expect to see from the winners, you will know who will win.

Sometimes it might be harder if you get cards that may not be as cut and dry as this. Go with your gut and with what looks like a "winner." The Colts did win.

2008—Giants vs. Patriots

Who has a better chance at winning?
New York Giants: Queen of Swords.

Who will win?
New York Giants: Four of Pentacles.

> These two cards combined showed to me clear and clever thinking with reasonable actions on stable grounds. Good plans and plays should be made. We have Air and Earth elements here. I felt clear thinking with stable roots.

Who has a better chance at winning?
New England Patriots: Two of Wands.

Who will win?
New England Patriots: Queen of Wands.

> These two cards showed me that they were thinking fresh and feeling like "we have it in our hands" as though they had already won. The fact that these two cards were of the Wands suit element Fire showed that they would play with a lot of energy. But how long could fire burn without it losing control or focus?

It's funny how both teams got a Queen card. This can show very different qualities between the two teams. These Queens reflect the action of thought and reason and the action of confidence and passion. I felt that the Giants had a great chance, because they seemed to have a good stable ground. They would have a good mindset and well thought-out plan. But will stubbornness be their downfall? If the time comes where their plan starts to fall apart, will they adapt or "stay the course?" If the Patriots win, it will be because of their new visions, fire, and energy. But like I said before, how long can the fire burn? How long can they be positive and confident? This year, it was very hard for me to make my choice as I felt it was very close or even. But I wanted to say Giants.

I was unsure with this reading, but when I had to pick one, I picked the Giants and, no, it's not because I am a New Yorker. I did not care who won. I just felt that Swords were a better element than fire in that situation. Like I said, the Patriots may have had the fire, but it might not have been enough.

This is a good example of a reading that is not as clear as to who will win. Nothing really screams to you, "HEY I AM THE WINNER." Intuition comes in handy and I was right. The Giants did win.

2009—Steelers vs. Cardinals

In this year's prediction, I pulled only one card for each team instead of two as in the prior years.

Who has a Better chance at winning?
Pittsburgh Steelers: Six of Wands.

The Six of Wands has a keyword of "victory" and would fit well when trying to find who would win and be victorious. Clearly, this was a sign that the Steelers would win.

Who has a Better chance at winning?
Arizona Cardinals: The Tower.

The Cardinals think they will win, but their false ideas would fall apart and they would be shocked. They would lose.

This is a perfect example of a clear cut-and-dry reading. The Six of Wands, without any doubt is a winner and the Tower represents downfall (failure). I predicted the Steelers would win and yes, they did.

2010—Saints vs. Colts

In 2010, I did not write out this reading in my blog. Instead, I made a video on YouTube for my prediction. Like in the previous year, I pulled only one card for each team.

Who has a better chance at winning?
Saints: Ace of Swords.

Who has a better chance at winning?
Colts: King of Wands.

My prediction from this reading was that the Saints would win, because the Ace of Swords is associated with victory. I did not realize until now as I am writing this that the Colts had the Ace of Swords back in 2007.

So twice now, the Ace of Swords has been proven to be a good sign for victories. Knowing this, I knew that the Saints would win. I ignored the King of Wands because I did not feel it "trumped" the Ace of Swords. If it had been another card that trumped the Ace of Swords, such as The Sun or The World, then I would have gone with the other team. The Saints won.

2011—Steelers vs. Packers

I pulled one card for each team, asking if they would win.

The Green Bay Packers: Ten of Wands.
The Steelers: Ten of Cups.

The Ten of Wands is known as the "Lord of oppression" and the Ten of Cups is known as "Lord of Perfected Success." Looking at the esoteric titles alone signals that the winner would be the Steelers. The Ten of Wands for the Green Bay Packers being "oppression" may have signaled that they would be challenged by the Steelers and oppressed. This was the first year where my prediction was incorrect. The Packers won the Super Bowl.

2012—Patriots vs. Giants

I pulled two cards, one for each team.

Patriots: The Tower.
Giants: King of Pentacles.

The Tower in situations like this will indicate failure and ruin as it did when the Tower came up for the Cardinals when they went to the Super bowl against the Steelers. I saw that Giants would win the 2012 Super bowl. This year, I was correct.

Celebrities

Celebrities occupy the news headlines, sometimes more often than is needed. However, readings on celebrities are a good way to practice your Tarot skills because you can follow the story as it develops in the media and see if the reading was right or wrong.

Here are readings I did on celebrities. Most of these readings are on celebrity deaths. (Sorry for the morbidity.) These deaths are often highly publicized, which makes it easy to follow the development and see how the reading matches up.

Anna Nicole Smith

Anna Nicole Smith was an American model, sex symbol, actress, and television personality. She died February 8, 2007, from a drug overdose. At the time, her death was the talk of the town. Her son died in September of 2006, five months before her and four days after she gave birth to her daughter. There were the rumors, allegations, topics of who said what, and what role did who play? What was the cause? Was she murdered? Who was the real father of her newborn baby, Dannielyn? I decided to do a reading on these issues to see what Tarot had to tell me. This is the original reading:

What killed Anna?
Card: The Devil.

> This was speaking loud and clear that the biggest influence on her death was drugs. In this case, The Devil is about addictions and drug abuse. On a non-psychical sense this card would say her loss of hope and faith and her depression (from the death of her son) killed her. I am not saying that she overdosed, though she may have. But if it was, let's say suffocation caused her death, but the drugs led to the suffocation; the drugs were the roots of this.
>
> Some readers might see this card as a negative relationship, that the foundations are not based on good things: like materialism, sex, money, etc. Or a relationship that is codependent in a negative way. I can see how the relationship between Anna and Howard is codependent. She needed him to satisfy her need for love and to have someone truly care for her. Howard may have needed her just for the money and all the material perks. So this all goes back to the relationship they had that killed her.

The influence over her death.
Card: Knight of Pentacles reversed.

> The media had been pointing to the husband Howard K. Stern and questioning his role in her death and the death of her son. This knight could represent Howard or some other man. Did he play a role? I didn't know and I wouldn't point my finger at anyone. Let the cards speak for themselves. If the death was planned and was murder, this card would indicate it was not planned out well and that the mistakes and errors would show sooner or later.

Who is the Father of the baby?

I pulled one card for each man involved.

Howard got The Magician reversed.
Larry got Four of Cups reversed.

The Magician reversed is said by many Tarot readers and myself to be a liar, con-artist, and "fast talker." So I felt that Howard was lying and was not the father. Larry got the Four of Cups reversed, which did not look promising. He may have been doing things just to gain attention or he could have been trying to expose the truth and change the way things were and how he was being cut off from his daughter. The media speculated that neither man was the father and that there was a third person. This could have been a highly likely possibility. As it turned out, Larry was the father.

What role did Howard play in Anna's death?
Card: The Chariot.

This card could imply that Howard was controlling Anna to do what he felt was the right thing to do, rather than what Anna wanted. This did not imply direct influence on her death, but he was a factor.

This reading highlighted some truths to the issue, as I could see them at the time and to my knowledge of the cards. It is reported from the official autopsy report that Anna died due to a drug overdose of the sedative chloral hydrate that became increasingly lethal when combined with other prescription drugs in her system. When asked about who the father of the baby was, the Tarot was 100% clear that Howard was not the father. However, I was confused with the Four of Cups reversed for Larry. Media reports influenced my thoughts on the issue, but my second reaction was the correct one, which should have been my first thought.

As you can see, this reading is a good example of how you can practice reading for issues in the media. Just be careful as to how the media impacts you. It is okay to be wrong or miss something. This is practice. You will learn from these readings. I look back at them now and learn.

Amy Winehouse

On July 23, 2011, British singer Amy Winehouse was discovered dead in her home at the age of twenty-seven. After hearing the news, I pulled out my deck and pulled three cards to see what the Tarot had to say about the influences and energies surrounding her death. At the time, no one knew what caused it. Drugs and alcohol were rumored to be the cause. Amy Winehouse was well known to have substance abuse problems and has been in and out of rehab many times.

Cards: King of Swords, Knight of Pentacles, and Eight of Cups.

We have two court cards: King of Swords and Knight of Pentacles. This can mean there were two people connected to her death or were significant in some form. As the investigation unfolded, this would make more sense. The Eight of Cups reflected her personally: her feelings and the main energy of her death. What I felt that the Eight of Cups was representing here was isolation, drained of energy, and burnout, lacking hope and letting go. It was an interesting card.

Cups can reflect addictions and drugs. Here, the Eight of Cups shows being drained and lacking energy and hope. Amy at her time of death was most likely weak and tired. This card is also about letting go and moving on, which makes me feel that Amy somehow, could have subconsciously known it was her time or she wanted to "move on," making me feel that intentional death by drug overdose was a possibility. This was a sad card and really represented her emotional state at the time. She might have been thinking about the deeper meaning to life, which is what the Eight of Cups shows a need to understand. She may have lost hope that there was more to life.

It was later reported that Amy had died alone in her bed, which reflects the isolation and loneliness of the Eight of Cups.

Conan O'Brien & The Tonight Show

In 2009, NBC removed Jay Leno as the host of their popular late-night talk show *The Tonight Show* and gave "Late-night" host Conan O'Brien the promotion to *Tonight Show* host. However, he was removed only a few months later to have Jay Leno put back after his failed attempt at prime time. It was big news in the entertainment industry. They were trying to work a deal out with Conan to keep him on NBC and have Jay on as well. There were time-slot speculations: would they move Conan an hour back and give Jay a later time slot? Either way, it was a mess. Conan's future was unclear, so I wanted to see what Tarot had to say. The following is a three-card reading I did:

Ace of Pentacles
Eight of Cups Reversed
Strength

I feel a strong possibility may be that Conan could leave NBC if they do not let him stay at his current time slot.

Ace of Pentacles shows new openings and avenues for money, another job offer.

Eight of Cups reversed shows him rejecting options presented to him by NBC (being put at 12:05 a.m. or any other suggestion).

The Strength card shows that his final action will take a lot of courage and strength to make. Leaving NBC will be a very hard thing to do and will take a lot of inner strength to make this decision.

This reading was 100% correct: Conan left NBC and, after a few months away from television, he was offered to host his own show on TBS.

In the News

The following readings were done for tragic events in the media. Both deal with gun violence. The reason I read for these topics was because of their cultural impact. They are non-trivial events that I wanted to use to test Tarot's ability to be used on heavy topics. In such events, we really learn how to apply Tarot cards to issues in which a Tarot reader many never face in a client reading.

Virginia Tech

On Monday, April 16, 2007, a student at the Virginia Tech University killed thirty-two people and injured many others. The student was Seung-Hui Cho, who had immigrated to the USA with his family at the age of eight. He had incidences with professors in college and students recount odd behaviors. Basically, he was disturbed and did not receive any help.

This event was a tragedy and true horror. Issues of this nature can push Tarot to its limits and push you as a reader to your limits. Can you handle the hard issues? How do you react to such horrible violence and senseless murder of innocent lives? I posted an entry on my blog about this incident. It was very hard for me to write that blog entry; my heart hurt and I cried for those families who had to be told their son or daughter had been killed while at college. This reading focuses on why the student did what he did and what repercussions this event may have on laws regarding firearms.

Concerning the shooter, I wanted to focus on the issues that were affecting him. The card I got for that was the Nine of Cups.

At first, it made no sense, because this is a "good card," but something just hit me while I was typing this entry. As many Tarot readers know, the Nine of Cups is the "wish card," and I would have to say, he wished this to happen; he had wanted to do this for a long time; and this was the one thing he desired. The thought that someone would wish for this, would cause so much pain, it hurts me. The Nine of Cups is also a card of satisfaction—killing people would give this man some sort of satisfaction. This, to me, is horrifying. The shooter sent NBC a package in the mail of a video of him talking. In one part, he says, "Your Mercedes wasn't enough, you brats... Your golden necklaces weren't enough, you snobs. Your trust funds wasn't enough. Your vodka and cognac wasn't enough. All your debaucheries weren't enough. Those weren't enough to fulfill your hedonistic needs. You had everything." All the things he listed are indicated in the Nine of Cups. He focused on all the material things the people at his school had and the "lust for more." Also, he mentions "debaucheries." The Nine of Cups, incidentally, can indicate debauchery when ill-dignifed.

How will this incident affect the federal government—Ace of Swords Reversed.

This card means that any attempt to change gun regulations on a federal level will fail or that changes made will not be the best ones. The reversal of this ace means error in judgment, so I see this as people making bad judgments on the issue. Thus, if the federal government makes no changes, then that's an error in judgment, in my interpretation of the card. If the energy of this ace is blocked, then we may see changes, but very slow changes.

How will this affect the state governments? The Judgment card.

I think that this is the wake-up call to tell the states to get up and start making some changes! The Judgment card is a good sign for progression. It is acknowledgment of changes that need to be made. So I say that we will see some states making changes in their gun laws. And like with most things, the more states that get involved, the more it will impact the federal government.

This was a tough reading to do, but I did it, hoping to gain something from it and to see if anything would change due to the tragedy. I also wanted to get in the mind of the shooter to see why he did it. This reading provided mainly a learning experience. I was touching on a subject that is difficult and, for some...they might not even go near it. I was also exposed to the Nine of Cups in a light that shocked me.

Arizona Representative Gabrielle Giffords

On January 8, 2011, in Tucsan, Arizona, there was an attempted assassination of Congresswoman Gabrielle Giffords. Twenty people were shot during the incident, six of whom died. Mrs. Giffords survived the gunshot to her head. Jared Lee Loughner was identified as the shooter. I wanted to do a reading on this event to understand why it happened, if Rep. Giffords would be all right, and what impact this event would have on politics. I did the following reading:

What promoted this shooting? I pulled the Ace of Swords.

> I ask this question to see why Loughner did what he did. Some keywords to the Ace of Swords are authority, intellect, obsession, and bravery. I do feel that this Ace of Swords is ill dignified, thus giving us the key words: injustice, tyranny, and instability. The news reports that Loughner held radical views on politics and religion. On his YouTube page, he is reported as saying, "don't have to accept the federalist laws," and accusing the government of brainwashing and mind controlling the American people. So far we can see the Ace of Swords in all of this, especially when ill dignified. He possibly views the government as tyrannical and unjust. Loughner was suspended from college due to complaints from classmates. They told Loughner that if he wanted to come back to the college, he would need to undergo mental evaluation. This correlates to the instability of the ill-dignified Ace of Swords. Loughner did what he did because he believed he was conducting an act of bravery (Ace of Swords) in the face of a government he saw as unjust. His actions may have been an act of rebellion against authority. It may also be an act of him trying to exert his personal authority onto others. Obsession is a keyword to the Ace of Swords. Loughner may have been obsessed with Gabrielle Giffords. It is reported that at an event three years prior, Loughner asked Gabrielle Giffords a question. According to two of his high school friends, the question was essentially this: "What is government if words have no meaning?" Loughner was angry about her response. She read the question and had nothing to say. According to these high school friends, "the question was classic Jared: confrontational, nonlinear, and obsessed with how words create reality." We see how the Ace of Swords relates to how his obsession with words (an aspect of Swords) created reality.

I am very optimistic that she will be fine. The Three of Cups is a card of celebration. She should get better, which will be cause for joy and celebration. She did recover in the end.

There was a website created by Sarah Palin with an image of the USA and cross-hair icons to denote "targeted" congressional seats. Gabrielle Giffords was one of those targeted seats. In 2010, after her office had been vandalized, Giffords had said:

We're in Sarah Palin's "targeted" list, but the thing is that the way she has it depicted, we're in the cross hairs of a gun sight over our district. When people do that, they've got to realize that there are consequences to that action.

The Three of Wands deals with what we have put into action, waiting on the results to see if what we put out will bring a return. Certainly, this buys into the idea of cause and effect. It has often been shown that politicians may say and do things that have negative cause and effect upon others. Further, it is likely that they do not take into consideration the consequences resulting from their actions. This then spurs individuals, like Loungher, who may not be able to understand the ideologies, to react with deadly force. This incident has brought some very heated discussion in politics. Both parties have called for a cooling off of political rhetoric.

TAROT EXPANDED

Education and Certification

Tarot and education and certification comes up every once in a while as an issue of discussion. I read a forum post from someone asking if a reader needs an education to read Tarot professionally. If so, what kind? Education is very important just as a general rule in life. However, when we approach education in Tarot there are mixed opinions. There are two ways of looking at this: the first is traditional education through college and the second is an independent education through courses/ programs specific to learning Tarot.

There are no college courses or degrees designed to teach you Tarot. If you want to incorporate a college education into your Tarot practice, there are certain degrees that can assist you and make you a well-rounded reader. They are as follows:

Psychology
A very popular degree option, psychology can provide you with a foundation for understanding the dynamics of the mind. Learning psychology will give you insights into personality theory, behavior, mental development, addictions, mental disorders, and more. These are good things to learn when doing Tarot. Tarot is not the same as a counseling and unless you are a licensed therapist you should not use Tarot as therapy. Transpersonal Psychology (spiritual psychology) integrates the spiritual and transcendent aspects of the human experience with the framework of modern psychology. This modality can be very helpful for a Tarot reader.

Sociology
Like psychology, sociology gives you insights into human behaviors, but looks specifically to the role of society and how it influences people. People who study sociology often become social workers (requiring a masters in social work). These people can do counseling when licensed by the state.

Philosophy/Religious Studies

This is my area of interest. I love philosophy and religious studies. Philosophy is often overshadowed by psychology in the Tarot world. However, philosophy has so much to offer the Tarot reader. Studying philosophy gives you a background in understanding some of the biggest questions that have ever been asked. What is the meaning of life? What am I here for? Ethics, logic, epistemology, metaphysics, and so much more is covered in philosophy. These areas of study can benefit you as a reader because philosophy can be applied in a Tarot reading. Many of the philosophical teachings can be found in the cards themselves, which gives you a deeper understanding of those cards. You can also apply these teachings as advice to your clients.

In religious studies, how does learning about religion apply to Tarot? Like philosophy, religious ideas are represented in the cards. So, once again, you gain a deeper understanding. Depending on the school, religion may be classified as a social science degree, in line with sociology and psychology. When studying religion you are studying people, their culture, ideas, and beliefs. As a Tarot reader, you encounter different people from different walks of life, and knowing about their religion is important. You understand their background and belief system. You would not necessarily talk about reincarnation to a Christian, but you would with a Hindu.

A formal education would be a wonderful thing to have, but is not essential for a professional reader—unless you will have a specific career (psychologist, for example) and will be conducting Tarot in conjunction with it (using the Tarot in counseling, for example), then you would need education/training/licensing. If your goal is to just be a Tarot reader, you could participate in independent study and could even audit college courses, if desired (which is cheaper, but you would not gain credit towards a degree).

Education specific to Tarot, such as a Tarot course/certification or training can be beneficial, but again is not essential. Many Tarot readers are self-taught and never go to any sort of class. However, as the Tarot gains popularity and with the accessibility of the Internet, it is easier than ever to learn Tarot in a formal setting. Some people enjoy the structure of a class and would benefit from taking a course. Education is always a good thing—you simply need to ask yourself if it is right for you, do you have the time and the money to invest in your Tarot practice? If you want to be a professional reader, consider it.

This now leads us to Tarot certification. Over the years, organizations have formed to offer certificates to Tarot readers after completing a training course. People are divided over this. Do we need certification? I do not think we need it, nor does any law require a reader to be certified. Clients hardly ask if a reader is certified, they don't care. Certification is solely for the reader, it provides them a way to develop their skills in a structured setting. It should be noted that organizations offering this kind of training are not accountable to any outside evaluation for their programing or materials as with an accredited college or trade school. In addition, having certifications can cause a divide between readers who are certified and not certified. This can lead to caste-system type scenarios.

Taboos

Fortunetelling

Over the years, fortunetelling has become somewhat of a taboo subject in the Tarot community. Many readers have discouraged the usage of the terms "fortuneteller" and "fortunetelling." It has come to a point where these words are demeaning and some are deeply offended when they are called this. Instead, there are alternative titles promoted, such as "advisor," "spiritual counselor," or "consultant." Some, though, embrace the title "fortuneteller" with pride.

Where did this attitude come from? Why are readers reluctant to call themselves fortunetellers or say what they do is fortunetelling? It could be a response to the many reports of fraudulent readers who scam large sums of money from people. It is the unethical readers who use the Tarot to scam people who are giving readers a bad reputation. In response, ethical readers have to present themselves as professional, ethical, and legitimate. This is achieved by dissociation with any terms that may give a less-than-desired picture of what a Tarot reader does.

Using alternative titles like "advisor" or "counselor" does not carry the same negative associations as fortuneteller. When someone hears "advisor," they think of someone who is going to give advice and help you. "Counselor" brings to mind a therapeutic image, but we must always be up front and clear that we are not doing psychological counseling (unless qualified to do so).

I have come across some attitudes about fortunetelling giving reasons for avoiding the term:

- Fortunetelling is "telling a client what he or she already knows." This is untrue. Fortunetelling by definition is the foretelling of future events. Telling a client what they already know (the present) is not fortunetelling (future). Telling certain things about a client's present is a part of a Tarot reading for validation that a connection is made between the client and reader. Reading the present does not make you a fortuneteller.

- Fortunetelling is a "trick" to "wow" the client. Fortunetelling is not a trick. You should not aim to "wow" and put on a show for a client. If I do pick up on something "wow," that's nice, but not something that I actively try to obtain. However, the reading should provoke a "wow" that says, "Wow, that was a very insightful reading" or "Wow, that reading really helped me."

- Fortunetelling "isn't empowering." It is a misconception that fortunetelling is not empowering, because knowing the future removes free will. This is true if you believe in predestination, that the future is set in stone. However, many readers, including myself, believe that the future is more fluid and changeable. With this view, fortunetelling *can be* empowering. It depends on the client. If, for example, you are going through some problems in your life and the outcome card shows a positive outcome, then that is good. That is a cause for empowerment. Then there are those who may become lazy, thinking everything will be fine and get off track. Again, the future is fluid. Your actions create your future.

- Fortunetelling can cause "psychic codependence." True and untrue. Everyone is unique. We can't jump to conclusions. Psychic codependence can be found in individuals with addictive personalities or insecurities. These people will become addicted to many things. Tarot is one possible thing. Someone who is codependent on Tarot or on people who are psychics is known as a "psychic junkie." These people typically either have little control in their lives or feel insecure about their future and choices. They feel they must get a reading to know what will happen. These people normally do not want advice, insight, and introspection. They only want to know the future. It is the responsibility of the reader to determine who they read for. I don't read for psychic junkies. You can't create a codependency if you don't supply the drug.

I feel that it is fine to use the word fortuneteller; it is all up to you regarding what you want to call yourself. The name is unimportant; it is your actions that are telling.

These arguments regarding calling one's self a fortuneteller are based on hasty generalizations. They are invalid arguments. It is improper to make generalizations, because everyone and every situation are unique. I also feel that the arguments are misplaced. Instead, these arguments should be directed toward fake and fraudulent readers.

Death Predictions

Using the Tarot to predict when someone will die is unethical. Tarot predicts death very rarely in readings and often indirectly from the question. Only two deaths have occurred in my experience with Tarot as an indirect outcome from the questions posed. You should not directly ask about death. If it is meant to come up in a reading, it will, but, again, it is very rare. The Death card, ninety-nine percent of the time, represents a metaphorical death of a situation or issue. Tarot will most likely point to a death that already occurred as an issue to be addressed in the reading.

THE MINOR ARCANA

The Minor Arcana is made up of fifty-six cards. They are grouped into four suits: Wands, Cups, Swords, and Pentacles. Each suit has pips titled ace through ten, as well as four court cards: Page, Knight, Queen, and King.

While the Major Arcana represents universal archetypes and major influences in our lives, the Minor Arcana represents the more mundane influences. They tell the story of our lives, our interactions with people, our hopes, dreams, fears, desires, anxieties, passions, conflicts, and talents. As well as showing us a wide spectrum of events that occur in life, the minors also represent the aspects in our lives we have more control over.

THE ACES

ACE OF CUPS
The Root of the Power of Water

Description

A hand extends forth from the sky, holding a golden cup with water springing from it. A dove descends from above into the chalice; below we see a large body of water with lily pads on the surface.

Symbolism and Meaning

The Ace of Cups embodies the beginning of new love and the first spark of attraction inside the heart. The flowing of water from the cup represents the flowing of emotions, expression of feelings, and openness of how you feel. This ace wants emotions and feelings to be shared; it does not like to be bottled up.

The esoteric title of the Ace of Cups is The Root of the Power of Water. This ace is connected to the element water. The main focus is love and romance. Outside of romantic relationships, the Ace of Cups represents how we connect with others: being open, loving, caring, and forgiving. It also suggests generosity and compassion. There is a strong connection to intuition here with the watery imagery. This card also suggests that you listen to your instincts. The dove descending into the chalice is seen as the Holy Spirit and the cup is representative of a vessel; with the two joining into one, this card can represent pregnancy, echoing Mary's conception of Jesus. The Ace of Cups also suggests healing and cleansing.

In a Reading

When the Ace of Cups appears in a reading, it can signal the spark of something new—as with all aces, a seed is planted. In life, you can experience the seed of the Ace of Cups as that first attraction to someone you meet. That first sign of desire, want, and love. The Ace of Cups advises you to open our hearts and express emotions. There are new opportunities awaiting you that may allow you to emotionally grow and develop.

When ill dignified, the Ace of Cups can represent an over-pouring of emotion, which can lead you to become emotionally dry. You may not be in touch with your spiritual side and closed off or shut down to your feelings.

ACE OF WANDS
The Root of the Powers of Fire

Description

A hand extends from the sky with a Wand firmly gripped. Leaves grow from the Wand. The landscape is open; trees are present, along with a river. There is a castle in the background.

Symbolism and Meaning

The Ace of Wands represents the beginning of new passions, inspirations, and life force. The Ace of Wands represents strong will, desire, and passion. There is a strong need to start new projects, new adventures, goals, and the like. The thumb is pointing upward as if it is a "thumbs up" from the universe. Go for it; just do it now.

The esoteric title of the Ace of Wands is The Root of the Power of Fire. This Ace is connected with the element of Fire, representing spontaneity, impulsiveness, and being forceful. Also, it is connected with confidence and courage. Being daring, energetic, and enthusiastic, there is a lot of optimism in this card. This Ace brings the gift of passion— about a cause, a goal, or a desire.

It also brings inspiration, being a visionary, and original. Leaves growing from the Wand represent life, energy, and growth. Taking a risk is suggested here.

While you are unsure of what will happen, the Ace suggests you take that risk, as it can lead to great adventure. The castle in the background represents the goal or aspiration to be attained.

In a Reading

When the Ace of Wands appears in a reading, it represents a seed of energy, power, and the potential for something to be created. If you cultivate the Ace of Wands properly, you will see a manifestation of the fire qualities.

When ill dignified, the Ace of Wands can either represent burnout, setbacks, powerlessness, lack of ambitions, and limited development or vision.

ACE OF SWORDS
The Root to the Powers of Air

Description

A hand extends from the sky, holding a sword. On the top of the sword is a golden crown with a two branches: one is an olive branch and the other is a palm tree branch. There are mountains in the background.

Symbolism and Meaning

The Ace of Swords represents the beginning of new ideas, thoughts, and concepts. New insights appear and are developed. New information becomes available as well as new solutions to issues.

The esoteric title of the Ace of Swords is The Root of the Power of Air. The element of this Ace is air, which is connected to matters of the mind, intellect, thoughts, and communication. The Ace of Swords cuts through right to the truth of the issue. The Ace of Swords is about clarity—seeing clearly and to the point. Along with this is the need for honesty and transparency.

The olive branch represents victory and the palm tree branch represents peace, joined together by the crown. The sword reflects our need to fight or bring peace. The Ace of Swords is connected to Justice, who holds a sword in the right hand and seeks to bring justice and fairness. The sword is a symbol of authority.

In a Reading

In a reading, when the Ace of Swords shows up, it can be a sign that you need to take control over the matter and bring direction to the issue. As a symbol of authority, it also represents facing challenges, not hiding from them. The Ace of Swords brings the gifts of logic, reason, and clarity, which aid in making choices.

When ill dignified, the Ace of Swords can be harsh and unfair. There can be confusion and lack of understanding. Something may be being kept secret. Authority can develop out of hand and become tyranny. There can also be distrust of others.

ACE OF PENTACLES
The Root of the Powers of Earth

Description

A hand extends from the sky with a golden coin in palm. Below is a garden with many plants. We also see a pathway and a gate.

Symbolism and Meaning

The Ace of Pentacles is the beginning of new opportunities for prosperity and physical wellbeing.

The esoteric title of the Ace of Pentacles is The Root of the Power of Earth. The element associated with Pentacles is earth, which represents growth, stability, the physical realm, money, possessions, and security. The Ace of Pentacles represents new opportunities regarding matters of career and money. It is the promise of continued wealth, growth, and expansion. Pentacles are the most physical and real of all the suits. The Ace of Pentacles represents the manifestation of what we desire in the material world. It is the only ace that is missing the Yods. The Yod is a Hebrew letter and is the first letter in the Tetragrammaton (four letter name of God); they signify the presence of the divine in the events that transpire in the cards. This ace is missing Yods, because the Pentacles represent the physical world, the lowest level, and the densest level.

The Ace of Pentacles, along with many of the Pentacles, deals with issues practically, playing it safe, being grounded, and looking toward the long-term goal. The Ace of Pentacles is about investments: what we invest ourselves into and what are our long term goals. It is the beginning of planning. The pathway to the gate represents that the next step after planning is taking action and walking out of the garden to create what we want. New business deals, contracts, jobs, promotions, salary increases—these are some of the things to be expected from the Ace of Pentacles.

In a reading, when the Ace of Pentacles appears, something new is bound to appear if you cultivate the Ace properly. You will need to plan and take the proper actions in order to reach your goals. Resources are at your disposal. You just need to tap into those connections you have.

When ill dignified, the Ace of Pentacles can represent misused money and resources. It can represent erroneous investments or decisions. Also, it can indicate greed and neediness, as well as materialism, loss, and failure.

THE TWOS

TWO OF CUPS
Esoteric Title: Lord of Love

Description

In a field, two lovers stand face-to-face, Cups in hand, reaching outward to the other. Above them are a winged lion and the Caduceus of Hermes.

Symbolism and Meaning

The Two of Cups is one of my favorite cards. What's magical about this card is its symmetry and harmony. Each figure in the card is equal in height and they are almost standing in the same positions. For this reason, this card is seen as the soulmate card. Two people are separate, but together are equal. A connection is being made here; the man on the right is extending his hand to the woman on the left. This is symbolic of reaching out, making a connection, courting, an offering, or a gift received.

The esoteric title of the Two of Cups is Lord of Love. In the Greek philosophical tradition, it is said that the force known as Eros (love/desire) is what unites the elements together. The Two of Cups represents this force. This is where we get the notion of unity in the Two of Cups.

In a Reading

In a reading, the Two of Cups represents agreements, seeing eye to eye, and understanding how the other person feels. This card is not about "me-me-me." It is about the other person. The questions you want to ask yourself are,

- Have I been listening to other people?
- Have I tried to take into consideration someone else's feelings?

Outside of love and romance, this card is about friendships and partnerships where there is mutual respect and equality among all. The winged lion and Caduceus of Hermes represents healing energy. On a deeper level this card can be seen as you looking into a mirror of self-reflection. Looking at surrounding cards may help reveal how you see yourself.

When ill dignified, the Two of Cups can represent rejection and separation (the opposite of unity). Instead of agreement, you have disagreements and arguments. Things have lost their harmony. Feelings may be tense between people. A partnership may have gone sour. Someone may be trying to gain dominance over the other instead of being equal.

TWO OF WANDS
Esoteric Title: Lord of Dominion

Description

A man stands alone behind a castle wall. He looks outward into the vast ocean before him, pondering possibilities. In his right hand, he holds a globe; his left hand holds firmly one of the two Wands.

Symbolism and Meaning

The Two of Wands is a card of envisioning the future, possibilities, dreaming of great adventures, and new worlds. The Two of Wands is reminiscent of Christopher Columbus. Understanding a little of Columbus will help to better understand this card. Columbus wanted to find an easier route to India, because the normal route was to follow the coastline of Africa all the way around the continent until he reached India. Columbus had an idea; he believed that if he sailed out west, he would come around to the other side of India. During this time, people did not know how vast the Atlantic was, or that it was not flat, and that he would not fall off. Columbus thought it was not as big as people thought and figured he could get to India in no time.

So how does this relate to the Two of Wands? Columbus had an idea, a vision, and he believed something that was true, but was not a commonly accepted belief. The Two of Wands suggests thinking outside the box, being different, and thinking differently. This card invites you to go out into the unknown; explore what has not been explored before.

As we see in the card, the man is facing left, looking out into the ocean. Behind him is a small town. This represents leaving what is known and safe to seek out that which is unknown. The Wand behind him is attached to the wall, while the Wand on his left, which he holds, is free to be moved. This represents our choice between that which is already established, or choosing to move onward and establish new grounds.

The esoteric title of the Two of Wands is Lord of Dominance, which tells us this card is about power, control, and will. All are Fire energy qualities. The Two of Wands indicates that you are in control and have the ability to make a change. As you see, the man holds the earth in his hand, which is symbolic of authority very much like The Emperor, who holds a golden globe.

In a Reading

In readings, the Two of Wands represents your inner power and self-reliance on your own capabilities. A strong desire to explore and create something of your own, this requires you to be visionary and to come up with new ideas to old problems—going against what is established and accepted by society, because that is how progress is made. It can also represent a choice between something safe versus something unknown.

When ill dignified, the Two of Wands can represent unrealistic ideas and plans. You may have big dreams but little ability to follow through with them. You may be limited in power or influence and feel put down by others. You may lack outside cooperation from others who are unwilling to help. You could also be lacking confidence.

TWO OF SWORDS
Esoteric Title: Lord of Peace Restored

Description

A blindfolded woman sits on a stone block. Two swords are in either hand, crossing each other in front of her chest. The scene is night; the crescent moon is up in the sky. Behind the woman is a large body of water with a mass of land in the distance.

Symbolism and Meaning

The Two of Swords represents our tendencies to replace intuition with intellect. As a result, you will end up with conflicts and indecisions. Swords are of the Air element, which deal with intellect. Two common symbols featured in the Two of Swords are water and the moon, representing intuition and emotion. Combining intellect (air) and emotions (water) does not work well with the Two of Swords. Your gut will tell you one thing while your brain is saying something else. You then become resistant to making any decision in fear of choosing incorrectly.

The woman is blindfolded, which, represented here, shows the inability to see clearly or not having any desire to see. The swords are crossing her chest; this is a sign that she is resisting change. The swords serve as a barrier between her emotion and her reason. This card represents our need to unite our intuition and intellect together, balancing the two, and coming to a conclusion.

The esoteric title of the Two of Swords is Lord of Peace Restored, which reveals to us that the Two of Swords represents momentary peace where a truce is established—in some cases, a stalemate where either side cannot progress. The Two of Swords can also be stagnation, as no movement is presented in the card. It can signify that you still yourself and become calm and composed. There is a certain amount of serenity here.

In a Reading

In readings, the Two of Swords represents confusion in the matter, being pulled by your heart and mind. Intuition or intellect—to which do you listen to? Think of when you are shopping for something. You are presented with a choice that is more logical and sensible, but you are also faced with another desire out of no logical reason—but you think it will make you happy. The Two of Swords is very protective of herself, always on the defense and not letting anyone near her. Also, this is a card of resistance. You may want to hold off on making a choice until you've weighed the pros and cons thoroughly.

When ill dignified, the Two of Swords can present itself as fear. The moon symbolizes unconscious fears as well as changing opinions and possibly mood swings. Clarity is lacking here. You do not see the reality of the situation. Procrastination is also a dominant feature, as no action can be made simply because there is no desire to take action.

TWO OF PENTACLES
Esoteric Title: Lord of Harmonious Change

Description

A man juggles two pentacles between his hands; the pentacles are linked together with the infinity sign. In the background, there is one small ship and one large ship riding large waves.

Symbolism and Meaning

The Two of Pentacles represents juggling different responsibilities in life. Work, family, school, cleaning the house, doing the laundry, painting, or even fixing that door that has been broken for five months because you have been too busy to fix it. The daily grind is represented by the Two of Pentacles. Because of all the responsibilities required of us, we need to become flexible. Adaptability is essential in this card.

The esoteric title of the Two of Pentacles is Lord of Harmonious Change; this card represents the ability to bring balance and harmony into the material world by practical means. The change brought here is not revolutionary or dramatic, rather it is subtle.

The Two of Pentacles represents weighing choices. What should I do? Which option is worth my time, money, attention, and investment? You are trying to weigh pros and cons and the long-term effects of one choice over another. This is suggested by the image of the pentacles joined by the infinity symbol. The ships in the background riding the waves represent our intention and action to pursue a goal, even when we feel conflicted inside. The Two of Swords was conflicted by the intuition and intellect, so no choice was made; the card is static. However, the Two of Pentacles is of the earth element, which water helps to develop. This card is in motion. However, it is the starting phase of motion. As you can see, the waves are rough. Moving forward is a challenge. The man is capable of juggling. No, it is not easy, but it is doable. As with life, it is hard, but we are capable of meeting the challenges.

In a Reading

In readings, the Two of Pentacles represents flexibility and balancing the everyday things in life. Many times, when I see the Two of Pentacles, it tells me that my clients are working multiple jobs or are balancing work and school. A need to be flexible in any given situation, you need to give a little to get a little. As you ponder the possibilities of one choice over another and being conflicted over which of the options is best, it is essential that you think things through before you make your choice.

When ill dignified, the Two of Pentacles can represent inability to cope and adapt to change and new demands. You may feel nervous and tense about a new opportunity or task. Also, you may be trying to multitask too many things and suffer as a result. It is best right now if you focus on one thing at a time. Things can be unstable at the moment. It isn't a good time to make change or try something new. Stick to what you are currently doing until circumstances are different. The Two of Pentacles can also signify distractions, particularly having your attention directed away from the real issue or problem and focusing on something irrelevant.

THE THREES

THREE OF CUPS
Esoteric Title: Lord of Abundance

Description

Three women join together in a celebrative dance in a circle with their Cups raised to the center, entwined. There are flowers as well as a pumpkin and grapes.

Symbolism and Meaning

The Three of Cups is a card of happiness, joy, fun, celebration, dancing, and indulgence. The Ace of Cups represented the seed and spark of love. The Two of Cups was the attraction, connection, and uniting. In the three, we get the first stage where the relationship becomes actualized. What is one way we actualize a relationship? A common way is by introducing our significant other to our friends or family. We bring them into our circle. This is what is happening here in the Three of Cups. This stage is where we make a relationship "official."

The esoteric title of the Three of Cups is Lord of Abundance. This title can be best explained and understood by the card's connection to the Three Graces of Greek mythology. The Three Graces are goddesses of beauty, charm, and nature, which symbolize fertility. The names of each of the graces are "Splendor," "Good Cheer," and "Festivity." In one tradition, their father is Dionysius, the god of wine, pleasure, and festivity. His cult included a lot of intoxicated dancing and sex. Because of the association with The Graces and Dionysius, the Three of Cups also represents blossoming and abundance.

The Three of Cups is a jovial card. It represents our desire to live freely and have a good time. There is a shared experience going on here. The focus is on the group, be it friends and or family. They are supporting and loving to one another. The Three of Cups is a card that appears to be very positive. However, it can have a downside, which is going to the extreme of indulgence and running wild. The female followers of Dionysius were called Maenads. These were crazed women who would yell and dance while intoxicated.

In a Reading

In readings, the Three of Cups represents coming together to celebrate, have fun, be happy, and express your wild sides. Dancing is a form of creative expression. The Three of Cups represents self-expression through personal creativity. The Three of Cups is lively and represents your inner self being brought out and manifested.

When ill dignified, the Three of Cups can represent excessiveness and the entering into a manic episode that can be self-destructive. What you perceive to be creative and amazing is actually harmful and not helpful. You need to be cautious that you are not getting too much of a good thing. You may become too focused on the pleasure and sensation and you can lose yourself from reality. The Three of Cups can also represent ill health or a warning of gossip and enemies in your circle.

THREE OF WANDS
Esoteric Title: Lord of Established Success

Description

A man holding on one of three Wands stands on a cliff, looking out at the ocean and watching three ships sailing off into the distance.

Symbolism and Meaning

The Three of Wands represents expanding outward, development, and progression. It is the birth of an idea and the first actions taken towards a goal. We see a man, possibly the same man from the Two of Wands, standing on a cliff. Both are looking out into the distance, out into the ocean. Both are holding onto a Wand, which is important to the meaning. We still have a part of the Two of Wands inside the Three of Wands. The Three of Wands is about exploration and doing research. The man is still stationary, holding onto a Wand, which means he is still holding onto something safe or that he has control over. They are no longer stuck to anything as they were in the Two of Wands; they are grounded in the earth, easily moved. This man is testing the water, sending others out to report back what they find. An example would be sending out your resume for a job. You have no job. Before you can get a job, you need to send the resume out and have people call you in. The little ships are like the resumes going off to different companies while you wait for a response back from one.

The esoteric title of the Three of Wands is Lord of Established Success. This title implies something successful has been established because the threes in Tarot represent the initial progress. In the Wands, the initial progress is establishing yourself in your journey by getting things in order first. Utilizing resources is an important factor of the Three of Wands. There is a lot of planning and foresight going on. Before making an action, you assess the environment, to make sure you are doing something that is not completely idiotic. The Wands are grounded in earth, which means that there is sensibility here; however, earth puts fire out, so there is an element of self-control going on.

In a Reading

In readings, the Three of Wands represents planning, taking things into consideration, doing research, and not making any real actions that have a profound effect. You need to think of the future and be strong and confident in yourself. Wait for results; if things look promising, continue onward. If your findings are not favorable, reformulate your plan. Look at your network and resources. People you know who have connections can assist you. Go through your phone contacts, post a tweet on Twitter/Facebook, anything to tap into your network or resources.

When ill dignified, the Three of Wands can indicate that you have not planned things properly. Go back and review your plans. Make sure you did not overlook something simple or small. It is the small details that can ruin the big ideas or plans. You may need to revise something and scale down if your aim is too high. There are delays and obstacles that you face.

THREE OF SWORDS
Esoteric Title: Lord of Sorrow

Description

A heart pierced by three swords floats in midair. There are dark rain clouds surrounding the scene.

Symbolism and Meaning

The Three of Swords represents sadness, pain, and sorrow. Depression and feeling blue are common feelings associated with this card. The heart is pierced by three swords, which brings our thoughts and feelings together. This is the only sword card that feels more akin to the Cups, because of the strong connection to emotions and feelings. In the Two of Swords, we saw a woman conflicted by choice. She could not make up her mind. The conflict was caused by a clash of intuition and intellect. In the Three of Swords, the choice is finally made and it is felt as a painful one.

The esoteric title of the Three of Swords is Lord of Sorrow; we are faced with sorrow and pain when we need to make hard choices, and the Three of Swords depicts a painful choice. This card can manifest as being honest with someone or yourself. It is hard for some people to be honest and speak from the heart. What we say may hurt the other person. Being honest with ourselves can be tough as well.

The Three of Swords promotes growth and development from these moments of adversity. We grow from these kinds of experiences. It is raining in this card, which is symbolic of cleansing and release. This can be associated with the release one has when they express themselves. Swords deal with analysis and communication; this card can represent our need to understand our emotions and feelings through critical analysis or discussing these feelings. The image of the heart emerging from the clouds can represent insights that are out of the blue or having a revelation of sorts.

In a Reading

In readings, the Three of Swords indicates situations where making a thorough choice is needed. Should you tell someone the truth? Even if it hurts, if it serves a good purpose, then yes, you should. Classically, the Three of Swords is related to infidelity and a cheating spouse. Pair it with the Two or Three of Cups and or Seven of Swords and you could be right. What may seem painful and complicated could just all be in your mind. There could be fear based off not much evidence. The issue at hand may be one that causes sad feelings. You may have a negative outlook or view of what is going on or of a person. Self-examination of these feelings would be helpful.

When ill dignified, the Three of Swords can represent a more severe degree of sorrow and sadness. It can also manifest denial and repression of troubled feelings and ignoring something important, which must be dealt with.

THREE OF PENTACLES
Esoteric Title: Lord of Material Works

Description

A man is at work, creating and building a large arch. Two people stand next time him, providing assistance or instruction.

Symbolism and Meaning

The Three of Pentacles represents foundations and creation of our ideas by our actions. In the Three of Pentacles, we see actual action being taken. You have finally picked the route you wanted, be it a job you wanted or a college program to which to apply. You have taken an action. The Three of Pentacles depicts a man working on a project he has been commissioned for. This represents our building of solid foundations in our lives. We are working towards a goal and making progress.

The esoteric title of the Three of Pentacles is Lord of Material Works. The Three of Pentacles is about creating something tangible or practical. The energy of Three is represented here as the birth of something that has an impact in your life. The creative aspects of the number three are represented here in the creative aspect of the Three of Pentacles; this card is filled with raw creative energy and is applied to the actual creation of something.

The two people at the side of the craftsman may be patrons. They appear to be giving instructions to the craftsman. The Three of Pentacles represents cooperation. The sculptor is not working. He has people helping in some form. He is looking at them directly. This shows he is open to discussing how the project should progress. Ideas are being shared. There is brainstorming, teamwork, and partnership. The arches can represent a passageway to new paths and opportunities.

In a Reading

In readings, when the Three of Pentacles shows up, it can be a signal that a new job may be heading your way. You may be free to allow your creative side to be expressed. The Three of Pentacles is the most actively creative card in the threes. This card can suggest stability and support. Study and concentration is important. If related to issues about education, it is signaling a need to study more and to get your hands dirty. Apply what you have learned to the real world, not just theorize ideas. When dealing with groups, it asks that you be a team player. Brainstorming is also advised if you are trying to come up with new ideas.

When ill dignified, the Three of Pentacles can represent people not cooperating or following orders. There could be disputes over how something should be done. Too many cooks in the kitchen, everyone has an opinion on the matter. Your performance at work may be lackluster. You could be lacking an interest in a hobby or a project you are working on. Your work environment may not be suitable for your talents or you are unhappy with your job itself or assignments.

THE FOURS

FOUR OF CUPS
Esoteric Title: Lord of Blended Pleasures

Description

A man sits under a tree with arms and legs crossed. He looks at the three empty Cups before him with a look on his face that reflects an apathetic mood. He is unaware of the cup that is emerging from a cloud next to him.

Symbolism and Meaning

The Four of Cups represents what happens when the element water is forced into structure. You get boredom, apathy, and withdrawal. Water does not belong in a state of order and structure. It needs to move and flow. The Four of Cups represents a lack of interest in things that bring you joy. Have you ever seen a commercial for depression medication? The symptoms listed describe the Four of Cups perfectly. This is quite the opposite from the Three of Cups and all the fun those three women were having. We might very well be seeing the hangover from a long night of partying.

The Esoteric title Lord of Blended Pleasures can imply the obtainment of a certain level of pleasure that may or may not continue. When something is blended it becomes combined. Blended Pleasure shows us that our pleasure is mixed and, in this mix, we've lost the original thing that gave us happiness—thus the discontent we see in the man. Emotions are unclear, blurred, or blended. We've lost the ability to distinguish one feeling from another. You can't pinpoint how you feel and why you feel a certain way.

Four represents stability and, inside the Four of Cups, it manifests by bringing order to our emotions. You contemplate, reflecting to try and understand your feelings. The man sits under a tree, like the Buddha who sat under the Bodhi tree seeking enlightenment. In the Four of Cups, we pull ourselves away from the things we love to indulge in (Three of Cups), and seek some enlightenment to some issue that is bothering us. The fourth Cup that bursts from a cloud is like the Ace of Cups. This can represent offerings; however, the man does not see it or ignores it. This can represent that we have narrow vision. The fourth Cup can also represent an epiphany, that *Aha* moment when something clicks inside and we gain insight.

In a Reading

In readings, the Four of Cups represents a lack of interest towards the issue or matter being asked. It represents your need to pull back and reflect. You may be feeling depressed or disappointed. You need to sort through the emotions and understand them to reveal insights. Oftentimes, the answers you seek are under your nose. You just don't know it because you have become blind to seeing it. There is resistance to help that is being offered.

When ill dignified, the Four of Cups remains much the same, perhaps reflecting a more serious tone. It can also represent daydreaming and becoming lost in thought. You may lose an opportunity if you stay apathetic.

FOUR OF WANDS
Esoteric Title: Lord of Perfected Work

Description

A couple stands together, arms raised and holding flowers. Before them are four Wands made into a canopy of flowers. In the background, we see a group of people dancing and a village.

Symbolism and Meaning

The Four of Wands represents celebration like the Three of Cups. However, in this card, the celebration is related to the achievement of some goal or the actualization of something. The Four of Wands represents the creation of something firm and stable for which we can continue to grow. The Four of Wands shows four Wands planted in the ground. They stand tall and are connected by a canopy of flowers. They can represent the establishment of something like a new home, a new job, or a new business. In the Three of Wands, we saw ships sailing out; the Four of Wands represents the return of those ships, bringing good news back with them.

The esoteric title is Lord of Perfected Work in which the Four of Wands represents the work that has been done and has led to some "perfect" result because of the harmonious unity of different elements to a singular goal. Things are as they should be.

The Four of Wands embodies solid ideas and strong foundations. When we channel our passion and energy in an organized manner, it strengthens the energy. Often this card represents invitations to weddings or parties in general. The atmosphere of this card is festive and joyous. In the background is a village up on the hill. The party is outside of the town, which can represent a freedom from society and what is expected. Like the Two of Wands, who has a figure with his back to the town, looking out to the sea and into the unknown, the Four of Wands celebrates innovations and uniqueness.

In a Reading

In readings, when the Four of Wands appears, it represents an achievement of some sort. You have obtained the thing you have envisioned and sought. You have made real what was only previously in your mind. It shows that things are moving in the right direction. Things are stable and are built upon strong foundations. Your actions will or have provided you with prosperity and wealth. Take your passion and manifest it into reality. Take pleasure in the work you do and aim for perfection.

When ill dignified, the Four of Wands can represent something standing in the way of reaching a goal. It can be the rain that ruins the outdoor wedding. Losing electricity when you need to finish that paper for class (which is due tomorrow). Usually, the thing standing in our way is a result of poor planning or a bad foundation, on which the plan/goal is founded. There may also be a fundamental problem with communication and bonds between relationships (personal or professional).

FOUR OF SWORDS
Esoteric Title: Lord of Rest from Strife

Description

Inside a church, we see a stone tomb with the sculpture of a man in a supine position with his hands together, praying. On the wall are three swords. The fourth sword is on the bottom of the tomb.

Symbolism and Meaning

The Four of Swords represents a retreat, pulling away from pain and strife. Taking time to suspend ourselves, rest, and recover. The events of the Three of Swords were strong and may have caused some sort of mental trauma that requires rest. You may have experienced something painful and all you wish to do now is hibernate and isolate yourself from others, or from the thing that has caused pain. Healing is essential within this card. Three Swords are hanging on the wall, which is a reminder of the Three of Swords. We are putting our problems on hold, hanging them on the wall, and putting them off for the moment. The Sword on the tomb, represents the Ace of Swords. We remove ourselves from the confusion by seeking clarity.

The esoteric title is Lord of Rest from Strife, which the image clearly depicts. After the heart-aching pain of the Three of Swords, we are offered respite in the Four. We are given stabilization of the mind, which helps us in putting our thoughts into order and grounding ourselves. The strife is not gone, but you get a moment to not worry about them. Think of it like taking a vacation from work. Yes, you will be away from the office for two weeks, but once the vacation ends, you will be returning to your job and the headaches.

The Four of Swords represents neutrality, staying out of the crossfire, refusing to be a part of a problem, and "playing dead" to the issue. The Four of Swords represents a need to take things into perspective and do some reflecting, almost like what we see in The Hanged Man. The Two of Swords can be seen in this card, which represents the refusal to face the issue. The two and four of swords also represent making diplomacy, the four signifying a walking away from the fight while the two symbolizes a stalemate.

In readings, the Four of Swords represents your need to recover from something painful. It is time for you to rest, to heal, and to rejuvenate. You need quiet time to be separated from everything else for a while. The Four of Swords cautions you not to make any decisions at the moment. You must remove yourself and consider your options. You need to be separated for the moment from others and focus on your emotional wellbeing and physical health. The Four of Swords also may advise that you "sleep on it" before making a decision. You may need to put something "to rest" and end an argument or a dilemma.

When ill dignified, the Four of Swords can show a short-lived rest, a vacation cut short, a nap interrupted, or not having the sick time from work you need to recover. You are unable to get the time you need to ground yourself and heal. It can also be internalized, where you yourself do not allow healing.

FOUR OF PENTACLES
Esoteric Title: Lord of Earthly Power

Description

A sitting man is tightly holding on to a pentacle in front of his chest. Beneath his feet are two other pentacles. There is a crown on his head and above the crown is another pentacle. In the background is the landscape of a city.

Symbolism and Meaning

The Four of Pentacles represents our need to hold on to what is ours: our possessions, property, money, and anything that we own. It also represents blockages, inflexibility, gain, greed, and being closed off. The Ace of Pentacles was the seed for new prosperity, the Two of Pentacles balanced responsibilities, the Three of Pentacles worked, made foundations, and allowed creativity to slow. We come to the Four of Pentacles and things close up and the focus is on gaining more and more, holding on to what we have created, and not wanting to share our wealth. Think of Ebenezer Scrooge from Charles Dickens's novel *A Christmas Carol*. The focus here is on "me, myself, and I."

The esoteric title of the Four of Pentacles is Lord of Earthly Power. The title and general appearance, as well as the aspects of control and power of the Four of Pentacles echoes elements of The Emperor, ruler of the material realm. He wears a crown, which may be reference to The Emperor. The Four of Pentacles is pretty much immoveable. Four is a structured number and pentacles are of the earth element, so you have yourself a very stubborn person. The Four of Pentacles manifests as the miser, the hard worker, control freak, and hoarder.

In readings, when the Four of Pentacles shows up, it talks about control and power—needing to be the one calling the shots. The focus will be about how things affect you. Can you turn this into something that can be beneficial? How can you make this work in your favor? The Four of Pentacles represents stability; are you making a stable decision and really taking into account the practicality of the issue? Like the Two of Swords, the Four of Pentacles blocks people out, preferring money and material items to the company of people. The Four of Pentacles protects himself and his assets. What are you protecting? What should you be protecting?

When ill dignified, the Four of Pentacles loses all sight of anything other than what is material. The Four of Pentacles expresses tunnel vision, inability to see the alternatives, and preferring his own perceptions/opinions. The Four of Pentacles retains much of its normal meaning, but with an unpleasant nature. Restriction and constriction become dominant.

THE FIVES

FIVE OF CUPS
Esoteric Title: Lord of Loss in Pleasure

Description

A person wearing a long black cloak with their head bent over grieves of the three spilled Cups in front of them. To their back are two Cups, which have not been knocked over. In the background, we see a bridge. On the other side, we see a castle. The sky is filled with dark clouds.

Symbolism and Meaning

The Five of Cups shows us a very sad scene. We see someone dressed in black, symbolizing that they are in mourning or that they are deeply depressed. We see what seems to the cause of this—the three Cups spilled in front of them, symbolizing something has been lost, has left, or has been removed. The two Cups remaining symbolize something that still remains, what we have that has not been lost. The two Cups seem to be neglected and/or ignored. The focus and attention is on what has been lost. The bridge connects two lands separated by a river. The river is our life experiences. You never step in the same river twice, as Heraclitus said.

The esoteric title of the Five of Cups is Lord of Loss in Pleasure, which speaks about spiritual growth. In the Two of Cups and Three of Cups, we saw such happiness and joy. The Five of Cups shows that it was not all it was hyped up to be. You begin to feel dissatisfied with the pleasures you experienced. In the Four of Cups, we saw a man expressing apathy. In the Five of Cups, we see the consequences of prolonged apathy. We may lose something from our lives. It could be a relationship, a job, or something that we love to do. The deep reflection of the Four of Cups may also bring about a desire to remove something from our lives that no longer is needed. We may feel that we no longer wish to be in the relationship and break it off.

In a Reading

In readings, the Five of Cups represents the challenge of knowing when and what to remove from your life, being emotionally able to let go, say goodbye, and move on. You may not be the one who chooses to let go. You might be on the opposite end of this and end up being let go by another. The challenge of both scenarios is moving on and not fixating on what was lost. You cannot ignore the two remaining Cups you still have. All is not doom and gloom in the Five of Cups. You still have something to walk away with. However, if you do not focus on what you have, you may end up losing that as well. The good news in this card is you are now open to new possibilities.

When ill dignified, the Five of Cups becomes more depressing than before. The Five of Cups may represent something that comes out of the blue and pulls the rug out from under you. It may start to ripple out away from you and start affecting people around you. Lies, distrust, and betrayal are also other qualities of an ill dignified Five of Cups.

FIVE OF WANDS
Esoteric Title: Lord of Strife

Description

Five men, each holding a Wand, participate in a good-spirited competition. Each is attacking the other, desiring to win.

Symbolism and Meaning

The Five of Wands shows a more playful and less painful scene in contrast to the Five of Cups. In the Five of Wands, we see five men in what may seem to be lighthearted rough housing. The positive energy of fire alters the influence of the number five. The energy in this card is resilient. Everyone is very forceful and energetic. You see a lot of enthusiasm and even optimism. Each person believes he will be the victor. They all stand on a small hill; each one is trying to be the king of the hill. The Five of Wands can be playful like a sport or more serious like a battle.

The esoteric title of the Five of Wands is *Lord of Strife*. At the core, this card is about struggle and strife. Strife can manifest within us or externally. It may be our need to take care of ourselves. In terms of "flight or fight," the Five of Wands is "fight." We might be struggling with different interests or passions that want our time and attention. We might be at war with ourselves, trying to do better than we did in the past. Strife can also manifest in our environment. When we go for a job interview, we must compete with other applicants. This is a real-life situation of the Five of Wands, where you have to compete against others, fighting to be the one who gets the job.

In a Reading

In readings, when the Five of Wands appears, it represents the challenge of competition. You need to get on top and be the winner. How do you do this? Wands deal with creativity and inspiration. The Five of Wands urges you to be unique, passionate, and have the desire to win. The Five of Wands has a tendency to mistake something that is harmless as a threat and makes it a reason for war. A harmless comment someone makes is interpreted as an insult, to which you insist on having a good old-fashioned duel. Your actions are actually reactions to some internal issue that has not been resolved and manifests as behaviors, like bullying and fighting. The Five of Wands challenges you to understand how you are reacting to situations. If you become violent, you need to take a step back and ask yourself why you are reacting in such a manner.

When ill dignified, the Five of Wands can represent violent outbursts and abusive behaviors. It can represent a short temper and argumentative disposition. Anger takes dominance in the ill dignified Five of Wands in that someone might be hostile in their interaction. In the realm of contests and competition Five of Wands can indicate cheating, sabotage of others, or poor sportsmenship.

FIVE OF SWORDS
Esoteric Title: Lord of Defeat

Description

The aftermath of a battle between three men reveals one victor. In the front, the winner gathers the swords forfeited by the losers. A grin can be seen on the face of the victor, which prompts us to question his victory.

Symbolism and Meaning

The Five of Swords depicts a victory, but a victory because of some advantage. The "winner" gains from the loss of others. He is seen as a cheater; he does not play fairly. The grin on his face is a clear indication that there is something shady or unknown about the circumstances to his gain, victory, and achievements. However, when we take into consideration the esoteric title, things appear differently.

The esoteric title of the Five of Swords is Lord of Defeat, not victory. Lord of Defeat implies that even if someone "wins," there is no true winner in the situation. Everyone is defeated; everyone loses. The Five Swords also link shame with the defeat/victory. No matter if you lose or win, you are still shamed.

In the physical world, defeat can manifest in the form of someone taking the promotion you wanted by presenting your ideas as their own. Shame can manifest in the form of the revelation of your cheating. In professional sports, the use of performance enhancement drugs, like steroids, brings shame to athletes, and along with their use of steroids, they also bring a self-defeat. All of their efforts to get ahead only return to harm them.

In the psyche of a person, the Five of Swords manifests as a self-defeating personality disorder. The individual will undermine any personal experiences that bring pleasure. Whenever an achievement is made, the individual will respond with thoughts of low self-worth such as guilt, shame, and depression. The individual will also reject help from others.

In a Reading

In readings, the Five of Swords shows that you may be faced with external forces working against your favor. You may be faced with gossip and slander from others. You desire to win, but should take a step back to understand the actions we are willing to take to win. Can you play fair? How will you feel if you twisted the rules to your favor? Can you live with the consequences? Deep down, this card suggests that it may not be others plotting against you, but that your own self-defeating behaviors are to blame.

When ill dignified, the Five of Swords expresses the saying, "cut off your nose to spite your face," which describes excessive self-destructive behavior in seeking revenge. The ends justify the means and the outcome as long as it is favorable to all that matters.

FIVE OF PENTACLES
Esoteric Title: Lord of Material Trouble

Description

An impoverished couple struggles through a cold winter night. The man has a wounded leg. The woman clings to her clothing to keep warm. They have no shoes on their feet. A large stone structure is seen at their side.

Symbolism and Meaning

The Five of Pentacles is to many the most troubling of all the fives. Pentacles represent the material world and all things physical, so we see the impacts of the Five in a very physical way. The Five of Pentacles represents material loss and challenges to finances. The image in the Five of Pentacles brings to mind the Great Depression and, even more recently, the economic downturn, nicknamed the "Great Recession." Up until now, the pentacles have been favorable. With the Five of Pentacles, the rug is pulled from under us and things change. The Five of Pentacles represents loss, hard times, instability, uncertainty, and a lack of hope.

The esoteric title for The Five of Pentacles is Lord of Material Trouble. This can manifest in our lives in the form of a lost job, being fired, or being laid off. You can lose money to a failed investment in the stock market. You may be evicted from your apartment or your home is foreclosed. These are extreme examples just so you are able to understand the energy of this card. The Five of Pentacles is about loss of security and stability in whatever it is you put faith in to take care of you. The Five of Pentacles also represents abandonment; you are left to care for yourself. You may need help, yet no one is offering assistance. The Five of Pentacles can also represent spiritual impoverishment.

In a Reading

Remember that pentacles are the most material of all the suits. The spiritual is not a natural association to it. So far, the pentacles have been focused on material things. The Four of Pentacles was fixated on worldly possessions, but in the Five of Pentacles, you see spiritual impoverishment. The building behind the couple is often viewed as a church, in which they seek assistance. This may be true, but they may be seeking spiritual assistance more so than material. The Five of Pentacles may also indicate a need to seek out Divinity in your daily life. You begin to ask if there is more to life than the material world.

An ill-dignified Five of Pentacles represents much of the same as it normally would. The only change would be the length at which this card expresses itself. There seems to be a feeling that the state that the two people are in will be prolonged in the ill dignified than it would normally be.

SIXES

SIX OF CUPS
Esoteric Title: Lord of Pleasure

Description

Two children are in a courtyard. The older child extends forth a Cup (gift) to the younger child.

Symbolism and Meaning

The Six of Cups often represents our past—childhood, to be more specific, or any period of time in our past we have very fond memories of. Traditionally, the Six of Cups symbolizes nostalgia, dreaming of a better time when everything was simpler, when we were taken care of and everything was wonderful. The children in the card can represent a few things: our innocence, our inner child, or the current children in our lives. In the card, one child is extending a gift to the younger child, which represents the things we inherit or what is given to us while growing up. The Six of Cups is closely linked to the experiences of our childhood, how we were raised, treated, what ideas, and beliefs were given to us. The Six of Cups also represents generosity, gifts, and caring for others. On the top left side stands a guard, which may suggest parentally protection or guarding something we cherish.

The Esoteric title of the Six of Pentacles is Lord of Pleasure. This indicates that the Six of Cups seeks pleasure and is about finding whatever pleasure can be derived from a situation. Combining the aspect of nostalgia and pleasure seeking makes the Six of Cups too idealistic. Even when we look back at our pasts with happy memories and a desire to relive them, the past is never as "perfect" as we remember it. That guard who protects the children may also serve as how we protect ourselves from reality or the "real world." The Six of Cups can manifest in our lives when we are seeing life as too perfect, seeking an ideal life where everything is happy and "utopian."

In a Reading

In readings, the Six of Cups represents your ideals and how you envision the world should be. Sixes represent a possible dependence of something. In the Six of Cups, it is the dependence of needing someone to nurture you or needing to be nurturing to others. The older child represents the need to give and the younger child represents the need to receive. There is a strong sense of innocence within the Six of Cups, which can represent pure intentions regarding your actions or those of others. There may be an offer of some kind given to you, an extension of generosity, such as a job from an old employer.

When ill dignified, the Six of Cups can represent naivety and gullibility. You may be too trusting, perhaps trusting the wrong person or thing. You may also be overly optimistic. You may be clinging to the past and resisting to step into the future.

SIX OF WANDS
Esoteric Title: Lord of Victory

Description

A man riding his horse is arriving home after a victory of some sort. The people gather around to cheer for him and his accomplishments. He holds one Wand with a circular reef attached to it while the crowd holds the remaining Wands.

Symbolism and Meaning

The Six of Wands depicts a celebratory scene. The victor is riding in on his horse. He is happy, confident, a bit boastful, but above all, proud of what he has accomplished. The crowd of people gathers in recognition for his hard work and achievement. They rally behind their hero to give support, acclaim, and notoriety. The Six of Wands represents having pride in yourself, being proud of others, and people being proud of you. This card is deeply rooted with recognition and acknowledgment. Your environment acknowledges you and your achievements. The only downfall to the Six of Wands can be the challenge of ego and becoming too full of pride in oneself.

The Esoteric title to the Six of Wands is *Lord of Victory*. Whatever you are faced with, you shall win. The Six of Wands is one of those "winner" cards that are very clear in its meaning. There is little that is vague about this card. The outcome of the Six of Wands is highly favorable.

In a Reading

In readings, the Six of Wands is seen as positive, especially with regards to outcomes. The Six of Wands brings with it the energy of success, winning, making a name for yourself, and having others reward, respect, and admire you. In life, the Six of Wands can manifest as a job promotion, winning an award, coming home from war, winning an election, or winning a competition. With all the sixes, there is a power displacement. With the Six of Wands, it is between the rider and the crowd. In some occasion, the Six of Wands can indicate a behavior of always praising others while never receiving praise of your own.

When ill dignified, the Six of Wands can represent jealousy and envy either by you towards other's success or vice versa. Pride or thinking you've won before the race is over will be the downfall. Do not be premature in your celebrations.

SIX OF SWORDS
Esoteric Title: Lord of Earned Success

Description

A ferryman carries a woman and child from one side of the shore to another. The woman is covered with a blanket and is slouched over. The child sits next to her. Six swords are pointing down, imbedded into the boat. To the right, the water is choppy. To the left, the water is calm.

Symbolism and Meaning

The Six of Swords depicts a somber yet peaceful scene. It shows the recovery and healing process after the battle in the Five of Swords. In the boat, we have three people: a woman, a child, and the ferryman. The Six of Swords reestablishes order and harmony. In this card, we see the rough water to the right of the boat. On the left and to the distance, the water is calm and still. This represents a transition. The boat is a symbol of a soul's journey through life's difficulties. The Six of Swords can indicate that our mind and heart are in alignment and that we know exactly what we need.

A new opportunity can be presented to you, but you may have to leave something behind in order to follow the new opportunity. The Six of Swords represents evolution and change in your soul and mind.

The esoteric title of the Six of Swords is Lord of Earned Success. The key word is *earned*. When we earn something, it is usually through very hard work and, specifically, hardship. The Six of Swords represents what we earned after a long struggle. Like the Six of Wands, who is a winner, the Six of Swords is also a winner, but the battle was tougher and more draining. Swords deal with intellectual aspects like thought, words, and anything concerning communication. The battle may be done with our mind, thoughts, words, and communication with others. There is little glory here in the Six of Swords as opposed to the Six of Wands. You've earned what you receive, but it is done quietly.

In a Reading

In readings, the Six of Swords indicates a need to transit, change, and move beyond the problem. This can manifest in the way of taking a vacation, moving to a new house, or removing someone or something from your life. The energy of this card is somber; things may feel depressed and can represent a low cycle or period. You will need to intellectualize, but also humanize the issue presented to you. As with all the sixes, there is co-dependence of some kind. In this case, the ferryman is helping the woman and child. If the primary association is with the ferryman, you may feel like you are obligated to help another. If the association is with the woman and child, you may feel like a victim needing help from others.

When ill dignified, the Six of Swords can represent feeling attached or stuck in a situation that won't change. You may try to leave, but feel the path to do so is blocked. On an internal level, you may be refusing to take charge. Instead, you stay on the safe side instead of making change or asking for help.

SIX OF PENTACLES
Esoteric Title: Lord of Material Success

Description

A wealthy, well-dressed man stands above two peasants who are begging for money. From his right hand, he distributes four coins to one of the beggars. In his left hand, he holds a scale.

Symbolism and Meaning

In the Six of Pentacles, we see possibly the same couple from the Five of Pentacles, whom were seen as poor and seeking assistance. Here in the Six of Pentacles, we see assistance being given by the wealthy man. It is from his right hand that he distributes his money. The right hand is the hand we use to give and share. In his left hand, he holds a scale. Sixes represent restoring harmony and the scale is the symbol that represents the act of re-establishing balance. The man uses the scale to share fairly and equally. There is not an excess or overabundance of giving, but just enough that you need at the moment. It is not the twenty-million-dollar prize from the lotto, but maybe 500 dollars from a scratch-off game that will let you fix the broken boiler. It is important to notice that it seems only one of the two beggars is being given money. Depending on surrounding cards, you may receive something or not. The scales, like the ones in Justice, represent fairness, even if it does not feel like it.

The Esoteric title of the Six of Pentacles is Lord of Material Success, which implies success in regards to money. The "Material Hardship" of the Five of Pentacles now becomes "Material Success." The Six of Pentacles is a sign of good outcome with regards to financial issues.

In readings, the Six of Pentacles manifests as opportunities to bring new balance and harmony to your physical life. There is a restoration of security. The four coins being giving out is making reference to the Four of Pentacles, which represents security. New money becomes available to you, loans are approved, someone lends you money, financial aid arrives from a government agency, or winning money are examples of possible Six of Pentacles situations. Generosity is at the core of the Six of Pentacles. As with all the sixes, there is co-dependence of some kind. In this case, it is the wealthy man and the beggars who are at odds. One gives and the other receives. You may be in the position to give or you are in the position to receive. Many times, with regards to relationships of any kind, there is someone who is or acts superior to the other and believes that the other needs them or vice versa.

When ill dignified, the Six of Pentacles can represent a lack of financial opportunities or support. The loan from the bank is denied or you may, in fact, owe a debt to someone that you cannot pay back. This may feel unfair and unjust; you are left with the short end of the stick. You may be offered assistance, but not enough to make a significant impact.

THE SEVENS

SEVEN OF CUPS
Esoteric Title: Lord of Illusionary Success

Description

In front of a man are seven golden Cups materializing out of the clouds. He looks both shocked and amazed. In each of the Cups are things the man desires.

Symbolism and Meaning

In the Seven of Cups, we see a man presented many options and possibilities. The setting of the scene appears as if the man is dreaming. Because of the dream association, the Seven of Cups is a card of illusions and delusions. In each of the Cups rises an image, each of which represents something the man desires and dreams of. The snake represents knowledge, wisdom, and possibly eternal life. The next chalice is covered by a cloth, which may represent the hidden or occult knowledge. The human face is for the desire of a romantic companion. The tower represents structure and home. The treasure is for wealth and prosperity. The laurel wreath is for fame, victory, and acclaim. Lastly, the dragon is for power and dominance.

The esoteric title of the Seven of Cups is Lord of Illusionary Success. This explains that the Seven of Cups shows the misleading idea of success. The man in this card is a dreamer and, without any concrete plans, his dreams won't materialize. Illusionary Success refers to the idea that there is a false perception of what we have actually accomplished. The man in this card is in the delusion that he might actually possess the images in the Cups. Illusionary success can also represent that the things we desire as signs that we are successful—fame, money, and power—are illusions and not true forms of success.

In theme with all the Sevens dealing with soul searching and isolation, the Seven of Cups is searching for his path in life. What does he desire most? What path does he want to follow, what goal should he work towards? The challenge is that everything is so tantalizing that he wants it all. Another challenge here is the possibility of procrastination and laziness. The man becomes disabled in coming down from this dream-like state that he does nothing and stays in this state of mind. With this in mind, there may be an association with mind-altering substances that provide you an escape from reality. There are other things that can aid you in escaping reality that are less harmful, like books and movies. The Seven of Cups depicts anything that takes you into a fantasy-like world.

In a Reading

In readings, when the Seven of Cups appears, it can refer to many options and paths to choose from. It represents an overly optimistic way of thinking: wishful thinking. There are no real solid foundations for what you are creating or planning. Make your decisions realistically. The Seven of Cup also represents an escape from reality into a dream world. Use the Seven of Cups as a source of motivation as it shows what can come true if you plan.

When ill dignified, the Seven of Cups can represent delusions and imagination running wild. You may become paralyzed by options or choices in front of you. You lose touch with what is real and immerse yourself in fantasy.

SEVEN OF WANDS
Esoteric Title: Lord of Valor

Description

On the edge of a cliff, a man with a Wand as his only defense, does battle with a mob below him.

Symbolism and Meaning

In the Seven of Wands, we see a man who stands at the edge of a cliff, holding a Wand in both hands in a stance of attack or defense. He seems to be protecting himself from people at the bottom who also have Wands that they are using to attack him.

The first impression we get from all this is the idea of defensiveness and protection. This is a card dealing with your need to defend what is yours (property) or defending what you believe in (ideas, opinions). This is a card that is empowering, because it tells you not to let people walk all over you. You are to be firm in your convictions.

The esoteric title of the Seven of Wands is Lord of Valor. Valor is strength of our mind and spirit that enables us to confront danger—or simply put, bravery. This card is about being bold and standing up for yourself. Fighting against that which is conventional in society is not an easy thing to do. It takes a lot of courage. The Seven of Wands is a card of going against what society says is okay, fighting the social norms. You "rock the boat" and do things your way. The problem is that you encounter the backlash of others who say, "No, you can't do this." However, you do not care for their opinions. You are fixed in your convictions and will not change, which can be problematic, because this card does not respond well to change or a need to be flexible.

If you pay close attention, you will notice that the man is wearing a boot on one foot and a shoe on the other. This can mean a few things. For one, it can represent independence and self-expression. Remember that he is fighting norms of society. Alternatively, the footwear represents two sides of society. The boot represents the working class (labor) and the shoe represents the higher class, so to speak. The shoes are a symbol of social class interactions or social mobility (i.e. fighting to work your way up the social ladder).

In a Reading

In a reading, the Seven of Wands represents that you should stand your ground. Do not given in or give out. You need to be persistent and resilient. Do not be afraid to defend yourself against a group against you. If your cause is true and honest, you will be the victor in the end. You do have the upper hand in the situation. Pay close attention to nearby cards as they can either support your position to indicate that your convictions are too rigid and you thus may need to compromise.

When ill dignified, the Seven of Wands can represent losing your footing and position or power. Your position may not be justified; you should allow new ideas in for consideration. You may also want to consider surrendering. This card could also represent conformity to a group or society norm.

SEVEN OF SWORDS
Esoteric Title: Lord of Unstable Efforts

Description

A shady-looking man sneaks away from a campsite, carrying with him five swords and leaving two behind.

Symbolism and Meaning

The Seven of Swords is a mischievous card. Traditionally, this card is seen as representing a thief. There is something unsettling about this card; the man looks like he is up to no good. He is sneaking away from a camp with swords in his hand. The thief concept here may not be as sinister as it appears. Hermes the Greek patron god of thieves was also able to transmute thievery into Hermetic inventiveness. Many figures in mythology stole for the benefit of humanity. Prometheus stole fire from Zeus and gave it to man. Eve "stole" from the Tree of Knowledge, which brought mankind to full consciousness. Much is to be pondered here in the Seven of Swords.

To fully understand the card, we must go beyond the face value, as with all the cards of the Tarot. In all of the Sevens in the Minor Arcana, we see situations where the main character is at focus and is often alone. Here in the Seven of Swords, the man is running off from the camp. Readers will often say he is stealing from others, that he is an outsider. Maybe, but he could also be a member of the group who has decided to depart and take what is rightfully his along with him. What is with the secrecy of his departure? He may feel it is best to leave without anyone knowing. The group might not want him to leave for what he owns (five swords) are more than what the group has (two remaining swords). If we look at the Seven of Swords in this manner, what does it mean? It shows us a need to leave the people we call "friends" or the people who we surround ourselves with. We learn that we are better off alone and going about our way rather than what the collective wants. It shows independent thinking. He could also very well be an outsider stealing from others, taking ideas that are not his, because swords represent ideas and thought.

The esoteric title of the Seven of Swords is Lord of Unstable Effort. This implies that the actions taken by the Seven of Swords are unstable, but why? Effort is what we attempt in doing something. The man here is attempting to go about things all alone. His efforts are unstable because he actually needs help from others. His intentions might not be in the right place. He is also seeking a fast and easy solution to problems that only cause more long-term problems. He may be trying to achieve too much too quickly. He carries too many swords, which cannot be balanced properly and causes instability.

In a Reading

In readings, the Seven of Swords can signal a need to look at what actions could be questionable. I see this card as about ethics, laws, and morals. This card can show that there could be some shady business going on. The Seven of Swords is a secretive card. He is hiding something, which can reflect that someone could be hiding something from you. It could also very well reflect that you are the one hiding something. Oftentimes, this is something you are ashamed of and wish to keep hidden. A good example of this card is indicative of politicians who are caught in a scandal. When near cards of romance, like Two of Cups, The Lovers, or Three of Cups, it can indicate affairs or secrets in relationships or business partnerships.

When ill dignified, the Seven of Swords can represent secrets revealed. Be careful who you place your confidence in. The motivations of others may be less genuine than they appear at face value. Protect your property from theft (this includes tangible and intellectual works).

SEVEN OF PENTACLES
Esoteric Title: Lord of Success Unfulfilled

Description

A hard-working farmer is tending to his crops. Leaning on his hoe, he examines and evaluates the progress of his efforts.

Symbolism and Meaning

In the Seven of Pentacles, we see a farmer who has been working on his crops. Right now, he is taking a moment to pause and look at the progress of his work and seeing what is being produced as a result. He rests on his hoe and has an expression of disappointment.

One of the things that the Seven of Pentacles represents is investment and return. What the Seven of Pentacles provokes us to do is review and evaluate what we have been doing and ask, "Is that which I am investing in worth my time, efforts, and resources?" This can relate to material investment. Are all your eggs in one basket? Where do you invest your money? Is what you invest in yielding anything in return or are you wasting your time and energy? Investment is not just in the physical and material realm of financial investment. Investment extends into the realm of love and relationship as well. I see the Seven of Pentacles appear many times in relationship readings where it signals that someone has been pondering if the relationship is worth their time and emotional investment. Are you getting anything in return in the relationship? Is there a future? Are things developing or is growth stagnant?

The esoteric title of the Seven of Pentacles is Lord of Success Unfulfilled. This means that success has not been obtained. This card is about the first signs of either the potential for success or failure. The facial expression of the man is a clear giveaway that things here are not wonderful and great. The look on this face appears to be disappointment or frustration. Why? Because what he was expecting is not forming in the way he wanted or had planned. Things may be taking too long to manifest, or he is not happy with the results. The look could also be in deep thought. Thinking of a way to turn things around is the evaluation aspect of this card.

In a Reading

In a reading, the Seven of Pentacles signals an important turning point. It is time to evaluate the progress of the situation and determine if you are getting any results from your investment(s). How are your actions affecting the outcome? Are you taking proper care and doing what is needed to get the desired outcome? Also, is what you are working for really what you desire or is it what you think you want? Take a good, long, hard look at everything. Is it all worth your time?

When ill dignified, the Seven of Pentacles can indicate the wasting of time and resources. It can indicate poor investment decisions and not thinking before doing something that bears importance for your future. The Seven of Pentacles can also indicate procrastination. You may be rushing and forcing a project to develop faster than it should.

THE EIGHTS

EIGHT OF CUPS
Esoteric Title—Lord of Abandoned Success

Description

In the eclipse, a man in a red robe walks away into the distance, leaving behind eight chalices stacked on top of one another.

Symbolism and Meaning

In the Eight of Cups, we see some sort of ramification or outcome from the events in the Seven of Cups. The Seven of Cups represented illusions, options, and our dreams. Because of these events, we see here in the Eight of Cups a desire to search for these dreams and illusions.

The Eight of Cups is a card very similar to The Hermit. This card is linked with isolation, withdrawal, self-reflection, and most importantly with seeking. The Eight of Cups seeks a deeper, more meaningful experience in life. He also seeks completion and wholeness to what is currently missing. In this card, the Cups are stacked on top of each other; however, there is a gap on the top stack. This shows that something is missing. An incomplete puzzle and our red-cloaked man leaves in search of that missing puzzle piece.

On the top left, we see the sun being eclipsed by the moon. This is a symbol of what is going on in this card. It shows a transition from light into darkness, switching from logic to emotion, feeling instead of thinking. It also shows an internal journey of the psyche sorting out all the emotions and baggage that has gone unexamined. It implies that a greater perspective is being achieved. Like The Hermit, who is on top of a mountain, the man in the Eight of Cups seeks higher ground for greater perspective.

The esoteric title for the Eight of Cups is Lord of Abandoned Success. This shows that there is an element of abandonment here, of giving up and deserting something or someone. The abandonment can be done due to dissatisfaction in what has been gained or what we have for the search of more.

In a Reading

In readings, the Eight of Cups shows the realization that something is no longer serving you and no longer holds any emotional meaning. This allows you to let go of emotional attachments. In terms of relationships, this shows that you have become distant and, on an unconscious level, you may have already departed from the relationship on an emotional level, even if you are physically with the other person. This says it is time to move on. The Eight of Cups is about letting go and putting the past behind you. You could stay where you are, which is safe and secure, but to obtain the real prize, the real treasures in life, you need to move beyond what is known and safe. That is how you grow spiritually and emotionally.

When ill dignified, the Eight of Cups can indicate that you remain attached to something you no longer need, but are afraid to let it go and move on. You may be trying very hard to keep a relationship going, even when the signs that it is over are clear. You repress the feelings of dissatisfaction and pretend to feel satisfied. Alternatively, the Eight of Cups can indicate a sense of non-belonging and wandering, seeking a place to fit in.

EIGHT OF WANDS
Esoteric Title: Lord of Swiftness

Description

Eight Wands quickly fly across the sky towards the ground. In the foreground there is a river.

Symbolism and Meaning

The Eight of Wands was always a tricky card for me to understand and apply in readings, mainly because there are no people in this card. Just about every card in the Tarot has at least one person in the scene. But here there are no people and we find ourselves looking at eight Wands flying across the sky. What does this mean?

The Eight of Wands is a card of fast actions, fast movement, and fast everything basically. The Esoteric Title of the Eight of Wands is Lord of Swiftness. When things are swift and move fast, it shows that there are little obstacles in your way. You are free and not limited in your direction. So the setting of a sky view is fitting because flight is symbolic of freedom. Birds are always seen as being free because they can fly away and go anywhere. It is here in the Eight of Wands the energy of Fire is not restricted and is let loose; it can flow free and open.

Which direction do the cards look like they are going? Look for a moment. Do they look like they have just been thrown and are moving up in the sky, or have they reached their max and are coming back down to earth? If they have just been thrown, it shows that plans are just starting to gain motion and progress is occurring. Something has been started. If you feel that they are heading back to earth, it shows that they have reached their goal and destination and things now are coming to a conclusion. Personally, I have always looked at this card as the Wands are coming back to the ground that they were thrown in the air with a specific direction in mind. A modern way to look at this card is electronic communications, like phone calls, email, text messages, social media, or sorts of communication where the message "flies across the air." The Eight of Wands can be arrows of love—look for supporting cards.

In a Reading

In readings, the Eight of Wands represents a moment of clear direction and having a goal and direction you want to head into. However, this card can at times be very wild, because, while the Wands are traveling in the air, they can change direction and the results are not the way you wanted. Make sure you are focused and your energy is guided and does not become scattered.

When ill dignified, the Eight of Wands can represent a frantic disorganization to your energy. You become unfocused and lack direction. Your ideas may get off the ground quickly, but do not maintain enough momentum to continue and fail soon after launch.

When ill dignified the arrows of love can become arrows of envy.

EIGHT OF SWORDS
Esoteric Title: Lord of Shortened Force

Description

Outside the city walls, a woman is blindfolded, tied up, and surrounded by swords.

Symbolism and Meaning

What is familiar about this image? Oh yes, it is the blindfolded woman that we saw in the Two of Swords! However, what is different is that it seems that the woman was tied up against her will, unlike the Two of Swords, who placed the blindfold on herself. The subject of this card looks to be a victim of a punishment.

Swords represent our mind and, in this card, it shows us what happens when we let our mind and thoughts take control over us. They bind us. The Eight of Swords is a card I have always seen as the games the mind plays on us. It represents, too, the traps our minds, our beliefs, and our attitudes place on us. In the background, we see a castle, that represents society. She is placed outside of society. She may be ostracized, isolated by others, and rejected. In legal issues, this can represent imprisonment or other fines and punishments.

The woman is tied up; she is restricted and limited in her physical movement as well as her awareness and perception of what is going on around her. Because she is restricted and the swords represent the mind and thoughts, the Eight of Swords indicates restrictive behaviors and self-limiting attitudes, much like what we see in The Devil, minus the addictions and materialism. What is similar here with The Devil is that she has limited understanding and awareness of her situation.

The esoteric title of the Eight of Swords is Lord of Shortened Force, which means that her "force" or awareness is "shortened" or restricted. Because her force is shortened, she is unable to make choices, make decisions, and is unable to solve problems. Her mental mind is not helping and is not a place to find answers. She needs to get creative to solve her problems. She is tied up, but her legs are free to move. She could walk away from the swords and seek help. She could back up to a sword and cut the ropes with the blade and become free. You need to take matters in your own hands, not wait for someone to rescue you.

In readings, the Eight of Swords represents that you are stuck in a situation and don't know which way to go or what to do. You are stressed, confused, and lacking an understanding of the whole picture. Someone has taken your power away or you have given it away (or given in to something else). Like Strength of the Major Arcana, you will need to find the inner strength to overcome this. Something unexpected may occur or has occurred that has caused this state of limitation. Often, when we are caught off guard by something we had no way to plan for, we become paralyzed. You also need to expand beyond your current understandings and do research beyond what you do know.

When ill dignified, the Eight of Swords represents much of what the normal meaning implies. The difference now is it could be a more dramatic manifestation. For example, it could represent punishment, such as imprisonment.

EIGHT OF PENTACLES
Esoteric Title: Lord of Prudence

Description

A craftsman is at work, creating pentacles. He is diligent and committed to his work, study, or craft.

Symbolism and Meaning

In the Eight of Pentacles, we see a man hard at work. He is laboring over his creations, making one pentacle after the other. He is focused and diligent in his attention to small details and wanting perfection.

As we saw in the Three of Pentacles, a man is crafting in a building. He could be seen as a master at his craft. Later on, in the Five of Pentacles, we see the loss of everything. Then, as we progress more, we see the regaining of what was lost in the Six of Pentacles. Now, in the Eight of Pentacles, he may be going into a process of having to learn new skills, maybe to do work that he is over-qualified for. He may be starting over from the bottom, working his way to the top once again.

This card loudly speaks to me about repetition, tasks that are done over and over. It shows little stimulation or variation in the events of the day and your job. I see this card as a "dead end" job or living in a way that everything is always the same. I don't want to make this card sound bad, as there is lots of good here. The Eight of Pentacles is a good indication of finding steady and continuous work if you're unemployed. It indicates you may need to learn new skills. It can show new interests in hobbies and things that you like doing, as the man is very into what he is doing.

The esoteric title for the Eight of Pentacles is Lord of Prudence. Prudence is one of the virtues; however, in this case, it is not applied in spiritual terms. Pentacles deal mostly with earthly matters more than the spiritual (though you can still find spiritual meaning). Prudence here is risk aversion. The man in this card is very cautious and reluctant to take risks. Prudence comes from the Latin *prudential*, which is from the Greek *Phronēsis,* and is better translated as practical knowledge. Thus, the Eight of Pentacles comes to mean common knowledge and practical application.

In a Reading

In readings, the Eight of Pentacles represents hard work and strong attention to details and striving for perfect results. It shows accomplishments, as the pentacles hanging up can be seen with modern eyes as awards, degrees, or trophies. Your hard work pays off with real physical results.

When ill dignified, the Eight of Pentacles can present poor judgment and errors. It can represent a lack of attention to details and decrease quality of work. It can also represent a lack of enjoyment or sense of meaning in the work or project you are engaged in. Lastly, it can indicate a false appearance of mastery in a craft or skill, a sort of faking it until you make it, if you will.

THE NINES

NINE OF CUPS
Esoteric Title: Lord of Material Happiness

Description

On a wooden bench, a wealthy man sits with an expression of happiness on his face. Behind him, on a covered, curved table, are nine chalices, a symbol of his accomplishments and possessions.

Symbolism and Meaning

The Nine of Cups is one of the so-called best cards in the deck. It is traditionally seen by readers as the "wish card," that if this card appears in a reading it means you will have a wish answered or get something you desire. This card is a most certain "yes" to any question asked. Likewise, if this card comes up reversed or ill dignified, it means "no" to your question.

If you recall from the previous card, the Eight of Cups, we saw a man leaving behind eight Cups stacked on top of each other with one space appearing to be missing. We saw that this card represented a search for what was missing and leaving what was safe and secure to find more. The Nine of Cups represents that you have found that which you have looked for. You completed the puzzle and can fill in the missing spot from the Eight of Cups.

The man in the Nine of Cups has accomplished much and he is very proud of what he has achieved. The chalices up on the table are like trophies on display for all to see and admire. He is fulfilled, satisfied, and simply happy with his life. He is confident in himself and is very secure in his identity. Pleasure is also important to understand when looking at the Nine of Cups. This card indicates pleasures of the simple nature, pleasure of life and living. He worries little and does not let things trouble him.

The esoteric title of the Nine of Cups is Lord of Material Happiness. This title would suggest the Nine of Cups leans more to physical/material energy here. The Nine of Cups comes close to the level of manifestation of a Pentacle. This may be due to the completion and manifestation of the element water. Water represents our emotions and, when our emotions manifest in a complete fashion, they become solid. Think of water turning to ice—it goes from a liquid to solid. It is still water but in a solid form. The same can be said of the Nine of Cups. Water (our emotions) manifests in the physical world, but because it is water, it is not corrupted by the material influence. Our emotions can be expressed fully.

In a Reading

In readings, when the Nine of Cups appears, it is a good and positive indication that you are happy. Everything is fulfilled and you have satisfaction in your life. It is also a great card to have in any "outcome" position of a spread, as it shows that you will have a favorable outcome and get what you want. The general sense of the card indicates that you are having fun. At the core, the Nine of Cups signals that you should have fun and enjoy yourself. Have pride in yourself and know that you are fulfilled, not just by material objects, but on an emotional and spiritual level as well.

When ill dignified, the Nine of Cups can represent a failure to obtain happiness and can indicate a setback or loss. It can also represent a haughty attitude and sense of entitlement. This card can represent the over-indulgence like no other card before could have expressed. The need for pleasure can be self-debilitating.

NINE OF WANDS
Esoteric Title: Lord of Great Strength

Description

A worn, tired, and wounded man stands next to a wall of Wands. The ninth Wand is held in his hands. The Wand may be used to support him, to help him stand, or as a barrier to protect himself.

Symbolism and Meaning

Here in the Nine of Wands, we see a figure that appears to be in some sort of defensive mode. He has a wall of Wands built up to separate himself from the outside world, from people who may serve to harm him. Conversely, he may simply think that someone is seeking to harm him.

The Eight Wands behind him represent the Eight of Wands. In the Eight of Wands, we saw those Wands as a symbol of communication, of messages flying across the sky. Here, however, the Wands are planted firmly in the ground. Communication has been halted. This can be a symbol that the man in this card is in no mood to talk, to express, or to vent. He would rather deal with the issue on his own, instead of letting others in.

The main themes of this card are defense, protection, will, stamina, determination, and, on a negative side, paranoia. The bandage on his head signals that he has been wounded in a previous battle. Could this man be the same man in the Seven of Wands, who fought hard against opposition and, in the end, was wounded? The Nine of Wands has learned from past mistakes. But right now, he is trying to recover and regroup himself. He is using this time to heal and to come back to full health.

The esoteric title of the Nine of Wands is Lord of Great Strength. This clearly expresses what this card is all about. The Nine of Wands is about not giving up and keeping to your goal and purpose. His "great strength" is found inside of him, within the element of fire's desire and passion. It is through conflicts when we are able to find our great strength.

One of the more negative aspects expressed by this card is paranoia: the feeling that someone is always trying to harm you. This can cause you to become over-defensive and close yourself off from others. This also turns things hostile and makes you lash out. This sense of paranoia is linked to the past wounds we mentioned. You have been hurt before in the past (perhaps many times), thus you feel you will be harmed again. You expect it to happen over and over.

In a Reading

In a reading, the Nine of Wands indicates you should take into consideration past failures when heading into future endeavors. Ask yourself, *why am I so defensive?* Are you attacking people who are trying to help? You may need time to heal and recover, so take time to recoup. Overall, the Nine of Wands tells you not to give in, but to push forward.

When ill dignified, the Nine of Wands can indicate that you are not protected as well as you thought. Your defense may be weak and you are open to attack. You may be letting your guard down when you should not. Alternately, you may be appearing weak or cowardly to your opposition.

ΠIΠE OF SΩORDS
Esoteric Title: Lord of Despair and Cruelty

Description

In the middle of the night, a woman is woken by her nightmares. The room is dark; she sits up in bed crying into her hands.

Symbolism and Meaning

Thought that Eight of Swords was rough? The Nine of Swords takes things to another level. This is a tough card to get in a reading, because it depicts an image people don't want to see. It shows a woman sitting in her bed, crying. She was sleeping, but was woken up by her nightmare. This is a very real card—more real than most of the other cards, in my opinion. Just about everyone has sat up in bed, worried about some issue. This is a very real emotion and maybe that is why many people cringe when they see this card. They can relate to it on a personal level. I know I do.

The Nine of Swords is mainly a card of mental anguish and exhaustion. The mind here becomes burdened by worries, by anxieties, and all sorts of thoughts that run in the mind that keep us from sleeping and finding peace. The swords are hanging in the background. They are the things that seem to follow us and haunt us. They represent the things in the back of our minds that seem to give us a feeling of foreboding. This is all a part of a greater cycle. The blanket, which is decorated with red roses and signs of the zodiac, represents our travels through the signs and the influences of the higher powers that place us into times of sorrow and joy.

The esoteric title of the Nine of Swords is Lord of Despair and Cruelty. This is a very harsh title and makes this card appear very harmful or negative. However, swords deal with the mind and this is where despair and cruelty is located. It is your mind that causes the cruelty and makes you feel despair. Your mind may be so focused on one thing or a number of things that cause you such turmoil, that it is simply self-inflicted cruelty. What needs to be achieved is the release of this cycle.

Because the setting is set at night and in a bed, this card is linked to our dreams and subconscious. Oftentimes, I see this card as an indication that my clients are having trouble sleeping. They may be troubled by nightmares or repressed negative emotions and thoughts surfacing in their waking lives. It is important to pay attention to these dreams, as they can offer insight into what is plaguing you so you can deal with it.

In a Reading

In readings, the Nine of Swords often indicates that you are more worried about someone else than yourself. In relationships, it can indicate fears and worries about your partner being unfaithful. Someone may be sick and you worry for them. Money may be tight and you are anxious about paying bills. The solution to this card is not to become isolated or hide these feelings. You may want to seek assistance in dealing with your anxiety or sleep troubles. You must also come to terms that you cannot control other people. You can only control your thoughts and when you realize this, you can move on from your anxiety.

When ill dignified, the Nine of Swords can indicate isolation and depression. There may be a lack of hope and fear for the future. Uncertainty eats away at you. Finally, there may be long-lasting grief.

NINE OF PENTACLES
Esoteric Title: Lord of Material Gains

Description

A wealthy woman spends an afternoon in her garden. Lush plants and grapes surround her and, in the distant background, a home can be seen. In her left hand, a hawk sits.

Symbolism and Meaning

The Nine of Pentacles is a wonderful card that is right up there with the Nine of Cups. It is here that we see the fruits of our labor finally being fulfilled and manifested. It was in the Eight of Pentacles where we slaved away at work for this time. The Nine of Pentacles is prosperity and material security at its best. Also, the Nine of Pentacles indicates that now we can finally enjoy our money, our possessions, our home, and our lives in general. She truly knows what she has in her life and enjoys it.

The main focus here is the self-sufficient nature of the woman in the Nine of Pentacles. She is an independent woman. She prefers to take care of herself rather than have someone else take care of her. She relies, also, on her resources. She is logical and practical in her judgments. She is not one to make a wrong decision; she has the experience and knowledge to make decisions that benefit her.

The esoteric title of the Nine of Pentacles is Lord of Material Gain. This is straightforward to its meaning. The Nine of Pentacles represents material gains, be it money, land, or possessions. Investments yield positive returns.

Out of all the cards of the deck, it was this one that I found great debate would stir. The debates deal with whether the woman is a lonely recluse or a woman of social interaction. Does she keep herself hidden away in her garden or does she interact with people? She seems to be very isolated in her garden, but the hooded bird is used to send and receive messages from outside her garden. So she is really not a recluse. However, I do feel at times that this can indicate seclusion. The symbol of the garden is often of a place separate from normal life. It is a sacred and special place for pleasure and contemplation. The garden is also a place of protection. So the question becomes, why does she need protection or what is she protecting? Another thing that would be asked is whether she is a kept woman, the mistress of a wealthy man or is her wealth the product of her own efforts? The snail at the bottom of the card is symbolic of self-containment and self-sufficiency. This is reflective of the Nine of Pentacles' self-sufficient nature.

In a Reading

In readings, the Nine of Pentacles indicates that you are prosperous and that your financial and material needs are met. It is from your self-discipline and self-assurance that you are able to come to this point. You can sit back and enjoy the fruits of your hard work. At times, though, you may feel lonely and want to get out and explore the world more. The Nine of Pentacles also advises that you take thing slow and easy, as the snail at the bottom left represents that a slow and steady pace wins the race. This card also indicates that your finances are in order.

When ill dignified, the Nine of Pentacles can indicate a lack of independence. You rely on someone else to assist you instead of supporting yourself. It can represent complications with properties (ownership) and arguments over finances. There may also be a squandering of resources.

THE TENS

TEN OF CUPS
Esoteric Title: Lord of Perfected Success

Description

Husband and wife stand together with arms raised, praising the rainbow in the sky. Their two children dance together on the side. A river and house are seen in the background. The rainbow holds within it ten chalices.

Symbolism and Meaning

What a wonderfully happy picture this is. A family is outside together in joyful praise. This image reminds me at the end of a fairy tale when they say, "And they lived happily ever after." The happiness and joy here is similar to the Nine of Cups, but the Ten of Cups goes a step further and deeper than the nine did. The nine was focused on the material success that he has acquired in life, totally happy and satisfied with his lot. The Ten of Cups goes further in that it shows a family (not just one person) being happy. This is a shared joy, a shared happiness. The focus has shifted from the individual to the collective as indicated by the children.

Because the image in this card features a family, the main themes expressed here are issues, events, and feelings that relate to the family and the home. Whenever this card has come up in a reading for others, more often than not, it represents a strong connection to the family. From the image, the sense of this card is that of gratitude and thankfulness for what the family has. Cups are the element Water, which is associated with emotions and our feelings. This family is grateful not for just the material things they have, but for the love they have for each other. The Ten of Cups strives to keep the happiness, which was experienced in the Nine of Cups, permanent and stable.

The esoteric title of the Ten of Cups is Lord of Perfected Success tells us that the Ten of Cups is a card that promises success. Since it is "Perfected" there is nothing left to do. How is the success perfected? The exchange of everyone within this family works towards this perfection. This does not have to be a family; it can be a group of people who work together to benefit each other.

In a Reading

In readings, when the Ten of Cups appears, it is a favorable card for many aspects. It shows, first, that happiness is the key factor. There is a lasting joy being experienced. There is sharing between people and wanting to ensure that everyone is happy and can share in the success of the group or family. There is a strong sense of family and belonging. This card is highly favorable in relationship and love readings.

When ill dignified, the Ten of Cups can represent a false appearance of exterior happiness. There are inner issues and problems inside the family; however, this is hidden from those on the outside. The Ten of Cups indicates arguments, dysfunctions, and disunity among the family members. There is a sense of disconnectedness and separation.

TEN OF WANDS
Esoteric Title: Lord of Oppression

Description

A man hunched over by the weight of the Wands he carries. In the background is a town or marketplace which he travels towards.

Symbolism and Meaning

The Ten of Wands represents burdens and responsibilities. The man in the card has taken too much onto himself. The Nine of Wands tried to separate himself from others to recover from some previous battle. The Ten of Wands seems to try to make up for lost time, lost efforts, and tries to do everything on his own.

The Ten of Wands reflects a personality of, "if you want it done right, you have to do it yourself" and "Only I can get this done." Another common trait to this card is a constant need to say yes to anyone who requests something be done. The man here always says yes and takes on more tasks and responsibilities than he can truly handle. Because of this need to do everything, the man overextends himself. He does too much, never refuses anything, and in the end, it can all come crashing down on him.

The esoteric title of the Ten of Wands is Lord of Oppression. This is the perfect title for this card. Because of his burdens, the constant need to take care of everything, the man here has become oppressed. He cannot do what he wants, go where he wants, and just be free. Wands are associated with Fire, which desires to be free and expand. However, he cannot do these things; there is a sense of being held down and back.

This card reminds me of the Greek myth of Sisyphus, who was condemned in Tartarus to an eternity of rolling a boulder uphill and then having to watch it roll back down again, only to push it back up again. Sisyphus' labor was a very frustrating one, rather like labor in the Ten of Wands. His head is buried inside the Wands, which may imply that he does not see exactly how much his burden is. This may also imply he might need assistance.

In a Reading

In readings, the Ten of Wands indicates that you may be weighed down by many responsibilities. You are burdened by all your commitments. You may be working overtime or saying "yes" to yet another project at work that your boss asked you to help with. It can show that you are spending too much time helping others. You pull yourself too thin and into different directions. You may do this out of the kindness of your heart or to make money. You may just love a new challenge and don't consider the other things currently on your plate you need to deal with. You feel some resentment, however, because, as a result, you cannot do what you want to do.

When ill dignified, the Ten of Wands can indicate a blockage in your life and little progress is being made. You may be halted in place and kept at bay. You may have taken on more than you can handle. Your hard work and efforts may be for nothing and wasted.

TEN OF SWORDS
Esoteric Title: Lord of Ruin

Description

On the ground lays a man with ten swords sticking out of his back. A pool of blood spills out. His right hand is seen making the sign of benediction with his hand. The clouds are gray with the sun breaking through.

Symbolism and Meaning

The Ten of Swords might give you a knee-jerk reaction much like Death, The Tower, and The Devil might have. The feeling that we get from this image is of sadness, dread, and despair. The man is dead. What else could this mean? Let me reassure you that, just like with the other "tough" cards (Death, The Devil, and The Tower), Tarot is a system of symbols. This card is not about death. Swords deal with issues of the mind, communication, and thought processes.

Taking a step back to the Nine of Swords, we saw a woman up in bed, crying, worried, and anxious. Something has been troubling her and an issue won't rest. Her mind kept circling around something. This leads us to the Ten of Swords, which shows two possible conclusions. Either the thing that the woman was so worried about came true, or she can finally put the issue to rest and let it go. The first view, that of ruin, is an older meaning. The second view, that of letting go/release is modern and softer. I feel both are valid and possible.

The esoteric title of the Ten of Swords is Lord of Ruin. This is clear to what it means. Things fall apart and the outcome is disastrous. Something external or internal can be to blame for this. You may feel that everything has fallen apart. This can go to a little extreme as thinking, "Life is over" and "why does everything bad always happen to me?"

There is a silver lining to this card that gives much hope. Swords deal with thoughts, thinking, and the mind. This card can represent a release and letting go of an issue, which has been a constant problem. Thus, the problem that the Nine of Swords was fretting about, can be let go. This card represents a need to break the pattern of negative thinking. In the background, the sunlight breaks through, which shows hope for something better. This card reflects the whole idea of cycles very well. Something ended and there is hope for a new cycle to start. If you pay close attention to the man on the ground, to his hand, you'll notice that he is making the same sign as The Hierophant. It is a sign of blessing. The secret message here is that bad things do happen, but there are blessings and good that can come from it. It is unsure if the sun is rising or setting. Are we in dawn or dusk? Dusk represents the psyche being blurred, the blending of conscious with unconscious. If dawn, it represents beginnings and renewals.

In a Reading

In readings, when the Ten of Swords comes up, it can show that you have come to a conclusion on a matter. You are ready to release something. This is the lowest point you can go. Now it is time to go up. Also keep in mind that risky adventures fail in ruin. This can be a warning card if it comes out in outcome and advice positions.

When ill dignified, the Ten of Swords can represent that more is to come. The worst is not behind you yet. Problems may linger around longer than they should. The Ten of Swords can also indicate humiliation. Not only does something fail, but it is put out for others to know about.

TEN OF PENTACLES
Esoteric Title: Lord of Wealth

Description

A wealthy family is in town, at a market maybe. Two white dogs accompany them. The child peeks from behind the mother, looking at the older man watching them.

Symbolism and Meaning

The Ten of Pentacles goes beyond the Nine of Pentacles that focused on the self and material needs of one person and goes on to look at the needs of the family, much like the Nine of Cups and Ten of Cups.

Early on in my studies, I found this card difficult to understand and apply into a reading. For one thing, it is similar to the Ten of Cups. They often appear together in readings because of this similarity. They talk a common theme relating to the domestic life and domestic affairs. To understand their difference, looking to the element helps. Cups (Water) deal with emotions and the Pentacles (Earth) deal with the material. The Ten of Cups showed a happy, loving family enjoying each other's company. In the Ten of Pentacles, we see a family who is more geared towards the physical, material, and tangible. However, it is not bad like the Four of Pentacles, per se. This card shows wealth, security, and prosperity on a grander scale.

The Ten of Pentacles looks for a way to make things last for a long time, to keep things permanent, and which can be passed down to the next generation. Because of the generational aspect of this card and its link to money, this is a card of inheritances, traditions, and sticking to what is established.

The esoteric title of the Ten of Pentacles is Lord of Wealth. This implies material wealth through money, investments, home, property, and anything physical. Wealth also refers to the abundance of these things. The focus here is heavily on the material, which can be good or bad depending on other cards. The positioning of the pentacles in the card is important to note as they form the Kabbalistic Tree of Life with each pentacle representing each of the Sephirot. The bottom one is Malkuth "Kingdom," our physical world. This reinforces the notion that the material is of concern and ruling this card. The downside to this is that the people in this card may become so accustomed to such a wonderful living that it is all taken for granted and that they may not appreciate the spiritual and emotional aspect of life.

In a Reading

In readings, when the Ten of Pentacles appear, it signals great and long-lasting success. It shows that you have created something, which you can build a life on and pass down. It can indicate the likelihood of a large purchase, like a house. It can also be seen as investing into the future and making long-term plans.

When ill dignified, the Ten of Pentacles can represent family problems much like the Ten of Cups. Both deal with domestic matters. The Ten of Pentacles can indicate financial matters, wills, trusts, estates are all sorts of things that family members can fight over. The Ten of Pentacles can also represent lacking a support system from family. It can also represent being disinherited or simply not being offered financial assistance in a time of need. It can also show ill health, especially with the elderly.

The Royal Families

Court Cards

In addition to the ten pip cards of the Minor Arcana, each suit has its own royal family called the *Court Cards*. The Court Cards are comprised of four characters. Starting with the lowest rank are the Pages, the Knights, the Queens, and the Kings. Some decks list them as Prince, Princess, Knight, and Queen—the *Thoth Tarot* is one deck that uses this system. Another system used is Princess, Prince, Queen and King. Within all the systems, regardless of the name, the main focus is the development of the particular suit element from the innocence/potential to maturity and full expression of the element.

The Court Cards tend to be a confusing issue for many readers. It is often an area of stress due to the ambiguity as to what is the proper way to handle court cards in a reading. To keep things simple, there are three key expressions that a court card could manifest itself as:

1. They represent a person that is not you, but someone around you who has an influence or will influence the question/issue being asked. For example, the Queen of Pentacles may represent your mother or boss.
2. They represent a personality: qualities or traits, talents, skills, and inner potential in regards to the question/issue. For example, the Page of Swords could represent an inquisitive nature and a tendency to gather information and learn.
3. Environmental influences and actions. For example, the King of Pentacles could suggest an investment is needed.

Traditionally, the courts cards would indicate people based on physical attributes such as dark haired or fair skinned. I do not favor this type of attributions to the courts as the main system to identify someone. It can be used, but is not something I put too much stock into. The same is true with gender. Does a King indicate a male or female? The gender of the court card does not always transfer into real life. Age is another way people try to identify people based on the courts. For example, the Page of Wands would be someone young in years. This is not always the case. The reason for this is because Tarot is a symbolic system and the people in the cards are not literal people. They represent elements and particular stages in development. Any person can be represented by any court card regardless of gender or age. However, you can use the gender and age in the court as a possible indicator. For example, I once did a reading for a man (using the Celtic Cross Spread) and the first two cards were Queen of Swords crossed by Death. I saw this as an indication of an older woman who had died. I asked the man, "Did an older woman, whom you looked up to as a sort of mother figure recently die?" I also applied character traits of the Queen of Swords to this woman, I said this woman was blunt, smart, someone who cut to the chase, and was very direct. He said yes, that there was an older woman at work whom he'd looked up to as a sort of mother-type figure and she had died recently. The death was on his mind and the reason why it must have come up in the reading. This is also a rare example that the Death card indicated death, but remember that this was death that had occurred already and was not a prediction.

I will break down the court cards to reveal to you who they are as if they were people, how they would behave in situations, what their habits are, likes, and dislikes. One of the best ways to understand the court cards is to understand the personality of the courts. A good exercise of this is to link them to people in your lives. Your husband may be a wealthy businessman, so he would remind you of the King of Pentacles. Your girlfriend may be the Queen of Wands, very attractive and charismatic. Your boss may be a Queen of Swords, a real bitch who likes to point out all your mistakes. Once you connect the cards to people you know, you will be able to better relate to them.

Court Associations: Elements and Qabalah

RANK	SUIT	ELEMENT	WORLD
Page	Pentacles	Earth	Assiah
Knight	Swords	Air	Yetzirah
Queen	Cups	Water	Briah
King	Wands	Fire	Atziluth

How do these elements influence the courts? The elements will have an impact on the court cards temperament and personality. The elements also have a deeper connection with Qabalah and the creation of the four worlds. Each rank is associated with one of the worlds.

Creation starts with Atziluth, the highest of the worlds, which is the world of emanations and archetypes.

Atziluth deals with ideas and concepts. It is the most abstract of the worlds.

Atziluth is associated with Kings.

Below Atziluth is Briah, the creative world where the ideas and concepts in Atziluth start to develop like a rough draft.

Briah is associated with the Queens.

Next is Yetzirah, the world of formation. This is the world where meanings and symbols exist and where details are formed as we get closer to manifestation.

Yetzirah is associated with Knights.

Finally, we end up at Assiah, the world of action, and our physical world. This is where manifestation occurs. Assiah is associated with Pages.

It is interesting to see that when we look at the cards through Qabala, the Pages represent manifestation while Kings are conceptual. Normally we see Pages as lower and represent the novice while Kings are higher and represent mastery. The Qabala give us another way of looking at the courts than we would normally expect.

Elemental Combinations

Each court embodies two elements. First is the element based on rank and second based on suit. For example, all pages are earth and Wands are fire. The Page of Wands then is "Earth of Fire." These elemental combinations help understand the elemental makeup of the court card.

	PAGE	KNIGHT	QUEEN	KING
Wands	Earth of fire	Air of Fire	Water of fire	Fire of Fire
Cups	Earth of Water	Air of Water	Water of Water	Fire of Water
Swords	Earth of Air	Air of Air	Water of Air	Fire of Air
Pentacles	Earth of Earth	Air of Earth	Water of Earth	Fire of Earth

The Pages

The pages are the youths in the courts, the children in the royal family that embody the feminine energy, but are not as developed as the Queens. Being the children of the royal family, they have a lot to learn. They take the element of their suit and wield it with little experience and understanding. But what they lack in experience they make up for in willingness to experience and learn.

Pages can represent something new entering into the situation, much like an Ace does. Because they are young, they are excited and ready to try new things. Pages are eager and want to experience as much as they can, much like a baby that wants to touch and sense everything around them. They are open vessels ready to receive all that life has to give them. They are optimistic and innocent.

In the New Testament, Jesus speaks about children as very important to entering into the Kingdom of Heaven. When asked in Matthew 18:3, who is greatest in the Kingdom of heaven? Jesus responds: "Assuredly, I say to you, unless you are converted and become as little children, you will by no means enter the Kingdom of Heaven." This parable deals with the selfish interest in worldly power, pointing to a little child as the model for the true virtues that allow one into the Kingdom of Heaven; one of these virtues is the willingness to love and be loved. The Pages express this willingness that Jesus teaches.

Elementally, all pages are rooted in the element of Earth. When expressed positively, Pages can be sensuous, persistent, and useful. When expressed negatively, the Pages can be unenterprising, afraid to take risks, and opportunistic.

As much as their youth is a benefit, it is also their downfall, which can make them immature and express negative qualities of their suit and element. They can be easily influenced and manipulated since they are gullible or they may be doing the manipulating.

Pages are associated with the World of Action (Assiah), where things become manifest and material. Alternatively, the Pages are often associated with the Archetypal World of Atziluth. However, that level of creation is beyond the Pages, who are young and lack the mastery needed to comprehend such archetypal concepts. They can, however, express archetypal ideals, but are not fully aware of their origin and full potential.

The Knights

After the Page, we encounter the Knights, who have a similar role as the Pages, but expand and develop on them. Knights can also represent news, but beyond that, they represent motion and a force of change. As the Pages were children, the Knights represent adolescence. They embody in themselves masculine energy, but on a less refined level than the King.

In psychology, the Knights relate to Erik Erickson's theory of coherent self-identity. According to Erikson, self-identity is gained through sincere and constant recognition of real accomplishments. These achievements must have meaning in their society or culture. What Erikson says applies to the Knights of the Tarot. The Knights venture out to accomplish something specific to their suit.

It is also in adolescence that a person is able to move from concrete thinking to abstract thinking. This aspect of abstract thinking relates perfectly to the Knight's association to Air. All the Knights express airy qualities in combination with their suit's element. Air deals with the mind, intellect, and thinking.

Knights are very goal-orientated. They each have a goal they are attempting to accomplish, but which can also make them single-minded or obsessed in meeting their aspiration.

Knights are associated with Yetzirah, the world of formation. The world where meanings and symbols exist and where details are formed, this again relates back to the change from concrete to abstract thinking.

As I mentioned, the Knights indicate motion and movement. It is highly important to note how each Knight is different in their level of motion:

- Knight of Pentacles is completely still. There is no movement.
- Knight of Cups—movement begins with the horse walking.
- Knight of Wands—movement picks up with the horse getting ready to trot.
- Knight of Swords—movement is at full force with the horse charging.

This observation in the different level of movement in the Knights has a lot of influence on the meaning of the cards' character and behavior, which will be explored in each Knight. In general, the Knight are about progress and moving forward, just at different speeds and intensity.

Astrologically:

- The Knight of Wands corresponds with Sagittarius.
- The Knight of Cups corresponds with Pisces.
- The Knight of Swords corresponds with Gemini.
- The Knight of Pentacles corresponds with Virgo.

The Queens

The Queens are the mothers of the royal family and much of their personalities and qualities reflect a motherly type role. This is because all Queens reflect the nature of The Empress.

The Pages and Knights manifested the immature or underdeveloped energy of the feminine and masculine respectively. The Queens and King manifest the feminine and masculine in a mature and developed manner. The Queens embody mature feminine qualities such as patience, understanding, nurturing, creativity, and creation. They offer encouragement and cultivate ideas.

The Queens correspond with Briah, the Creative World where the ideas and concepts begin to take shape, emerging into an undeveloped form.

Elementally, all Queens are rooted in the element of Water. Water, when expressed in a positive way, can manifest as protecting, nurturing, and empathy. When expressed in negative manner, water can manifest as overprotecting, overemotional, insecure, and deceptive.

Queens co-rule with the Kings. Queens have their own authority and power, but express it in a subtle manner. They use their powers of persuasion rather than brute force. They work behind the scenes, influencing people without the other person really being aware of it. This can also manifest as manipulation in some of the Queens.

As people, the Queen can represent an adult female figure that you may look up to, respect, or is an authority figure. They can also be any person who embodies the qualities of The Queens, be it male or female. Queens generally desire to help and assist people who come to them for help. A Queen can easily befriend you and be a benefactor as well as becoming an enemy if ill dignified.

Astrologically, the Queens are associated with the following zodiac signs:

- Queen of Wands corresponds with Leo.
- Queen of Cups corresponds with Scorpio.
- Queen of Sword corresponds with Aquarius.
- Queen of Pentacles corresponds with Capricorn.

The Kings

The Kings are the father figures in the royal family. They are husband and co-ruler with the Queens. The Queens and Kings balance each other out as the Queens represent, in some fashion, The Empress. The Kings, in turn, represent The Emperor.

The Kings are outward and forceful in their authority. They represent the mature and developed masculine energy as opposed to the Knight's immature and underdeveloped masculine energy.

Kings correspond with Atziluth, the highest of the worlds, which is the world of emanations and archetypes. Atziluth deals with ideas and concepts. It is the most abstract of the worlds.

Kings represent the mastery of their element. They command respect and honor for their knowledge and experience. They are authority figures, wielding power to make decisions as a leader.

Elementally, all Kings correspond to the element Fire. When expressed in a positive manner, Fire can be expressed as self-confidence, enterprise, independence, inspiration, and optimism. When Fire is expressed in a negative manner, it can be impatient, aggressive, and unrealistic.

Astrologically, the Kings are associated with the following signs:

- King of Cups corresponds with Cancer.
- King of Wands corresponds with Aries.
- King of Swords corresponds with Libra.
- King of Pentacles corresponds with Taurus.

THE PAGES

PAGE OF CUPS
Element: Earth of Water

Description

A young boy dressed in a tunic decorated with lotus flowers holds forth a cup that has a fish springing from it. The Page examines the fish with interest. In the background, there are rough waves.

Symbolism and Meaning

The Page of Cups is a very sensitive person, someone who is connected to his or her emotions and feelings—someone who may be a little too connected at times. This connection to his emotions allow the Page of Cups to be very imaginative and creative. However, remember that this is a Page, so he is lacking the full control and understanding of his emotions. We are in an early stage of emotional development; the love expressed here is innocent.

Like the Ace of Cups, the Page of Cups expresses the element Water, which represents love, intuition, feeling, and emotions. The Page of Cups is thoughtful and kind, someone who makes kind gestures of friendship and affection. He wants to spread joy and make people smile. He has an overall good nature and pure spirit.

The fish that comes out from the cup may or may not be real. The Page of Cups is highly imaginative, so this fish may be a figment of his imagination. Fish themselves symbolically represent fertility and creativity in Pagan traditions, because the fish is one of the symbols of the Divine Mother. The fish also represents happiness and transformation. One of the things that the Page of Cups aspires for is spiritual meaning and seeks to learn and develop his spirituality. This is the transformative aspect of the fish that the Page is trying to understand.

In Jean Piaget's four stages of cognitive development, the Page of Cups represents the second stage of Assimilation. This is a child who interprets new experiences by incorporating them into existing schemes. The Page of Cups then is seen as experiential and receptive.

In a Reading

When the Page of Cups appears in a reading, like all pages, can indicate messages and news heading your way. The message or news may deal with the birth of a baby, a romantic encounter, or news from loved ones. As a person, it can represent someone who gives emotional support and offers humble gestures of love. As an inner personality trait, it can represent intuition. It can also represent dreaming and fantastical ideas. Lastly, it signals a need for self-love.

When ill dignified, the Page of Cups expresses negative traits such as narcissism, focusing only on outer aesthetics, and lacking emotional depths. It can also represent insincere gestures and apologies.

PAGE OF WANDS
Element: Earth of Fire

Description

A young page is dressed in a regal tunic, decorated with salamanders, and stands in an arid desert with three pyramid-like structures behind him. He grasps his Wand with confidence, looking forward with motivation and optimism in his direction.

Symbolism and Meaning

The Page of Wands is a very enthusiastic individual who is willing to go on an adventure and experience life. He desires to seek new paths and avenues of experience for self-growth and exploration of his identity.

According to developmental psychologist Jean Piaget, there are four stages in cognitive development in children. I associate the Page of Wands with the first stage, Scheme, the organized pattern (framework) of thought that is constructed by a child to understand the world around them. Within this psychological view, the Page of Wands can be seen as having a certain framework of understanding the world that is innate and pure without much influence upon it. This makes the Page of Wand's thinking "idealistic," which comes from the Fire element of Wands.

The Page of Wands is confident in himself. He is willing to take risks and jump onto any opportunity that involves travel, adventure, and cross-culture contact. The Page is similar to The Fool and The Sun symbolically, because of a common symbol they share, which is the feather on their head. This symbolizes life force and energy, which again is rooted in the element of Fire. The Wand he holds is taller than the Page, which shows that the Page needs time to develop and grow to fully channel the energy of the Wand.

In a Reading

When the Page of Wands appears in a reading, it can be seen as a positive sign. It can represent news coming your way, a proclamation that will be made, and an invitation to an event, and all other sorts of messages. It can indicate the start of a new phase or project that is being developed. As a person, it can represent someone who offers you encouragement and support. As an inner personality trait, it can represent optimism and eagerness. It also can represent a playful nature, one that seeks fun and adventure. You may need to take some risk and overcome the fears that hold you back.

When ill dignified, the Page of Wands is expressed negatively by acts of immaturity, refusing to grow up, or take responsibility. This is the person who parties every weekend. It can also mean delays and hesitations.

PAGE OF SWORDS
Element: Earth of Air

Description

On top of a small hill stands the Page of Swords in an offensive position. Swords are held high behind him, ready to strike. His hair flows in the wind. Clouds in the distance rise high up from the land to the sky. The clothing of this Page is not as regal or luxurious as the previous Pages.

Symbolism and Meaning

The Page of Swords is an intellectual person with high mental activity. He is a student seeking knowledge and information, but above all, truth. He is a fast talker and fast thinker who can—or at least thinks he can—multitask many mental activities.

Like the Ace of Swords, which stands for mental activity, justice, and truth, the Page of Swords embodies these qualities through action. The Page of Swords is curious and wants to figure things out by analyzing problems and looking for logical solutions.

In Jean Piaget's four stages of cognitive development, the Page of Swords represents the third stage of Disequilibrium. This stage involves a child having an experience that causes an imbalance or contradiction between the new experience and an existing scheme. This imbalance or contradiction leads to change of knowledge and allows cognitive growth. The stage is associated with the Page of Swords because swords can represent mental conflicts. The Page of Swords may then indicate something that you find conflicting with what you already know and forces you to adapt your cognition.

In a Reading

When the Page of Swords appears in a reading, it can indicate that you need to look at things intellectually and logically, but to be cautious not to jump to conclusions.

Use your observational abilities to gather information from others. Be careful, however, as your analysis of the situation may be premature and not really cover the deeper reasoning. Like all Pages, the Page of Swords can indicate messages. Since this is a Sword dealing with communication, expect it more so in this Page. The message may be a warning or a heads up to something that you were not aware of. Vigilance is important. As a person, the Page of Swords may be someone who is learning and likes to get into conversations on great matters. As an inner personality trait, the Page of Swords can represent inquisitiveness and wanting to learn. You may also be looking for practical ways to apply your knowledge.

When ill dignified, the Page of Swords may be someone who is working against you, spying, or has malicious intentions. It can indicate trickery and malice. There is misinformation that could be unintentional. You may also be feeling frustrated and annoyed from a lack of understanding.

Page of Pentacles
Element: Earth of Earth

Description

A boy dressed in green and red stands in an open field. He holds up high his Pentacle as he gazes into it. In the background is a small farm.

Symbolism and Meaning

The Page of Pentacles is a practical and serious student who learns hands-on through real experience. He is an ideal student who wants to learn by actually doing physical actions, not just theoretical or conceptual.

As with the Ace of Pentacles, which represents the material world and earthly qualities like practicality and prospering, the Page of Pentacles embodies these qualities through actions. The Page of Pentacles looks at things realistically and with a practical common sense approach.

Because the Page of Pentacles is of Earth, we have a grounded person who is cautious. He does not take many risks. When deciding something, he studies all the angles and details.

In Jean Piaget four stages of cognitive development, the Page of Pentacles represents the fourth and final stage of Accommodation. It is in this stage when a child changes their scheme to integrate and adapt a new experience. There is equilibrium when this occurs that matches up with the Page of Pentacles's love for learning and study. As he learns, he is adapting new knowledge and experiences into previous mental frameworks.

In a Reading

When the Page of Pentacles appears in a reading, it can, like all pages, represent a message. Being a Pentacle, the message may indicate financial matters dealing with money, career, and educational opportunities. Job offers or acceptance into a college or training program can be indicative of the Page of Pentacles. As a person, the Page of Pentacles represents a student or apprentice. He is someone who is generous and helpful when it comes to projects and work. As an inner personality trait, the Page of Pentacles can represent diligence and persistence with whatever matter is at hand. The Page of Pentacles can also represent being trusting or trustworthy.

When ill dignified, the Page of Pentacles can represent laziness or inertia. It can represent a lack of motivation to do physical activity, a lack of interest in what you are studying, or in your job. There could be news regarding financial matters or that your career is unfavorable. You may be having trouble getting your ideas developed, being delayed due to funding, or other roadblocks.

THE KNIGHTS

Knight of Cups
Element: Air of Water

Description

Walking at a steady pace, the Knight of Cups rides on a white horse. He holds a cup, extending it outward. On his helmet and feet are pairs of wings.

Symbolism and Meaning

The Knight of Cups is our archetypal romantic person, someone who is in love with love. Often seen as the "Knight in shining armor," the Knight of Cups takes off where the Page of Cups left off by taking steps to delve deeper into the unconscious and develop his emotions.

Astrologically, the Knight of Cups is associated with Pisces, a water sign that is mutable. Exploring the astrological aspect of the card will reveal what makes this Knight's heart tick. Being a water sign makes this Knight of Cups sensitive, compassionate, and empathetic. He is sensitive to his feelings and the feeling of others. His gentle nature is evident by his slow pace. The horse bows its head. His bare hands are exposed, which, as a Knight, is dangerous to getting hurt. This exposure of the hands signals his character is gentle and tender. He is a lover, not a fighter, as the French would say.

Being a mutable sign, much like the Knight of Wands, he is capable of change and learning. The change and learning he deals with is in the realm of emotion, feelings, imagination, and creativity. The type of change this Knight brings is methodical. He is not fast to act like the Knight of Wands. Instead, he examines his feelings and tries to see if what is being presented sits right with him.

According to Erikson's psychological theory, the Knight of Cups seeks accomplishments often in romantic relationships as well as creations of creativity like art, music, or dance.

In a Reading

In a reading, the Knight of Cups asks that you take a moment to reflect on decisions before determining anything. Is it the best time to act or is it better to wait? When you are hit with a block, interject some creativity and imagination into the equation to get better results.

When ill dignified, the Knight of Cups expresses negative water traits. He can be insecure, secretive, shy, and clingy. His emotions may be scattered and unfocused, unsure of what to make of a matter emotionally. He may be a seducer. He can become moody, irritable, and highly introverted. He can become jealous and easily offended when criticized or ignored.

KNIGHT OF WANDS
Element: Air of Fire

Description

On his golden horse, the Knight of Wands dashes off to another adventure. He is dressed in armor and covered in decorative salamanders like the Page of Wands. From his helmet, plumes of fire extend outward.

Symbolism and Meaning

Looking at the Knight of Wands, we see him moving in a fast pace. He is off to seek adventure; his fiery nature being a Wand makes him energetic and progressive. While the Page of Wands thought of goals and plans, it is the Knight that takes actions to get closer to his goal.

Astrologically, the Knight of Wands represents the sign of Sagittarius, which is the base for much of the personality of the Knight of Wands. Sagittarius is a sign that is associated with individuality, travel, adventure, courage, spontaneity, and being active. Sagittarius is a mutable (adaptable to change) sign, which manifests in the Knight of Wands through learning and preferring change. The Knight of Wands, being a traveler, learns along the way out in the open, not in the classroom-type setting. Being a catalyst for change, the Knight of Wands changes for the sake of changing. Overall, the change presented here in the Knight of Wands is that of the impulsive kind.

As a mutable sign, he does not like repetitive tasks and will become easily bored. Sagittariuses are physical people who are athletic or are constantly moving. I worked once with a Sagittarius who always had to go outside on her break to walk: rain, snow, or blistering heat. With a Sagittarius rising myself, I fidget a lot. I do not like sitting in the same position too long.

According to Erikson's psychological theory, the Knight of Wands seeks accomplishments often in athletic arenas. This would be the star athlete or the high school quarterback who has a room full of trophies.

In a Reading

In a reading, the Knight of Wands indicates a new adventure awaits you. It is time to take action and get a move on your projects now. Focus on how to advance and promote your dreams and desires.

When ill dignified, the Knight of Wands can express negative qualities such as being hot-headed, impulsive, impatient, pushy, chasing a false dream, unfocused, and scattered with his energy. He can become full of himself and over-confident in his ability, boasting his accomplishments and adventures. One of the more dominant factors is unfocused and scattered. These two negative expressions can be the downfall of the Knight of Wands. Without focus, all the energy of the Knight of Wands is misplaced, misused, and wasted.

KNIGHT OF SWORDS
Element: Air of Air

Description

Rushing into battle, the Knight of Swords rides his horse. The sky is gray with the storm rolling in. One hand is gloved while the other hand is not; in this hand he holds his weapon.

Symbolism and Meaning

Out of all the Knights, the Knight of Swords is the most aggressive and active of them all. The image we have here is very fast-paced; the wind is blowing as we can see by the trees and clouds in the background.

Astrologically, the Knight of Swords is associated with Gemini, an Air sign that is mutable just as the previous Knights were. As an Air sign, the Knight of Swords is intelligent, knowledgeable in concrete facts, and is alert to his surroundings. This knight's mind is very versatile. He is able to deal with complex mental tasks. Also, he is very quick-minded and fast with his words, which makes him very clever

According to Erikson's psychological theory, the Knight of Swords seeks accomplishments in either education or knowledge or in areas of the military service.

In a Reading

In readings, the Knight of Swords serves as a sign for caution and to be alert with your environment. As a catalyst for change, the Knight of Swords represents assertive changes. Immediate actions needs to be made in the present moment; you do not have the comfort to reflect on the issue like the Knight of Cups. Put aside your feelings and follow what is logical. Your mind will be your ally; use your cleverness to your advantage. The Knight of Swords may indicate a need for mental stimulation and challenge, as he can be restless with his mind and need stimulation.

When ill dignified, the Knight of Swords paints an unpleasant picture. The Sword is double-edged. The hand in which the Knight holds his Sword is bare. This represents skill in his use of the sword. However, it is equally skillful when ill dignified. The Knight of Swords can become hostile toward others and defensive to other's criticism. He can become detached from the world and his emotions become too airy. He can lose sight of things, becoming nearsighted towards the long-term ramifications of his actions. He may meddle in affairs that have nothing to do with him. His skill with words can be used abusively, and, thus, hurt people.

KNIGHT OF PENTACLES
Element: Air of Earth

Description

Sitting on his black horse, the Knight of Pentacles is motionless. He gazes forth to a field, which has not brought a harvest. A green plant grows on his helmet.

Symbolism and Meaning

We have reached the last Knight—the Knight of Pentacles. This Knight is stationary; he does not move. Being that Pentacles represent Earth, this would make sense since Earth can be fixed and unmovable. However, the Knight is motionless because he reveals a lot when we compare it to the other Knights.

The other Knights all had some sort of speed to their movement. The Knight of Pentacles does not, so this shows that he lacks the enthusiasm of the Knight of

Wands, emotion of the Knight of Cups, and the bravery of the Knight of Swords. So what does the Knight of Pentacles have that the other Knights do not? A plan.

The Knight of Pentacles would be the only Knight who has a true plan of what he wants and probably has the material, connections, or means to get it done. While the other Knights were motivated intensely, The Knight of Pentacles is motivated extrinsically for a specific outcome.

Astrologically, the Knight of Pentacles is associated with Virgo. Being a Virgo gives the Knight of Pentacles such qualities as being patient, productive, hardworking, and dedicated. He is patient, for he waits for the harvest in the field. He is also cautious because Earth signs are slow to decide and use discernment in all things.

According to Erikson's psychological theory, the Knight of Pentacles seeks accomplishments in areas regarding money, career, and reputation.

In a Reading

In readings, the Knight of Pentacles indicates you need to take things slowly. You may need to protect something that you feel is your "investment." There may be someone who will represent or helps you succeed in life. It is time to make a commitment and get all your ducks in a row. Keep a serious attitude with matters dealing with money and work.

When ill dignified, the Knight of Pentacles represents laziness and non-productivity. There is stagnation with projects, career, and material growth. On the flip slide, you may be overcommitted to too many responsibilities. You may not have a solid, pragmatic plan. You may abandon your obligations for something enjoyable.

THE QUEENS

QUEEN OF CUPS
Water of Water

Description

The regal Queen of Cups sits on her throne, which is on the shore of a sea or ocean. She gazes deeply at the chalice in her hand.

Symbolism and Meaning

The Queen of Cups is the Queen that embodies the pure essence of the element of Water. She is Water of Water. This allows us to understand her to be an emotionally connected Queen.

The personality of the Queen of Cups is caring and loving. She is someone you would go to for comfort and a sympathetic ear. Cups are a receptive element, which makes the Queen accepting of others and receptive to all sorts of things. Her open nature makes her a natural psychic or someone very interested in spiritual matters. She listens to her intuition, to her dreams, and has a good grasp over her feelings. She is naturally very nurturing, giving support for those she loves and cares for. She gazes intensely at her chalice, which is the only chalice in the Tarot that is this ornate and has a lid. So ornate this chalice is that it appears to have a religious appearance. This associates this Queen with matters dealing with the spiritual realm and, to me, a reference to her possible role as a symbol of the Divine Feminine. The Queens correspond with Briah the Creative World, where the ideas and concepts begin to take shape, emerging into an undeveloped form. The Queen of Cups focuses her creative forces as her source of creation.

Astrologically, The Queen of Cups is associated with the sign Scorpio. Scorpio is the most probing of the signs, which could explain her staring at the chalice. It's closed and she wants to know what the heck is inside. The Queen of Cups is not all lollipops and rainbows as it may appear from my description. She is someone you should watch out for. This will be explained when she is ill dignified.

In a Reading

In readings, when the Queen of Cups appears, she can represent a person who may be able to help and give you advice regarding the matter at hand. The kind of advice she gives is more about allowing you to understand how you really feel about the particular issue. The Queen of Cups as an influence and not a person represents when our heart is aligned in what we are doing. This is when we are in a place or love that is at the center of the matter. She may be reminding you to follow your heart, listen to your intuition, and go deep beyond what is seen on the surface.

When ill dignified, she manifests the negative side of Scorpio. She can be secretive, deceptive, very jealous, and above all, manipulative. Her manipulative powers are strong because of her ability to be so connected with emotion; she can use that power to get the upper hand on someone else: pretending to be a friend, gaining the trust of others, and then turning around and betraying them. In her ill dignified aspect, she can be untrusting, bitter, and gossipy. She can also show that you are emotionally dried out, the sea is dry, and you have lost your connection to your feelings.

QUEEN OF WANDS
Water of Fire

Description

The fiery Queen of Wands sits on her throne, which features the heads of lions. In her left hand she holds a sunflower, in the right, her Wand. A black cat sits attentively at her feet.

Symbolism and Meaning

The Queen of Wands mixes the positive qualities of Fire with the inward focus of a Queen to produce a very positive figure. The Queen of Wands is one of the more benevolent Queens.

The personality of the Queen of Wands is energetic, enthusiastic, confident, and cheerful. She is very outgoing, sociable, and popular with people. All eyes are fixed upon her dominating presence. It is easy to understand why everyone loves the Queen of Wands; she is associated with Leo, the Zodiac sign that is commanding, egocentric, entertaining, and grandiose.

The Queen of Wand is seated and facing us, which shows her dominance, power, and focus. She is looking forward to the future, showing her ability to create new directions, ideas, and put them into action. She develops and grows ideas with her enthusiasm and inspiration.

The Queen of Wands has a clear understanding of her Self. This clear sense of Self gives this queen the ability to look beyond the surface of things. She explores what is underneath our outward persona we show to the world. The persona is the false Self, the person we appear to others in our lives. The Queen of Wands is authentic in her sense of self.

In a Reading

In readings, when the Queen of Wands appears, it can represent a person in your life, possibly an adult female who possesses the qualities of the Queen as well as a male. This person may offer you encouragement and helpful advice to help you see what is really going on in the situation. She will also push you to take action even if you feel that you are not ready yet. As an influence and not a person, she represents that it is a good time to move forward with whatever plans you have made.

When ill dignified, the Queen of Wands can express herself through jealous, vindictive behaviors. In Greek mythology, she would be Hera, queen of the gods and wife of Zeus. Hera was a very jealous Goddess; you see Zeus was a man whore who had many extramarital affairs. Hera could not hurt Zeus so she took her anger out on his children. Some of the most well-known of these incidents were her attempts to kill the baby Hercules with snakes. Lesson: remember to not piss off the Queen of Wands.

QUEEN OF SWORDS
Water of Air

Description

The compelling Queen of Swords sits on her throne, looking right. In her right hand, she holds her sword that points up. Her left hand is raised, a gesture of greeting.

Symbolism and Meaning

The Queen of Swords is Water of Air. As we learned, water is receptive and is inward in nature. Air is related to thought, speech, and knowledge. With the Queen of Swords, we see these two elements combine and give us a Queen that is very intelligent.

Her intelligence comes from her receptive water nature, which allows her to observe her surroundings. Combined with air qualities, she is able to turn those observations into opinions, especially critical ones. She is a quick learner and can adapt to new information and new ways of thinking. This makes her a fast thinker—a witty one in fact, for she does have a sense of humor that is the intelligent kind. In the background, we see a large grouping of clouds that cover about half the card. However, her head is above the clouds, which shows she thinks clearly. Her crown is made of butterflies. This serves as a symbol of the element Air. It also signals that her spiritual evolution is through serious contemplation, which is the essence of Water of Air. She is seated looking right, which may suggest she is forward thinking and progressive.

She is depicted with her sword pointing up, which alludes to the Justice card. There is the possibility that she is judging someone or telling someone to rise up. Either way, she is an authority figure. I often call the Queen of Swords the queen who thinks she is king. She is independent and rules on her own terms. I associate her with virgin queens, those queens who rule alone without a King, such as Queen Elizabeth I, who was called The Virgin Queen. The Queen of Swords has often represented a widow. She is simply independent; she could not subject herself to the will of another.

Astrologically, the Queen of Swords is associated with the sign Aquarius. Aquarius represents qualities, many of which I've already described in her, such as progressiveness and independence. The Queen of Swords can become aloof and detached from practical matters if she intellectualizes too much.

In a reading, when the Queen of Swords appears, it can represent a person who has authority. It can be someone like your boss or a judge. Oftentimes, when you have a mean boss, this Queen will represent that person. The Queen of Swords is the perfect person to seek the most objective guidance from, free of personal bias or agenda. She looks at facts and evidence, so she will only give you the truth. She is honest and authentic. As an influence and not a person, the Queen of Swords tells you to really think things through, to consider the evidence and facts at hand. Evaluate what is knowable and objective. She can serve as a reminder that you should be truthful and honest.

When ill dignified, the Queen of Swords can become harsh with her words—her constructive criticism turns to destructive. The best reference to the ill-dignified Queen of Swords is Lady Macbeth from Shakespeare. Lady Macbeth represents the symbol of the anti-mother figure, which is apparent when she talks about smashing in the brains of a baby that is feeding from her breasts. Lady Macbeth also defied gender roles by deviating away from her femininity in order to push her husband's political career. The Queen of Swords can become very demanding and domineering. She can also be someone who is picking at every detail, looking for errors and mistakes. Lastly, she can be unwilling to compromise and must have things her way.

QUEEN OF PENTACLES
Water of Earth

Description

The earthly Queen of Pentacles sits on her throne in a lavish and luxurious garden.

Symbolism and Meaning

The Queen of Pentacles is Water of Earth, a very good combination. Water and Earth go together well like a horse and carriage. They give us a Queen that gives us a likeness that is closest to The Empress.

While all Queens embody The Empress in some way, the Queen of Pentacles represents it most directly. Both are situated in nature with a lot of greenery around them. The Empress represented abundance and Pentacles present the material, thus this emphasizes the Queen of Pentacles as material abundance. She lives in an environment that is warm, earthly, comfortable, and secure. If we were to have an archetypal mother contest between all the Queens, it would be a close tie between the Queen of Cups and Queen of Pentacles. However, I give a slight edge to this Queen, because I see her as the archetypal housewife. She loves her home, her family, and takes care of it all. She is a domestic queen for sure, a real Martha Stewart or Betty

Crocker. If you were having a bad day, this queen would fix you up something to eat to make you feel good. All this reflects the earthly nature of the Pentacles with the inwardness of the element of water. Aside from domestic affairs, the Queen of Pentacles is a great businesswoman; she has a realistic mindset that comes in handy. Organizing and gathering resources is easy. She is great with money and investments. This is because she has her intuition, but applies it to real-world matters.

Astrologically, the Queen of Pentacles represents the sign Capricorn. Capricorn is material, worldly, managing, and responsible.

In a Reading

In readings, when the Queen of Pentacles appears, it can represent a woman who supports you, either with money or real-world advice from experience. She offers comfort by physical means, like food or gifts. As an influence and not a person, she reminds us to be grounded and not to let emotions rule us. We should invest ourselves in things where we can see a real change happen or real manifestation of our goals.

When ill dignified, the Queen of Pentacles can become overbearing in nature. Instead of mothering and nurturing something to grow, the energy is smothering and growth is debilitated. She becomes nitpicky at all sorts of little details and interferes in the natural progress. The prime focus and attention when ill dignified is the material and worldly possessions. She has trouble seeing beyond the physical. She also becomes mistrusting in others or in herself (second guessing your own instincts).

THE KINGS

KING OF CUPS
Fire of Water

Description

The King of Cups sits on a throne that is floating in the sea. In the background to the left, we see a whale and, to the right, a ship.

Symbolism and Meaning

Kings represent mastery of their suit and element. They are the mature development of masculine energy and this does not fit well with the water nature of Cups. His demeanor is that of seriousness. After all, he is a King.

There is a difference between the King of Cups and Queen of Cups. She may have created her cup, which symbolizes her creative powers. The King of Cups holds his as a symbol of power. His cup is more practical than hers, which could explain his cup being normal and not ornate. What does this translate to? It shows that his emotional side is controlled by masculine influences. This is a man who is connected to feelings, but not overwhelmed or ruled by them. This notion can also be observed by the strong waves surrounding him. However, he is calm and cool where the currents do not move him.

Again, this masculine influence does not sit well with Cups and the element Water. Water likes to flow and be free. Being that the King, which is structured, and that the King of Cups is Fire of Water, we've got an unsettling combo. These conflicting influences manifest strongly when he is ill dignified.

The whale and ship in the background are symbolic of a few things and imply something to the nature of the King of Cups. The whale serves as a symbol of the hero's journey where he enters the belly of the whale, encounters death or great fears, and overcomes them. The ship symbolizes the soul's journey from this world into the afterlife. Cultures such as the Egyptians would place Abydos boats in the tombs of pharaohs, so they could use them to travel through to the afterlife. Later in Egyptian history, there was the creation of solar boats, which would allow the pharaoh to travel with the Sun God Ra down the Nile during the day. What does this have to do with the King of Cups? It all translates to a deep layer of understanding. The King of Cups has been through a long journey of transformation of the soul, which results in deep wisdom

The personality of the King of Cups is that of a person who expresses unconditional love and care. He is a counselor, the kind that is best to talk to about religion, spiritual matters, and issues regarding the heart. He listens and gives you a feeling of security. He looks for ways to get people to work together, to understand one another, so this makes him a very good mediator in a dispute. He is very patient before committing himself to a thing or to a person. He is slow to open up to. He wants to know that he can trust you. Trust is important to this King.

Astrologically, the King of Cups is associated with the sign Cancer, which is protective of the home and family. They are sympathetic and gentle, but also moody.

In a Reading

In a reading, the King of Cups can represent an older male figure or any person who offers guidance, compassion, and love. This can be a person interested in the arts. This also is typically someone who supports you.

The King of Cups as an influence can be a sign to apply your creative interests and abilities in a practical manner. Do not get swept up in the emotions of a situation. Understand how you and others feel. When you find something you love, do not get attached and invested right off the bat. Play it out and see if this endeavor is secure, safe, and trusting.

When ill dignified, the King of Cups becomes a person who holds grudges for a long time if his trust is betrayed. He may, in fact, be someone who betrays someone else in a matter regarding love. I view the King of Cups, when ill dignified, as a liar, someone who does not have true love for someone else or even for himself. He will fake affection and love for his own gain. He can become biased when he cannot separate his emotions from his reason, being swayed by the appeals of others through emotion.

KING OF WANDS
Fire of Fire

Description

The King of Wands sits on his throne with his Wand in one hand. His cloak is covered with salamanders.

Symbolism and Meaning

The King of Wands is a very successful person, as all the Kings represent success and mastery. The King of Wands has gained his success through his sheer confidence, willpower, and influence over others.

In contrast to the Queen of Wands and how she used her influence quietly, the King of Wands is more direct with his influence. He is vocal and blunt with what he wants and gets people to do what he wishes. He does not need to use force; he is charismatic, confident, and persuasive.

The personality of the King of Wands is expressed by his Fire of Fire nature, which gives him strong fire qualities. He is energetic, full of spirit, life force, and power. He is also confident of his identity and purpose in life. This Fire of Fire nature makes the King of Wands a natural leader of people, companies, or nations. The King of Wands is highly enthusiastic and motivated. He has many ideas and plans that he visualizes perfectly the way he wants it done. He has strong beliefs, values, and morals.

The salamander, which is depicted all over the King of Wands's cloak, is a symbol of what the alchemist Paracesus called one of the four elemental spirits. The salamander is the living manifestation of the element Fire. It also represents a person who can retain composure during adversity. The King of Wands thus is a man who, even under pressure, can keep calm. In fact, he may indeed live off that pressure.

Astrologically, the King of Wands is associated with Aries. The sign Aries is pioneering, assertive, leading, independent, and headstrong. The King of Wands is goal-orientated and gets results.

In readings, when the King of Wands appears, it can represent a male figure of any person who embodies qualities like the King of Wands. They are someone who is magnetic, socially lovable, and commands attention from others because of positive reputation. This person would be a leader. They can be your boss or person who has a strong influence over you. If not a person, the King of Wands as an influence reminds you to stay optimistic and focused on a goal. Visualize your goal and how you will obtain it. Be determined and work for it. You will see results. Facing blocks? Be inventive and creative. Your answer will be found outside the box, not inside.

When ill dignified, the King of Wands can become a zealot, an extremist for his own cause or beliefs. He can use his power of persuasion for negative means. This leads to abuse of power. He can be intolerant and argumentative. These are the negative sides of Aries and a Fire of Fire nature. Other qualities would be having total lack of confidence in yourself and feeling inadequate.

KING OF SWORDS
Fire of Air

Description

The King of Swords seated on his throne looks directly at us. Sword in hand, he embodies authority.

Symbolism and Meaning

If the Queen of Pentacles was the closest representation of The Empress, then the King of Swords is the closest representation of The Emperor.

The Emperor is the archetype of authority and power. The King of Swords embodies those qualities more so than the other kings, mainly because swords are symbols of authority, rule, and justice. The Emperor is a figure of reason and logic. This carries over to the King of Swords. Swords deal with intellect and mental processes. The King of Swords is very intelligent; he is great with critical thinking and processing difficult amounts of information. He conducts research before coming to any conclusion. He wants to see facts and theory put into practice. The King of Swords also resembles closely the image of Justice with his sword. Justice represented law, order, judgments, decisions, etc. The King of Swords acts justly and with responsibility.

His nature is Fire of Air, which go together. Air feeds into fire and makes it strong. Fire's power lifts Air's intellect higher up as representative of the two birds on the right side of the card. The King of Swords is able to go beyond the norm and see from new perspectives.

Astrologically, the King of Swords is associated with Libra, which represents fairness, diplomacy, and balance. Justice is ruled by Libra as well, so we see yet another connection to Justice with the King of Swords.

In a Reading

In readings, when the King of Swords comes up, it can represent a male figure or any person who expresses qualities of the King of Swords. They may be a person who advises on matters from a place of what is ethical, legal, and just. This is a person with more reason and thinking skills than most people. They are balanced and see fairness for everyone. Also, they are interested in keeping people equal and providing people with what they need. As an influence and not a person, the King of Swords tells us to remain logical and look at the facts. Look at things from different viewpoints and rise above the rhetoric. Be just and honest with what you are dealing with. Take control and authority or listen to authority when you are told something.

When ill dignified, the King of Swords can go from commander to tyrant. This is someone who is harsh and cruel with his authority, which he uses to help himself and hurt others. John Locke said it best in his argument against *Divine Right of Kings* where he defines tyrant as someone who exercises power beyond their right, making use of the power one has, not for the benefit of others, but for their own private advantage. This makes the King of Swords manipulative of facts and twisting the words of others around. Simply put, he can become ruthless and cold.

KING OF PENTACLES
Fire of Earth

Description

The King of Pentacles sits on a lavish throne surrounded by his wealth.

Symbolism and Meaning

The King of Pentacles is my personal favorite court card, because he is the essence of material earthly success. His card screams money, wealth, security, and abundance.

We see in front of us a luxuriously dressed King of Pentacles. This throne has decorative bull heads, symbolic of the sign Taurus. The King of Pentacles represents material success from your own efforts. He has excellent financial experience, and is great at savings and investments. He created his own fortune. He could be a CEO, a business owner, or any person who generates his or her own prosperity, but not necessarily.

The King of Pentacles is Fire of Earth. Fire and Earth are neutral elements that do not impact each other. This shows that fire has no real influence here on the earth nature of this King. He has a positive disposition, but his earthly nature is dominant. He is reliable, hardworking, and favors routine rather than adventure.

His personality is that of someone who works slowly and steadily toward his goals. His mood is stable and almost immune to mood swings. He is generous with his time and resources. He will offer a helping hand to someone who needs it.

The King of Pentacles is clothed in luxurious clothing that has grapes depicted on them. Grapes are the symbol of the Greek god Dionysus as well as the bull. An interesting belief about grapes is that the best wine is made from grapes that are grown in difficult soil. This alludes to King of Pentacles obtaining his riches and success from real work and not by sitting around waiting for it to come to him. He endured a lot to get to where he is.

Astrologically, the King of Pentacles is associated with Taurus. Taurus is earthly, stable, productive, practical, and dependable.

In a Reading

In readings, when the King of Pentacles appears in a reading, it can represent a male figure or any person who embodies the qualities of the King of Pentacles. They may be a businessman, executive, CEO, or someone who is self-employed, but generally well off financially. He is generous and supportive of other people's goals and desires and encourages and offers assistance. This is a person who avoids risks and stays on the safe course. They are well disciplined and well mannered.

The King of Pentacles reminds me of King Midas from Greek mythology. He was gifted with the ability to turn anything he touched to gold. Now as nice as that sounds, the downside is that he could no longer eat or drink, as those would turn to gold as well. His desire for wealth led to his daughter turning to gold after he accidently touched her. This myth connects well with the King of Pentacles who has the golden touch, but when he is ill dignified, this King could learn a few things from mythology.

When ill dignified, the King of Pentacles can become greedy. He will no longer share with others what he normally would. He saves everything for himself, fearful that people may be using him. His materialistic nature can turn to obsession with material objects, food, alcohol, and sex. His main concern would be pleasure and feeling good. The negative side of Taurus expresses inflexibility and stubbornness. He becomes skeptical, but with cause.

The Major Arcana

The Fool

"It is better to remain silent and be thought a fool than to open one's mouth and remove all doubt."

—Abraham Lincoln

The Fool is numbered zero. Depending on the deck used, it may be the first card placed before The Magician. Or it may be the last card, after The World. This is because The Fool is not part of any sequence; he is almost outside the rest of the majors. This is because philosophers have debated over the centuries about whether or not zero is a real number.

Zero is formless and uncreated. It has no substance, no order, and no structure. On the flip side, zero has all the potential and possibilities within it to become any other number. In a way, zero is nothing and everything at the same time. It is a paradox in Tarot. Pythagoras stated that zero represents "perfect form." In Buddhism, zero stands for the concept of Sunyata or emptiness, the concept that everything in the world is empty of any absolute identity. Objects in the world exist neither in the physical form nor in the mind, but only through our *perception* of any given object. The Fool represents the ultimate reality that everything is devoid of any true identity. In Kabbalah when a number ends in zero it is increased tenfold, which strengthens the power of any given number.

The Fool is linked to cosmology myths through the association with ether, chaos, and the cosmic egg. Chaos is depicted as a vast, never-ending ocean representing infinity. It has within it all the elements of creation—in an unformed state. In one Greek creation account, out of Chaos, the Great Goddess Eurynome emerged, dancing on the water. Ether came in the form of the south and north winds, spinning around her. Enrynome took hold of the winds and formed them into a snake called Ophion. Ophion impregnated her and she gave birth to the cosmic egg. Ophion wrapped himself around the egg and cracked it open, releasing all things into creation.

In Genesis you see a very similar vision of creation:

In the beginning God created the heavens and the earth. Now the earth was formless and empty, darkness was over the surface of the deep, and the Spirit of God was hovering over the waters. (Gen. 1: 1-2)

In Genesis, you see that things were formless, there were vast waters, and this is Chaos. The Spirit of God (Ether) hovered over the waters (chaos). It is a similar story using similar elements, but in set in a different religious setting.

All of this is embodied in The Fool, who represents everything before creation: the eternal void, the chaos, never-ending. The Fool is the cosmic egg, holding all the potential of life and creation. The cracking of the egg by Ophion is, however, not present in The Fool. The Fool is not creation, which is what the cracking represents.

Astrologically, The Fool is associated with Uranus. Uranus embodies within it freedom, change, originality, spontaneity, individuality, and unpredictability. The planet Uranus rotates on its side, the only planet to do this in our solar system, representing uniqueness and individuality on a cosmic level. The characteristics of Uranus are fundamental to The Fool. The Fool seeks freedom from limitations, as it does not like to be restricted to one place or thing. The Fool is standing at the edge of a cliff, the edge of the physical world or of the mental world. This reflects boundaries and seeking to expand beyond them. The Fool shows change that comes in the form of new opportunities, adventures, offers, and possibilities. The Fool, in his desire to be unique, dances to his own beat, and does his own thing. He does not care what society thinks or expects from him. In that sense, it appears The Fool stands for rebellion, but not truly. The Fool does not want to change the world. He only wants to change his own world. The Fool is unpredictable because there is no real reason behind the reasoning; he does things freely without care or worry.

The Fool stands on top of a mountain, which is symbolic of being in the presence of the Divine. To the ancient Greeks, the Olympian gods lived on Mount Olympus. In the Bible, Moses climbs Mount Sinai to obtain the commandments from God. Mountains become a place where the divine can reveal itself to humanity. It acts as an *Axis Mundi*, a spiritual connection point to the divine.

The Fool is on a journey. He is going someplace, or at least it appears so. A. E. Waite writes in *The Pictorial Key to the Tarot*, "He is the spirit in search of experience." This can mean that The Fool is representative of the human soul waiting on the other side to be born into the physical world to experience life. Behind The Fool the sun shines brightly. This may represent divine knowledge or divine protection. Having Divine knowledge may suggest that the Fool is not dumb as often thought. The Fool has knowledge. However, once incarnated into the physical world, it is forgotten. This is the concept of recollection or reminiscence, which Plato taught. One must experience life (i.e. each card of the Major Arcana) to relearn what he already knew before birth.

In a Reading

In readings, The Fool appears to inform you of new adventures and fresh starts. He represents a time when you can do anything desired and that limitations shouldn't stop you. Through this energy, you feel optimistic and worry-free. Things look positive and joyful. Often, The Fool advises to take a leap of faith. Don't think. Don't try to rationalize what is going on. Just go for it. The goal of the fool is to experience life, both good and bad. Taking risks is one of the only ways you can do that. The Fool says you have potential; you just have not formed it yet. It may say you need to tap into your unused skills. You should express your uniqueness and do what makes your soul sing.

When ill dignified, The Fool can represent actual foolishness. You may make an error in judgment and be reckless in your behavior. It can represent hesitation and fear. Fear results in indecisiveness. It can also signify resistance to change. The Fool, when ill dignified, can indicate immaturity, as well.

The Magician

"Whatever you think you can do or believe you can do, begin it. Action has magic, grace and power in it."
—Johann Wolfgang von Goethe

As card number one, The Magician is where the Major Arcana truly starts, not with The Fool. The Fool represented Chaos, the void, and the unformed world. Eurynome, the Great Goddess, gave birth to the cosmic egg, which Ophion cracked to bring about the world. The cracking of the cosmic egg is not represented in The Fool as previously stated; it is found within The Magician. It is in The Magician we see the act of creation. The Magician is the beginning point, the first of everything.

One is the number of creation. The Magician represents the first action or cause that sets the world into motion. Around the waist of The Magician, you will notice that there is a snake. This snake serves two purposes: one, it represents Ophion, who cracked open the cosmic egg, two, it represents the Ouroboros, the self-eating snake and the first creature, as stated by Plato, to be created into existence. The Ouroboros is self-sustaining. It gives life to itself by consuming itself. To the Gnostics, the Ouroboros represents eternity, infinity, and constant creation.

In Genesis, creation is performed by the spoken word of God.

And God said, "Let there be light," and there was light. (Gen. 1:2)

God only has to speak and His words take form. The Magician is the spoken word, creating whatever it is he desires to create.

Pythagorean philosophy states the number one represents the Monad, what the Pythagoreans called God. The Gnostics regard the Monad as The Absolute, Supreme Being of the universe. The number one is highly active and in constant motion. In scientific terms, The Magician represents kinetic energy, which an object possesses while in motion. The energy can't be destroyed, but only transferred into another form.

According to the Greek philosopher Empedocles, all matter is comprised of four root elements: earth, air, fire, and water. The four suits of Tarot are then seen as the basic elements that are the building blocks used in the creation of everything in the world. On his table are the four suits of the Tarot, which he influences to create through will and desire. The Magician stands in a position with one hand pointing to the sky and the other pointing to the earth. He creates a connection to the spiritual realm and is channeling energy to earth. This represents the Hermetic concept of "as above so below." This concept states that all levels of creation are interconnected. The spiritual, mental, and psychical worlds are one.

The Magician is associated with Hermes/Mercury. Hermes is the patron god of travelers, thieves, and liars. Hermes is clever and witty, which earns him a reputation of being a trickster.

Another association can be made between The Magician and Phanes, who was one of the firstborn deities. Phanes is said to be the deity created from the cosmic egg. He created day and become associated with light. His wife Nyx created night and is associated with darkness.

Astrologically, like in mythology, The Magician is associated with Mercury. Mercury rules over communication, intelligence, skills, and dexterity. As the fastest moving planet in the solar system, Mercury is always on the go. The Magician embodies these astrological characteristics. With all the four suits on the table, The Magician is viewed as a jack-of-all-trades-type of person. He is very skilled and able to accomplish anything when given the right tools to work it. Like Mercury, The Magician is heavily connected with mental process. He can solve any problem, from fixing the leaky pipe to repairing a broken engine. The lamniscate above his head suggests his mind works differently than that of "normal" people. He can think about complicated issues or problems and come to solutions easily.

What The Magician represents is the conscious aspect of the mind. He is fully consciouss of his actions, understanding what he does and why. Carl Jung believed the ego was at the center of consciousness. It is associated with our identity, self-worth, and confidence. People who are overconfident or cocky are said to be egotistical.

In a Reading

In readings, when The Magician appears, he represents taking things into a new direction. He advises you to examine the tools you have before you (your skills, talents, resources) and see how you can put those to use regarding your situation.

He's also a man of action. As such, when he appears in the reading, it's suggested that you'll need to be the leader, take control over the situation, and communicate. Be very articulate and clear. You're also asked to fully examine the situation, understand what it is that's going on, and figure out your motives. Take into consideration, too, any possibility for trickery. Are you dealing with reality? Or is it just an illusion? The Magician in a reading can indicate what is being acted upon, looking at nearby cards to determine where your will and desire should be directed.

When ill dignified, The Magician can represent trickery, manipulation, illusions, and sleight of hand. It can also represent lack of knowledge and poor training. As he is represented by Hermes, the God of thieves, The Magician gets the reputation of being like a used-car salesperson. Also, he can steal from you. As he has a way with words, he will manage to convince you that you'd said he could have whatever it was he'd swiped from you.

The High Priestess

"I would rather trust a woman's instinct than a man's reason."
—Stanley Baldwin

The High Priestess is card two of the Major Arcana. She is on the other side of The Magician as his equal counterpart. While The Magician represented energy that is masculine, active, and conscious, The High Priestess is passive, feminine, and unconscious. Together, The Magician and The High Priestess represent a father god and mother goddess relationship. They are the co-Creators that build, construct, and maintain reality through the balance of each other.

As The Magician was associated with the monad in Pythagorean philosophy, The High Priestess is the dyad. The dyad represents the "nous" or the divine mind. In Eastern Orthodox context, nous is the mind of the heart. This translates into Tarot as intuition.

On another philosophical level, The High Priestess represents Sophia (Wisdom), the female principle of God in Gnosticism, who gave birth to the Demiurge. Ashamed of what she had created, she exiled him. The Demiurge was ignorant to the existence of his mother or any other higher level of reality, believing instead that he was the highest level of reality. Thus, he created our universe, but his mother, Sophia, infuses a spark of herself in everything he creates. She is within everything and it is the goal of the Gnostic to seek her in everything to achieve salvation. The High Priestess's robes flow like water and spill into the rest of the Major Arcana. This symbolizes the embodied wisdom that is hidden in every event in our lives, much like the way Sophia is embodied in everything.

In Egyptian mythology, The High Priestess is associated with Isis/Hator. Her triple moon crown makes this association. Plutarch, the Greek scholar, wrote the following about Isis:

She is both wise, and a lover of wisdom; as her name appears to denote that, more than any other, knowing and knowledge belong to her.....that the shrine of Isis in Sais carried the inscription "I am all that hath been, and is, and shall be; and my veil no mortal has hitherto raised."

Isis is connected with motherhood and many other female qualities. The Moon at her feet shows her connection to its powers. She is often seen as someone who is psychic or interested in divination. If anyone in the cards would be a Tarot reader, it would be her. The veil behind is decorated by pomegranates, which is a symbol connected to the divine feminine. Behind the Pillars and curtain, we see a calm body of water, symbolizing the unconscious mind and her control over emotion and intuition.

In Greek mythology, she is Nyx (night), wife to Phanes (The Magician). Nyx represents the darkness, the shadow side of life. She is the mother of Hypnos (sleep) and Thanatos (Death). The High Priestess has a great understanding and connection to the realm of sleep, dreams, death, mediumship, and general ruler of all things mysterious. She is also associated with Persephone, the daughter of Demeter who was taken into the underworld by Hades.

Astrologically, the moon is associated with the High Priestess. The moon symbolism is heavy in this card. The triple moon crown on her head and the crescent moon at her feet establish a firm connection between her and the moon. The High Priestess concerns herself with cycles of the moon, the cycles of women, intuition, and psychic abilities, as we have already come to understand.

The two pillars beside her are black and white and show the Letters "B" and "J." This is a reference to the temple that King Solomon built in Jerusalem. He was known to be the wisest of all men. The High Priestess is the guardian of the temple, the guardian of wisdom.

The High Priestess is Major Arcana number two. In numerology, two is the most sensitive of all numbers. It represents duality, balance, the feminine, empathy, love, and patience. Two is passive as compared to the active energy of one. The High Priestess is passive and non-active. She is an observer, aware of everything, but does not react to it impulsively.

In physics, the energy of The High Priestess is potential, while The Magician is kinetic. Potential energy is the energy that is stored inside an object in a state of rest.

The High Priestess manifests in our lives when we rely on our intuition to guide us. When we listen to our inner voice, our gut, and our dreams, this is how we know we are experiencing The High Priestess.

In a Reading

When the High Priestess appears in readings, it can mean that you need to withdraw from the situation. It is not time for you to act, but only to watch and take notes. Watching is a passive action. You are not ignorant to what is going on around you, but you are not active in the situation. The truth to the situation may still be unknown. The mystery of the High Priestess means that you may not have a full and complete understanding of what is going on. You might only have a "feeling" or clue to the whole picture. The truth may be distorted because of your perception of what you feel is going on. This is the influence of the moon at work. When everything is known, however, you keep silent to the fact that you know the truth. It is better to let others think you know nothing, while you actually do. The full potential of the given situation has not been fully developed. Things are currently in a stage of figuring out what the emotional connection is.

When ill dignified, the High Priestess can represent your intuition is in a haze. You are not sure what to make of a situation. You are unable to get a "read" of a person. You may reject your gut instincts. You may be paranoid and suspicious of others. You may also be experiencing a psychic attack or disturbed dreams.

The Empress

"The future destiny of a child is always the work of the mother."
—Napoleon Bonaparte

After encountering The High Priestess, the symbol of the virgin mother or Goddess archetype, we come to The Empress, the symbol of the earth Goddess. While the High Priestess is a virgin, The Empress is usually interpreted as pregnant. The High Priestess expresses the feminine energy, which is secret, passive, and unconscious. The Empress, however, is the feminine energy more active and conscious. She is more closely related to the physical realm than the High Priestess.

The Empress is the third Major Arcana. The number three has some significance to understanding The Empress. The Pythagoreans viewed three as the first real number, because it is the first number that allows you to create the first real structure—the triangle. The tripod, for example, is a three-legged stool that allows one to sit on something firm. The oracle at Delphi sat on a tripod. This number is associated with knowledge and understanding.

In mythology, The Empress can be associated with a handful of Goddesses. The first one we can see, based on the sign over the heart, is Aphrodite/Venus. Other Goddesses associated with love, like Inanna and Ishtar, can also be affiliated with the card. They connect The Empress to beauty, which was, according to the ancients, harmony in proportions. Thus, she is beauty from harmony.

The love Goddess is just one of the many connections. There is a more profound Goddess connection here: that of the great mother Goddess. In the Greek pantheon, mother Goddesses included Hera (queen of the gods and wife of Zeus) and Demeter (Goddess of the harvest and fertility of the earth). And of course Gaia the primordial Goddess, the oldest of them all. The Romans referred to their earth Goddess as Terra Mater—"Mother Earth."

My main focus when talking about the earth Goddess connection is mostly with Demeter/Ceres. As we saw when reading The High Priestess, who was associated with Persephone, the daughter of Demeter, we return to the story of her abduction and rescue from Hades. When dealing with The Empress and Demeter, we relate this myth to the love and devotion Demeter showed in her search for Persephone.

The final Goddess I want to bring into this conversation is Hecate. Hecate is known as the triple Goddess, Goddess of the crossroads, and of magic. She played an important role in helping Demeter search for Persephone. Also, she is the guardian of the household and protector of newborns. Together, Persephone, Demeter, and Hecate were seen together as the triune Goddess and represented the cycle of vegetation. The Empress is then connected with cycles of growth and decay.

The Empress's robes are adorned with pomegranates, another symbol we saw first with The High Priestess. The pomegranates symbolize the eternal renewal of the life of the world (the crops). On the head of The Empress is a crown of twelve stars, which are associated with the zodiac signs and the heavens. The Empress is Queen of Heaven on earth.

Astrologically, The Empress is associated with Venus and Taurus. Venus relates to attraction, beauty, and indulgence. Taurus relates to the earth and what is material. Thus, The Empress is the embodiment of the earth and beauty.

In a Reading

In readings, The Empress symbolizes abundance, growth, and prosperity. She also signals a new time of potential. She can indicate something is manifesting or has manifested in the real world. Being pregnant, she represents gestation in some circumstance or the creation of something. Happiness and comfort are represented in this card and can indicate positive events that benefit you. Time is right for investment and to start something new. She shows love and caring feelings towards others. In relationships, she is the caregiver and may act in a motherly fashion to her lover.

When ill dignified, she can represent slow growth or decay. The Empress can become overbearing and smothering other people with too much attention. She herself may become attention seeking, feeling unwanted and alone. She becomes lazy and indulgent in luxuries.

The Emperor

> "Organizational effectiveness does not lie in that narrow-minded concept called rationality. It lies in the blend of clearheaded logic and powerful intuition."
>
> —Henry Mintzberg

Leaving the lush gardens of The Empress, we find her counterpart and balance, The Emperor. So far, we are seeing a common theme of balancing forces: The Magician and The High Priestess and The Empress with The Emperor. While the first pair represented the divine or heavenly parents, the second represent our earthly parents.

We can see the opposition between The Empress and The Emperor in a few ways. Firstly, by the image itself: The Empress looks comfortable whereas The Emperor is tense and aggressive. He screams seriousness. The Empress was the first introduction to the psychical world through emotion. The Emperor is the second phase and balances the Empress's emotion and femininity with logic and masculinity. She is about being joyful and happy. He is serious and has to follow the rules.

As the fourth card, The Emperor embodies the number perfectly. Numerologically, four represents order, systematic thinking, and planning. It builds and preserves, gives formation to thoughts and ideas. Also, the number allows us to create a square, which relates to different structures of the world, such as the four seasons, four elements, and four directions. The mountains behind The Emperor represent this order in the world, as well as boundaries.

As we have seen, The Empress is the mother figure of the cards, which means The Emperor, is the father figure. So think about how the father archetype would apply to this card. The father is supposed to be strong, a leader, logical, makes the rules, and enforces them. The Emperor is all about power and authority.

In mythology, we can associate The Emperor with the great father gods—first with Oranos (Uranus), husband of Geia (The Empress). Oranos was the father of all the Gods, Everything came from him and his wife. In older decks, the Emperor has a shield at his feet with an eagle on it, which was a reference to Zeus and, again, the idea of supremacy over all. In his many depictions, Zeus can be seen seated in majesty, which is what we see with the Emperor. There are also rams on the throne, which symbolize Aries. This gives the Emperor a strong connection to the fire element. Aries is the god of war and tells us the Emperor is the first to stand up and fight...or send his army to do it for him.

Astrologically, Aries is also associated with The Emperor. Aries represents qualities, such as pioneering, assertiveness, impulsiveness, leadership, independence, eagerness, and being headstrong. Impatience, carelessness, aggression, arrogance, and overzealousness are some negative traits. Because he is usually seen as being too masculine, too rigid, and the archetype of authority, The Emperor tends to get a bad reputation.

The Emperor is not a bad card. There are no bad cards. There is only our perception of what the card means. Some of the concepts provided about The Emperor are good. He gives order and formation to the world. Also, he is the representation of real manifestation that The Magician was channeling into this world, that which was being birthed by The Empress. This is a very positive thing. He is a good ruler. The Ankh in his right hand symbolizes wisdom. In his left hand, he holds the globe of dominance, which symbolizes his right to rule. This can also denote he is a wise ruler. He turns thoughts into reality. He is also a protector and preserver; he protects that which he creates and builds from destruction and decay.

However, there are some issues with The Emperor. The fact of life is that everything changes, dies, and decays. It is interesting to note that the Death card is number thirteen. One plus three equals four—The Emperor. Thus Death and The Emperor are connected and represents a desire to hold on to what we own or create, resisting death and decay of those things.

In a Reading

When The Emperor appears in readings, he indicates many positive things, such as security and stability. Things are working and operating, as they should be. You may be developing your leadership abilities, taking charge and command of the situation. Show that you are responsible and serious. Using your logic and pragmatics is essential.

When ill dignified, he can be a tyrant, using his power and authority for his own means. He can be strict, unemotional, uncaring, and ruthless. Also, he can be stubborn, unwilling to change. Accepting new information may challenge his views. He holds on to what he owns or what he views as "his." His logic and reason become the only things he has access to, as he lacks any emotional connection or intuitive input. The Emperor can also signify a lack or total loss of control, self-control, or control of others or a situation. His personality can go into two extremes: either total aggression to show his dominance or total passiveness to show his weakness.

The Hierophant

"God has no religion."

—Mahatma Gandhi

From one authority figure (The Emperor) to another, The Hierophant takes us from the material world and up into the religious and spiritual. The Emperor ruled the earthly world. His word was law and authority came from God. He was limited by one thing and that was the Divine. This is where The Hierophant comes in. He is the representative of God on earth, the spiritual authority as compared to the earthly authority of The Emperor. Because of this, they balance each other, reflecting the Hermetic "as above, so below" that we saw in The Magician.

In older decks, The Hierophant was titled The Pope, which has different connotations than Hierophant. Historically, The Pope was more than a spiritual leader. He was also a political figure, a King. After the fall of Rome, the power shifted from Rome to the east in Constantinople. This left a void open in Rome, where the Pope was able to gain political authority and power. As history continued, The Pope lost most of his power as land was taken away from him and was only left with Vatican City, of which he was the sovereign ruler. The Papacy is a monarchy.

The Pope exercises principal legislative, executive, and judicial power.

Pope and Hierophant are both rooted in Greek words. Pope comes from the Greek *pappas* meaning "father." Hierophant is a compound of two Greek words: *Ta hiera* "The Holy" and *Phaninein* "to show or appear." Hierophant is someone who reveals or shows you the holy and sacred. They interpret the sacred: teach spiritual lessons and more. The Hierophant was the title used by the priest of the Eleusinian Mysteries, a cult to the Goddesses Demeter and her daughter Persephone.

Why the change of titles? Why shift this card from The Pope to The Hierophant? It is all in the name. Pope brings with it too much baggage. It is selective to Christianity and Christian dogma. Plus, the political aspects also weigh down this card with material earthly associations. In contrast, Hierophant is a non-Christian title, harkening back to an ancient time of the Greek Mystery cults: a time of lost knowledge and secret spiritual teachings. It must have been an attractive title for the Hermetic Order of the Golden Dawn, when our modern Tarot decks (*Rider Waite Smith* and *Thoth Tarot*) were being created.

But why does The Hierophant still retain so much Christian symbolism in it? The use of these symbols are kept to keep the spiritual aspect of The Pope associated with the card, as well as to allow lay people of the time of the deck's creation not to think twice about the pagan title.

The trinity appears in hidden style and occurs in three forms. The Hierophant has three crosses on the trim of his robe. On his head, he wears the Papal tiara, a three-tier crown. The symbol of the crown represents the Holy Trinity, as well as the authority of the Pope on three levels as the Supreme Pontiff. In the last few decades, the Papal Crown is hardly worn, opting instead for the miter. In his hand, The Hierophant holds a Papal Cross, a cross with three arms. This also represents the Holy Trinity. Although these symbols appear Christian on the surface, they have other meanings. The Holy Trinity alternative is Mind, Body, and Spirit. Trinities also appear in Paganism as the three aspects of the Goddess, Maiden, Mother, and Crone. In actuality, the Trinity, as most people know in Christianity, comes from Paganism adapted for the Christian faith. In the end, it does not matter how you look at these symbols. The goal is to serve as symbols that The Hierophant is wielding a higher knowledge and authority than us.

Next, below the feet of The Hierophant is a set of crossed keys. These are the Keys of Saint Peter, the keys to the gate of Heaven. Again, this is a symbol used to associate the Pope with authority as the successor of Saint Peter, the first Pope. However, we need to look beyond this Christian symbol and see that, for the Hierophant, the Keys are used to unlock spiritual teachings and the doors from this world to the higher spiritual world. The Hierophant is a teacher who leads us into a spiritual quest for wisdom. In the Gnostic tradition, it is Sophia "wisdom," who leads us to salvation.

The Hierophant is the first step we take to find that wisdom within us. The focus, on the other hand, is more on authoritative teachings, as we see with the two figures below The Hierophant who are learning from him. What does he teach? He teaches you lessons that The Empress (your mother) and The Emperor (your father) cannot.

The main subjects he focuses on are matters of philosophy, morality, metaphysics, and ethics. This is in contrast to The Emperor, who dealt with social issues and the law of the land. The Hierophant deals with what is morally correct rather than legally correct. If someone would hit you, for example, The Emperor would say, "Hit back." The Hierophant would say, "Don't do it. Be the bigger person and walk away. It is wrong to hit back."

There are aspects to this card other than spiritual. Morality and ethics are connected to this card. Religions are one place where we learn morals. The Ten Commandments of Judaism and Christianity, the Eight Fold path in Buddhism or the Wiccan Rede all teach how one should act. In psychology, The Hierophant represents a stage of moral reasoning development in child development. The stage that The Hierophant represents is heteronymous moral judgment making. In this stage, children view rules as unchanging. If mom says not to do something, you must not do it ever, no matter the circumstance. In The Hierophant, when he says something, it is given, unquestioned authority.

Morality here is based upon the standards of a group, a society, anything that has structure and organization to it. The individual is lost to the group. Because of this concept, the more negative traits of The Hierophant come out. Qualities like dogmatic law and antiquated beliefs may hold people back from progressing on an individual level. The Hierophant is heavily focused on keeping the status quo, keeping people in line, and sticking with tradition. This is why many readers probably dislike The Hierophant and The Emperor. They represent order, structure, and authority in its negative aspect. Many readers, like myself, have "untraditional" religious beliefs that run counter to the norms within society.

In the positive light, The Hierophant is the person who passes down traditions from one generation to the next: teaching children their culture, faith, morals, and knowledge. The Hierophant imparts to us the structure to use when venturing out into the world using what those who are older than us believe we need in order to function in society. We are to take the time to learn whatever we can from The Hierophant, good or bad, and then apply it ourselves in the world.

Astrologically, The Hierophant is associated with Taurus. Taurus is stubborn and conservative, which relates to The Hierophant's reluctance for change or progression.

In a Reading

In a reading, when The Hierophant appears, he may implore you to stick with tradition and what many would consider safe. Do not upset the status quo, try not to be a rebel or go against the grain. Follow the group you are in and integrate yourself rather than set yourself apart from the crowd. You may need to seek the assistance from someone you trust as a teacher, mentor, and adviser—someone who can guide you and show you the way regarding a problem. The Hierophant states that it is time for you to listen and learn. Be quiet and do not speak, but instead listen to the other person who is wiser and more knowledgeable. In relationships

The Hierophant can represent a wedding and marriage. But he also can represent a struggle between sticking with tradition or not as some couples have arguments over religion or family traditions. For young people, The Hierophant symbolizes higher education and training, as well as conflicts over their birth faith and exploring faiths outside of their culture.

When ill dignified, The Hierophant embodies ignorance at its highest potential. As wise as he may be, if he elects to ignore new information, his knowledge will become obsolete one day. If people follow this leader with outdated knowledge, then they will be ignorant as well. Such can lead to fundamentalist groups like hate groups, terrorists, or any other form of extremists. An ill-dignified Hierophant also shows that you are following too close to someone else's will or ideals rather than your own. You run the risk of losing yourself to the collective group.

The Lovers

"Every heart sings a song, incomplete, until another heart whispers back. Those who wish to sing always find a song. At the touch of a lover, everyone becomes a poet."

—Plato

If you thought The Hierophant was loaded with Christian imagery, here is a card that is ripped straight from the pages of Genesis. The Lovers depict Adam and Eve, the first humans created by God in the Garden of Eden. Eve stands to the left. Behind her is the Tree of Knowledge with the serpent wrapped around it. To the right is Adam. Behind him is the Tree with flames coming from the branches. This is the Tree of Life. Between the two is a mountain. Above them is the Archangel Raphael, whose name means "God Heals."

The Lovers has a lot of meaning to it, but for many, the imagery of Adam and Eve, the Garden of Eden, the snake, and the rest may need some explaining. The Lovers is more than just a representation of the Garden of Eden. There is always something deeper with the Tarot below the surface of the Christian image.

Genesis is the first book of the Bible. Genesis is a Greek word for "origin" and, as such, the book tells the story of how the world came into existence. In the beginning, Adam and Eve lived together in the Garden of Eden, a perfect paradise where there was no suffering and nothing to worry about. They lived in accordance to God's commandments. Although Adam and Eve were free to do what they wished, there was one thing God had forbid and that was to eat from the Tree of Knowledge of Good and Evil. They were allowed to eat from the Tree of Life, which gave them immortality, but not the Tree of Knowledge, "for in the day that thou eatest thereof thou shalt surely die" (Gen. 2:17).

But one day, the craftiest of all God's creatures, the serpent, tempted Eve to eat from the forbidden tree. He told her she would not die, "For God knows that when you eat from it your eyes will be opened, and you will be like God, knowing good and evil" (Gen. 3:4). Eve ate from the Tree and gave Adam a bit of the fruit as well. When he eats, something interesting happens. They see that they are naked and they cover themselves.

It is this part of the story that is most important in the theological aspect and has a connection to The Lovers of the Tarot. Before eating the fruit, Adam and Eve were innocent, their minds and souls pure. After they ate the fruit, they gained the Knowledge of Good and Evil. At the moment of eating the fruit, their consciousness shifted. They recognized their nakedness and were ashamed of it. They did not know of shame, much less discomfort, until this time because they lived in utter perfection and bliss. Adam and Eve were unconscious because of this.

It is in the Kabbalah that you find an explanation that Satan (the adversary) was created to test us and make us earn Eden, instead of it simply being handed to us. The temptation was a gift, in a way. It woke us up and humanity is now conscious. However, returning to the Bible, God finds out what Adam and Eve did and evicts them from the Garden. In traditional Christian theology, it is from their act that death and sin enter the world. In the West, primarily from Saint Augustine, we get the notion of original sin, which is that all mankind is born with the Sin of Adam. In the Eastern Churches, (orthodoxy) the theology differs. Man is not born with the actual sin attached to them. We are, however, born into a corrupted world. We are born into a world of death and sin, instead of the Garden of Eden.

Theology aside, the important concept to take away from this story is the part on the consciousness shift. It is a shift from unconscious to conscious and from innocence to corruption. Look back at our previous card—The Hierophant—the teachings and lessons were given from an authority down to the followers. Daddy or Mommy was telling you what to do and how to do it. I brought up the psychological development of moral reasoning. The Hierophant represented a heteronymous moral judgment process. In this stage, children view rules as unchanging. In The Lovers, the rules change. Questions are asked. Rules are broken! We now develop to the autonomous morality stage. Law does not come from above, but from within us. Children at this stage learn to take into consideration the feelings and needs of other people and try to cooperate with others. Cooperation means communication and The Lovers is a card of communication and relating to others.

There is also another psychological connection in The Lovers. It represents the Freudian view of the structure of the mind. The Id, Ego, and Superego. The male (Adam) represents the Id, the pleasure principle. It is the part of the mind that is instinctive and pensionable. The woman (Eve) represents the Ego, the reality principle. This part of the mind looks at things realistically and with reason. The Angel represents the highest part of the mind, the Superego. The Superego seeks what is ideal and perfectly moral. It retains all the morals we learn from parents (The Empress and The Emperor) along with society (The Hierophant). It is the job of the Ego to balance between Id and Superego and allow an identity to rise into consciousness. The Lovers is then seen as a blueprint for human consciousness coming into its own authority, becoming liberated by the control of some other controlling force, like The Hierophant.

Now Freud's theory was created during the time the *Rider Waite Smith Deck* was created. Was the Golden Dawn drawing from this theory? Maybe, but Freud's theory is actually older and more ancient. In Platonism, there is a theory of the three-part structure of the psyche. Though Plato and Freud do not match up perfectly, there are close parallels. Plato categorized them as the Eros (self-gratification), Thymos (motivation, emotion, and ambitions) and finally, Logos (the mind, reason, and thought). The Golden Dawn probably drew upon the Platonism more so then Freud.

The Lovers is a lot like the teenager finally getting freedom when they go off to college after having lived under their parent's strict rules. They are free! They can do what they want. Do anything. The world can be so tempting in this time of their lives. Sex, drugs, and parties—all sorts of things are tempting factors. The Lovers is a card of temptations, of lust, and pleasure. It is a card simply of choice. Do I or do I not? Should I or should I not? These are the fundamental questions The Lovers should make you ask yourself when it appears in a reading. In older decks, the image was of a man choosing between two women with cupid above at the center. Denoting choice and dilemmas between different options. Between what we are expected to choose and what we actually want. Desire arises from The Lovers; an attraction is inherent in this card between the two figures. However, there is a conflict here between their morals and their desires.

Astrologically, The Lovers is associated with the sign Gemini. Gemini is communicative, dualistic, sociable, and adaptable. These qualities resonate with The Lovers aspect of balance and harmony. The Lovers seek to find a balance, between two things.

In a Reading

In a reading, when The Lovers appears it often, if not always, represents decisions between different choices. You are faced with a dilemma, often a struggle between a desire for pleasure versus the more rational and difficult. The Lovers can signify matters relating to the heart, romantic relationships, but many times The Lovers just represents relationships of any kind between people, from love to work. On the personal level, The Lovers makes you question your personal beliefs and values. You may find yourself tested and tempted. You need to think for yourself and not simply follow what others have told you. All this leads to a clearer understanding of your own values and beliefs. It allows you to clear out the outdated notions. With romantic relationships, The Lovers advises you to be open and experience the relationship purely and full-heartedly.

When ill dignified, The Lovers becomes overtly focused on pleasure, sex, and all sorts of naughty stuff. Love turns to lust. You can lose sight of your morality, blurring the lines between what is right and wrong. You may become confused as to what you believe in, making improper decisions and choices. Harmony and balance are upset. Things are not equal or in sync.

The Chariot

"There is nothing impossible to him who will try."

—Alexander the Great

In The Lovers, we were introduced to desire, lust, passions, wants, and a need to balance and harmonize all these emotions. The Chariot continues the story of human development. So far, we met the divine polarities: masculine (The Magician) and feminine (The High Priestess). We met the material manifestations of these polarities as mother (The Empress) and father (The Emperor). We were raised in society and taught rules, morals, and ethics (The Hierophant). We then grew up and began to think for ourselves, desires arose; we challenge the status quo (The Lovers). The Chariot is the young adult in the story. Finally, we are independent and on our own to make a life for ourselves.

We see a returning theme that often runs through the Tarot, the theme of opposites and the balance between them. We see it in the pairings of masculine and feminine majors Magician & High Priestess and Empress & Emperor. However, after these cards, we see opposites appearing in singular cards: Hierophant, Lovers and now Chariot. This shows a process of cosmic forces uniting together into a singular force through different stages.

With The Chariot, we see a general or a commander riding on his chariot. In front of him are two sphinxes. One is white and the other, black, just as it was with The High Priestess, who had two pillars of the same colors. This represents two opposite forces. Those forces represent a struggle for control. Psychologist Carl Jung called it the "balance of shadow and light." The Shadow is a term used by Jung to represent our hidden self, the dark and secret self we do not know is there. It is the unconscious mind and the unreaped potential we have. The Light is then the opposite of The Shadow. It is our conscious mind, what we are aware of about ourselves. The Chariot combines shadow and light to become fully aware of one's nature. It taps into both aspects of the Self and masters them, allowing one to reach higher potentials. Successful integration of different aspects of the psyche to form a complete and whole persona is represented. This wholeness of the psyche embodies a healthy ego, one that is sure of itself without any neuroses or complications.

The Chariot depicts the mythological figure, the son of the Queen of Heaven. "Queen of Heaven" was a title given to many ancient Goddesses. Some of the more well known ones are Isis, Innana, and Hera. The title is also used in the Catholic Church and, to some extent, the Orthodox Churches for Mary, mother of Jesus. The symbol of the Queen of Heaven is the starry sky, which in turns becomes the canopy covering The Chariot. The Star on his crown represents the world above, while on his chest, a square represents the earthly world, signifying his place in both. The two crescent moons on his shoulders are symbolic, again of his heavenly mother, who, alongside as "Queen of Heaven," was known as the Moon Goddess.

Another mythological figure depicted in this card is the god Helios, who is shown riding a chariot across the sky driven by winged horses. Helios, being the god of the sun, represents light and the ability to see, in this case, enlightenment. Specifically, The Chariot brings enlightenment about your inner self and what you are actually capable of. What you are able to do when push comes to shove and you have to act. Historically, the Chariot is associated with great leaders of the past, such as Alexander the Great and Julius Caesar. These leaders were educated and smart, and the Chariot embodies intelligence, skills in the battlefield or in situations required to be a leader. The Chariot is one of the most forceful of the Tarot cards. He is determined and goes after his desire.

The Chariot holds a Wand, which may be a reference to The Magician's Wand. However, in this card, the Wand is not being used. It is merely being held, not activated. This is because The Chariot has already manifested that which he desired.

Astrologically, The Chariot is associated with Cancer. Cancer is a "touchy-feely" sign of the Zodiac. It is emotional, which is an odd association for The Chariot—a masculine, forceful card. He is hardly the type to touch your heart. He is more likely to bash your head. But there is the small spark of Cancer, the aspect of protection. Cancer is protective of what it loves; it will defend it to the death. So does The Chariot. He puts on his armor and runs into battle to protect his home and family.

In a Reading

When The Chariot appears in a reading, he represents clear focus and intention. Things are on the move and going forward. Gain control of circumstances, which you are able to control. The Chariot takes control the old fashion way—by force! You need to push yourself to your limits and the limits of others to get what you want. The Chariot is a clear sign of victory and accomplishment. Be determined in what you want. The Chariot has a strong will and is very dominate.

When ill dignified, The Chariot manifests in harsh ways. He becomes pushy, mean, bullying, hurtful, and violent. He can explode with rage when things don't go according to plan. The movement energy of The Chariot can slow down or come to a screeching halt. Thus, the ill-dignified Chariot is a card of blockage, delays, and resistance. Instead of victory, we see failure. When I asked the Tarot in 2008 if Hillary Clinton would win the Democratic nomination, I pulled The Chariot reversed, thus representing her failure. You may be wasting energy on projects or plans that do not manifest or progress. It feels as if you're spinning your wheels. No matter how much you press on the gas, all you get is loud noise and burning rubber, causing smoke. Slow down and figure out what is wrong and where to focus your energy better.

Strength

"Courage doesn't always roar. Sometimes courage is the little voice at the end of the day that says I'll try again tomorrow."

—Mary Anne Radmacher

The gentle Strength card counterbalances the fast charge of The Chariot. As we have already noticed, most of the majors come in balancing pairs. As we have seen, the Tarot is very dualistic in its nature. The Chariot is the masculine energy, which is aggressive and active. Strength is the feminine energy—passive and reserved. The image of Strength is supposed to give a sense of calmness, serenity, and peace. She is assertive and strong, but does not flaunt her power and abilities like the Chariot. She does not want to control others, but only to control her inner self.

Strength is a soft card. It is quiet, speaks low, and moves gracefully. However, within this card is a hidden power. It is a source of raw power that is kept under wraps and in control, not by force or brute strength like The Chariot. On the contrary—it is kept in check by internal means instead of external forces. Strength is able to do what The Chariot could not: show self-control. Self-control is the ability to control your emotions and behavior. It is also known as self-regulation and impulse control. The Chariot was impulsive, often charging into battle and reacting quickly. Strength, however, responds properly by holding itself back from acting on emotion.

Strength was originally named Fortitude, one of the cardinal virtues. Plato was the first who wrote about the Virtues, ascribing them to different classes within society. Strength (Fortitude) was associated with the warriors. So gentle and kind as she may be in this card, she has the spirit of a warrior in her.

Examining the image, we see a maiden standing over a lion. Her hands hold the lion's mouth shut. The lion can mean a few things. It could represent the animal side in us. It tells us that we need to regulate it and keep our desires in check. The closing of the mouth can be very literal in life, in that it tells you to keep your mouth shut, meaning: speak when spoken to; do not give opinions or advice when not asked or you could regret it.

This imagery leads to the association with compassion and empathy. In Buddhism, compassion and wisdom leads us to enlightenment. The Buddha said the following: "Compassion is that which makes the heart of the good move at the pain of others. It crushes and destroys the pain of others; thus, it is called compassion. It is called compassion because it shelters and embraces the distressed." This makes the image of Strength different. Instead of forcing the lion's mouth shut and maybe causing pain, she is doing something for the lion's benefit. This is why, in some newer decks, the woman is healing the lion of some physical problem. For example, removing a thorn from the lion's paw.

In mythology, Strength brings to mind the story of Hercules and the Nemean Lion. The Nemean Lion was named for the town it had terrorized. This lion was special, for no weapons could pierce its thick skin and kill it. But Hercules killed the lion by wrestling with it as one of his twelve labors. After the lion's death, Hera placed it in the stars as the constellation, Leo. In the myth, the lion is a force of destruction and raw animal power and Hercules's wrestling with it is a representation of the wrestling we do with ourselves: our animal needs, demos, desires, and so forth.

A similar story is present in Genesis when Jacob wrestles with an angel all night. The angel triumphs over Jacob by touching and laming his leg. Jacob demands a blessing and is renamed "Israel," meaning "one who has striven with God and has prevailed" (Gen. 32:28). This story speaks about transcending and gaining redemption from struggle. Strength echoes this message. As the maiden "wrestles" with the lion, it provides a struggle, but with the goal of transcending human nature.

Astrologically, Leo is associated with Strength. The sign of Leo is a fire element and is said to be the more energetic of the fire signs. The lion in this card represents negative qualities such as aggression, hubris, extravagant living, and short temper. However, this card is not a "negative" card. The maiden represents the earth element and is able to temper the lion's fire element, with stability and control. The vines wrapping around, connecting the woman and lion, show the overpowering of the fire element. To be more specific, the woman represents Virgo, which follows after Leo. Virgos are known to be slow moving. They do not react quickly and they develop skills that will befit them. We can see these qualities here in the Strength card. Virgo is controlling Leo. Maybe she is trying to develop the fire energy for her personal benefit, to learn new skills or traits that is opposite to her nature. The two elements also represent a balance and a sense of harmony. This harmony and balance is only brought about through self-control and will. You have to actively try and obtain this harmony.

In a Reading

When Strength appears in a reading, it asks that you evaluate your reactions and behaviors. Regulating yourself is number one. Check how you speak, how you think, and how you behave. You cannot control others. You can only control yourself. Do not let others get the better of you or fire you up. Strength asks that you be patient and compassionate to others. Look for ways to help someone else, instead of seeking that which only benefits you. Practice compassion and have empathy for those suffering and in need of assistance. Offer your support and aid. You may require some discipline regarding something. Practice makes perfect. You should not throw in the towel just yet.

When ill dignified, Strength can become weak and lacking control or restraint. You give into your desires by embracing your animal side. You doubt yourself, because you may not see any progress or growth in an area of your life. You lose motivation and start slacking on goals. The fixed energy of Leo may make you fixated and obsessed over something, allowing you to focus on just one thing while losing sight and control over others. When it comes to communication, Strength ill dignified can show a lack of a verbal "filter." You say what comes to mind without regard of others' feelings.

The Hermit

"The mind can weave itself warmly in the cocoon of its own thoughts, and dwell a hermit anywhere."
—James Russell Lowell

All the cards of the Major Arcana so far have corresponded with themes dealing with human existence and human development. Our divine principles (The Magician and The High Priestess), our parents (The Empress and The Emperor), our teachers (The Hierophant) and coming into ourselves (The Lovers) and then independence (The Chariot). The Hermit continues in this developmental story and also ends it, with a new story to be told with the remaining Major Arcana.

The Hermit is card number nine, which is often the number of completion and perfection, so it is fitting that The Hermit be placed as the ending point in the first "chapter" of our examination of the cards. The Hermit represents the highest of human consciousness, curiosity, knowledge, and wisdom. The Hermit is a seeker of wisdom, a searcher of knowledge. He is a philosopher seeking to answer the deep questions pertaining to life.

The word hermit comes from the Greek ἐρημίτης, which means "of the desert." In the religious context, a hermit is a person who lives a monastic style. They live outside of society and make no contact with it. They seek unity with God by rejecting the pleasures of life, living simply and humbly. They are searching, seeking, learning, and growing spiritually.

The Hermit in the Tarot reflects this theme perfectly. We see a bearded man in a long robe, alone in the dark with a lantern and a staff. He has the classic hermit look to him. He is at the top peak of the mountain. As mentioned in the chapter about The Fool, mountains are referred to as an *axis mundi*—the point at which the higher "divine" realm is connected with the earthly realm. They can be made in nature, like Mt. Olympus or man-made like the pyramids of Egypt. The Hermit stands at the top of this *axis mundi*, seeking the higher level, seeking God, truth, wisdom, and understanding—whatever it may be. It is dark around the Hermit, which gives the impression that what he is searching for is not going to be easy. It is not clearly seen or may never be known, because The Hermit stands on top of what is humanly possible and cannot reach beyond that. If anything is going to become known to The Hermit, it must come down to him from above or from within himself. The Hermit stands facing the left, extending his lantern out into the darkness. This is reflection on the past, bringing up old issues for evaluation and understanding. The Hermit, because he is wise, is seen as a mentor and a spiritual guide. Unlike the Hierophant, who tends to stick with more traditional means of spiritual guidance, the Hermit is more practical and easier to relate to. He speaks universal truths that do not tie in with one religion or one ethnic group. He represents all humans and our search for meaning.

He appears to be very pensive, introspective, and reflects on everything. This card can be a bit difficult for many people to grasp, especially extroverts and anyone who is always on the go—which can be just about everyone in the Western world. How do we connect with a card so isolated, quiet, and pensive? It is quite opposite to what we normally experience. You can experience The Hermit yourself in two methods: an external or an internal way. Externally, The Hermit manifests as behaviors, such as withdrawal and isolation: wanting to be alone, researching, studying, and reading. Internally, The Hermit manifests as introspection (self-examination) and reflection. The external behaviors often lead to the internal reactions; however, they are not mutually exclusive. You can be introspective without being isolated.

As previously mentioned, the only other card that appears similar to The Hermit is the The High Priestess. Many even see these cards as almost identical, but differences can be discerned between the cards if you dig deeper into their meanings. The High Priestess is intuitive and emotional, whereas The Hermit is more intellectual. He is more open to subjective experiences as a means to gain knowledge and wisdom. The High Priestess operates internally by nature. The Hermit, on the other hand, also operates internally, but it is not his natural nature. Another big differences between these cards is that The High Priestess withholds what she knows, whereas The Hermit shares whatever he knows with whomever seeks to learn.

In Astrology, Virgo is associated with The Hermit. The Hermit is analytical, disciplined, unselfish, and can be skeptical. Virgo is humble and who is more humble than a hermit? On the flip side, Virgo can be narrow-minded, picky, and critical.

In a Reading

When The Hermit appears in readings, he advises that you pull away from the situation at hand. Sleep on it and let the choices or dynamics of what is going on sit in your mind for a period of time. The Hermit does not act fast. He knows it is better to be patient and really figure things out first. The Hermit signals a need to examine the situation or examine your own motivations, feelings, and attitude towards what is happening.

The Hermit may advise you to withdraw and be left alone. Oftentimes, when The Hermit appears, it shows a reduction in social activity and increase in solitary activities. This withdrawal occurs because often there is a feeling or need to work on inner matters of the self. Generally, The Hermit represents a quest or journey of the soul, seeking understanding and meaning. You may ponder religious and philosophical matters or even more earthly things, like which career or educational path to take.

Being symbolic of a guide or mentor, The Hermit oftentimes represents someone we go to for guidance. The Hermit is the archetypal old wise man who can teach us many things, which we may not receive from normal education or common knowledge found in society.

When ill dignified, The Hermit can become overtly isolated and rejecting all of society, living inside your head and or becoming unsocial to people. You become distant to others and relationships break apart because of a lack of interaction. The Hermit's desire for knowledge can become one of obsession, seeking information endlessly, and never being satisfied. Alternately, you may reject knowledge, leaving yourself ignorant. An ill-dignified Hermit can also represent hidden knowledge and concealment of things. You may also be pretending to know more than you do. As an outside force, it may represent a person who is a false teacher, someone who is not genuine in his or her guidance and knowledge.

The Wheel of Fortune

"Anyone who is prosperous may by the turn of fortune's wheel become most wretched before evening."

—Marcellinus Ammianus

The Hermit represented the final stage of human development that started with The Magician. As we move above and beyond The Hermit, we enter a new series and set of cards that starts to deal with archetypes of greater increasing abstractness and spiritual meaning. The Wheel of Fortune is a transition card between these two sets of groups. The Wheel of Fortune is one of my favorite cards, both because it is a powerful image and also because it can be ambiguous in meaning, so when it appears in a reading pay extra attention to it.

The Wheel of Fortune is one of those "good" cards clients may love to see. A majority of the time, this card is seen as positive, but the card's meaning is deeper than just about fortune and luck. The Wheel of Fortune is the first card we encounter in the deck without people and the setting is up in the clouds. The subject of focus clearly has shifted from man to divine and is the main reason The Wheel of Fortune starts a new group set in the Majors. The removal of people and the sky/cloudy scene give us the impression that this card represents something higher than mankind and is outside mankind's control.

This card is directly associated with the Roman Goddess Fortuna, who was the personification of luck and fortune. With the rise of Christianity and the fall of Paganism, Fortuna's image was kept alive in the middle ages. Philosophers and theologians removed her divine status, demoting her to a servant of God and a vehicle of His divine will. Fortuna is often depicted with a wheel, which she spins. The wheel is called "Rota Fortuna,"—wheel of fortune. Fortuna would turn the wheel and would cause great losses for some and great gains for others. In older

Tarot decks, the image is a wheel with a man on the rise and a man on the descent. A man sits on top of the wheel. At the center is Fortuna. Fortune, like Justice, is also blind. It does not matter what you do and how good you are. Fortune comes and goes. It builds you up and knocks you down. In the religious context, the wheel was used to remind people of how quickly you can lose fortune and how unimportant it is. It was a reminder to people to focus on the larger issues, like the salvation of your eternal soul.

The image of the wheel is symbolic of turning, change, and movement. Movement is in the sense not that you are moving between places, but movement in that the situation is gaining motion and is changing. Change is a core concept of The Wheel of Fortune. It is the crux of the image and a concept, which goes back to the original meaning. The Wheel of Fortune is a fluid card. Things are not fixed or static, but ever changing and flowing.

Numerologically, The Wheel of Fortune is connected to The Magician. The Wheel of Fortune is a card ten, one plus zero equal one—the number of The Magician. Thus, The Wheel of Fortune is infused with some ability of the higher divine manifestation. Because of this connection and the fact that this card follows The Hermit, the ways of The Wheel of Fortune are not easy to understand by reason. This card does not follow logic or reason. We cannot analyze the Wheel or understand it with our minds. This goes back to the notion that The Wheel of Fortune is random. What the wheel hands out to mankind can be capricious and unjust at times. That is the nature of the Wheel—unknowable change.

Do not start to think that this card is wicked and that it should be avoided. No card should be avoided. They all have lessons to teach. I am only stressing early on that this card is ambiguous and you need to focus on it when it appears in a reading, because you need to determine if it signals a change that is either favorable or not. If the Wheel came up paired with The Sun, it would indicate a good change in fortune. But a pairing with The Tower or The Devil would be ominous.

The Wheel also suggests cyclical time, which is how the ancients believed time operated—repeating itself through patterns, like day and night and the changing of the seasons. The ancients called it the wheel of time. Inside the wheel, we see the Tetragrammaton, the Hebrew letters that spell the four-letter name of God. In Kabbalah, the Tetragrammaton is the source for all creation. We can see the four letters as the four elements that all things are comprised of. The Latin letters spell the word *rota*, which means "wheel." This represents that God/creation is a wheel/circle that never ends. Again, this gives the card a sense that it represents something beyond our control. We cannot control time or the changing whim of fortune, so we should not be too comfortable where we are. Things can change. In the *Rider Waite Deck*, the Wheel is golden. This is often seen as a symbol of the sun. In the center of the wheel, there are eight spokes. They represent the Solstices, Equinoxes, and the midway points between them, which are the eight Sabbaths. Again, this relates to cyclical time and changes, following patterns and structures.

On top of the wheel is a sphinx, which is a symbol of the Guardian of Life's secrets. This notion goes back to the Riddle of the Sphinx. A Sphinx used to stand outside the city of Thebes and asked a riddle to all who would pass by. Answer incorrectly and you would be cursed to die. The riddle was: "What goes on four legs at dawn, two legs at noon, and three legs in the evening?" The only person to answer this riddle was Oedipus, whose answer was, "Man, who as a baby crawls on four legs, then walks on two legs as an adult, and in old age with a cane as his third leg." The sphinx, frustrated that the riddle was answered, committed suicide by throwing herself off the cliff to the sea.

Is is possible that the sphinx in the Tarot's Wheel of Fortune is telling us we need to answer the riddle of our own lives? To the left, a snake (the god Typhon) is descending the wheel. Snakes are often a symbol of wisdom and transformation, as well as eternal youth. Being on the descending side of the wheel, the unfavorable side, we must learn to be flexible, adapt to the new change, and prepare for the transformation when we come to the ascending side. The figure of Anubis is pictured on the ascending side, Anubis was the Egyptian God associated with mummification and the afterlife. It can be seen as a sign of death or rebirth, however you wish to view it.

In the corners of the card, we have four winged figures. They are the fixed signs of the zodiac: Aquarius, Scorpio, Leo, and Taurus. Also, they are the stable signs of the elements air, water, fire, and earth. What's interesting about this is that these signs are reading blank books. This can represent that with fortune, you can't calculate what will happen, or learn anything that can prevent it. In a way, this is a mocking of the elements (the fixed signs), making them useless in a way. It can also represent a futile effort to rationalize chaos.

Astrologically, The Wheel of Fortune is associated with Jupiter, the great benefactor. Jupiter and The Wheel of Fortune is a perfect paring because Jupiter is the planet of good luck, success, and generosity. Jupiter is also connected with the concept of expansion, abundance, and wealth. It is all about increasing and expanding, giving you more of something. It is because of the Jovian nature that The Wheel of Fortune is associated with good fortune. When it appears in a reading, you may want to ask yourself, "What am I getting too much of?"

In a Reading

When The Wheel of Fortune appears in readings, it symbolizes a turning point in the situation at hand. It can represent a turning of bad fortune or a reversing to good fortune. If you pay attention to The Wheel, it may give you new insights to underlying influences at work within your situation. Like The Fool, there is risk here within The Wheel of Fortune. It is a card about chance and taking a gamble. When you are confused about the situation and The Wheel appears, it advises you to take a step back and try to see the bigger picture and all the interconnecting influences, people, and variables that relate to you and the issue.

When ill dignified, The Wheel of Fortune can represent stagnation and delays. Things appear to be going nowhere. There's no progression and no development. The wheel is not spinning. Instead of expansion and abundance, you have contraction. You may be experiencing a streak of bad luck or unfavorable events. Also, you may feel frustrated because your efforts are yielding no results. Remember, too, that the wheel represents that which is out of control. Attempting to control something over which you have no power will lead to frustration. If failure is pending, you may need to consider returning to the drawing board to rework a new idea.

Justice

> "The virtue of justice consists in moderation, as regulated by wisdom."
> —Aristotle

After The Wheel of Fortune, we encounter the first card that starts the next group of the Major Arcana. Recall that The Wheel was a transition card. This second set represents spiritual and religious concepts and archetypes of the cosmos.

Inside the Major Arcana, we see a repeating theme of certain pairings of cards, which balance each other or reflect a relationship of opposition. Justice is paired with The Wheel of Fortune, because both cards deal with cause and effect. The Wheel of Fortune dealt with this in a cyclical fashion, while Justice corresponds with it in a more direct, linear way. Justice balances The Wheel of Fortune as a cosmic system of check and balance. The main balancing factor is from the control of Fortuna erratically spinning her wheeling, dealing good luck or bad on a system based on worthiness and fairness. The Wheel was unfair with the way it gave its "verdicts." Justice, meanwhile, is fair. It looks at the facts before issuing a verdict.

The image of Justice brings to mind "Lady Justice," who can be found in any courthouse. She is blindfolded and holds a sword in her right hand and scales in her left. The picture comes from the Greek Goddesses Themis or her daughter Dike. Themis was the daughter of Gaia and Oranos. A Titan, she was the second patron Goddess of the oracle of Delphi, the personification of divine order. Her name means, "law of nature, that which is put into place or in action." In some ancient depictions, Themis was not blindfolded because of her prophetic abilities. Dike dealt with human justice based on customs and norms of the society. These two Goddesses dealt with two separate types of justice but I feel Justice in Tarot depicts both forms in the one card. Themis and Dike have been depicted with a sword and or scales or neither. Themis sat next to Zeus on Olympus giving him advice.

In the card, Justice is not blindfolded. Justice wears a crown encrusted with a jewel in the center. This is symbolic of the third eye and the connection to Themis' prophetic abilities. The jewel is square, which means she keeps her abilities under her control. While it is said that prophecy is attributed to her, Justice in nature has a higher level of perception that is on a grander scale. She is able to perceive the cause and effects, all things, which appear to be prophetic. This is revealed to us through the connection to The High Priestess. Justice is card number eleven. One plus one equals two, The High Priestess. Being connected to The High Priestess reinforces the notion that Justice has an almost psychic way of understanding the issue at hand and making a decision. However, Justice sees things clearly and does not become overwhelmed by any emotion or empathy or subjectivity.

Behind Justice are two columns. A curtain is attached, covering the background. We have seen this already with The High Priestess, which connects us to the idea of uncertainty and the unknown. Unlike the columns of the High Priestess, which were white and black, the ones in the Justice card are the same in color. This represents that equality is the structure and foundation of Justice.

The Hindu idea of Karma, the cause and effect law of the universe, can be associated with the Justice card. Karma means action and determines the type of rebirth you will be dealt when you reincarnate. Good actions lead to good rebirths; bad actions lead to bad rebirths. However, in the Tarot, we are not focused on the concept of reincarnation. We are focused on the relationship of cause and effect, reward and punishment in this life.

Astrologically, Justice is associated with Libra. When Dike left Earth, she became the constellation Virgo and her scales were placed into Libra. Libra is the zodiac sign that deals with balance and beauty by way of Venus. Libra embodies justice, fairness, and diplomacy, as well as cooperation.

In a Reading

When Justice appears in readings, it often is indicating a need to become aware of our actions and their effects. You may need to apologize to someone or resolve some mistakes you have made in the past. Neglecting to take responsibility can have negative consequences. When dealing with other people, Justice reminds you to be fair and impartial. Set aside your personal views and subjective emotions. Stick with facts and make an objective decision. Justice can indicate having choices to choose from. However, Justice advises you to weigh all options, list the pros and cons, and choose the practical. On a deeper level, Justice informs you to look at the connections between events and to find the cause of the issue, not simply the after-effect of the symptom. Truth and honesty is expressed by Justice, much like the Ace of Swords. Justice's hand with the Swords harkens to the ace and urges us to be authentic and truthful. Justice plays an important role in legal questions, as it can indicate rulings in your favor.

When ill dignified, Justice can be vindictive. If Justice appears in a negative manner, you should ask where you are blind in a situation or issue. What are you overlooking or taking out of context? Justice ill dignified can represent denying or forgetting your responsibility and not taking account for your actions. You may be blaming others for your failures and not seeing your own participation in the situation. Justice ill dignified represents unfairness, a balance that has been disrupted, and things feeling off base. Others may be treating you unfairly or you may be treating others unjustly. With regards to legal questions, Justice in an ill-dignified light can express rulings against or an unjust ruling and delays in judgment.

The Hanged Man

"The important thing is this: to be able, at any moment, to sacrifice what we are for what we could become."

—Maharishi Mahesh Yogi

The meanings of The Hanged Man have shifted over time. At first, the card was seen as betrayal. The image of The Hanged Man has stayed constant with a man hanging upside down by his foot. In older decks, coins fell out of the man's pockets. The Hanged Man is depicting a scene from Renaissance Italy, that of the *Pittura infamante*, meaning "defaming portrait." It is a form of character assassination. People such as thieves or traitors would be drawn in humiliating scenes to bring shame onto the person. These drawings would be placed in public places for the townspeople to see. One of the common depictions was to draw the accused hanging by one foot. The tradition of the hanging upside down comes from the *Last Judgment* fresco by Giovanni da Modena in the Basilica of San Petronio. It depicts dammed souls hanging in the same position of The Hanged Man card. This fresco was created before the creation of the Tarot and is a direct influence on the creation of the Tarot image of The Hanged Man.

The story of Jesus's betrayal by Judas Iscariot is also viewed as a possible influence on the card. Judas betrayed Jesus to the high priests for thirty pieces of silver, after which he felt remorse and killed himself by hanging, according to Mathew 27:5. However, looking at the redrawing of the card in the *Rider-Waite Deck*, it does not give us the sense that we are looking at Judas or someone from a *Pittura infamante*. The traditional meaning and view of the card has changed with Waite. He is depicting something different altogether. In his work *The Pictorial Key to the Tarot*, Arthur Waite tells us:

> It has been called falsely a card of martyrdom, a card of prudence, a card of the Great Work, a card of duty; but we may exhaust all published interpretations and find only vanity. I will say very simply on my own part that it expresses the relation, in one of its aspects, between the Divine and the Universe. He who can understand that the story of his higher nature is imbedded in this symbolism will receive intimations concerning a great awakening that is possible, and will know that after the sacred Mystery of Death there is a glorious Mystery of Resurrection.

Waite says that he feels the card deals with the understanding of the "sacred Mystery of Death" and the "glorious Mystery of Resurrection." What is Waite referring to? To a Christian, it is eternal life after death. However, this is not the case. Waite is making a direct reference to the dying god cults of the ancient world.

The motif is recognized as a metaphor for the cycle of vegetation. The god sacrificed often is hanged on a tree and or there is the cutting of the genitals. This god is then resurrected to represent the renewal of the earth. These myths are closely related to the Great Mother Goddess. A god-king dies and is brought back to life in one way or another. These myths originated in the Fertile Crescent, where the cycle of vegetation was important. This cycle is related to the Great Mother Goddess. Often, the god is viewed as a surrogate to the actual king and is killed in his place to ensure the survival and renewal of the lands. It is during the springtime or summertime when most of these gods are celebrated for the death/sacrifice and resurrection.

In Egypt, the motif appears with Osiris and Isis. In Greece, it appears with Dionysus and Demeter, as well as Adonis and Aphrodite. In Phrygia, it is Attis and Cybele. Osiris was a living god-king who was murdered by his brother Set. Isis, his wife, grieved his death in so much sorrow that the sun god Ra sent Anubis to aid in the revival of Osiris. Osiris was resurrected in the underworld and became the god of the underworld, ruler of the dead, and the lord of eternity. His resurrection assured that the soul would live on after death.

Dionysus was born to Persephone by Zeus. Zeus transferred kingship to his son. Hera ordered the Titans to murder the child and Dionysus was killed violently. Pomegranates sprang from his blood. What happens next differs by tradition. Some say Zeus raised his son from the dead or that he arose after burial on his own and ascended into heaven.

Adonis was the child of Myrrha, who, at the time of pregnancy, was made into a tree by the gods. Venus fell deeply in love with Adonis. One day, when he went hunting for boar, he was struck by an arrow in his groin and mortally wounded. Venus knew that he was in trouble and went to his aid. Adonis died and, from his blood, red anemone sprung as a symbolic resurrection from the earth. Aphrodite promised that every year his death would be reenacted with lamented cries that would imitate her own cries for him.

Attis was hanged by a tree and lost his genitals. Violets sprung from his blood. The worship of Attis and the Great Mother Cybele included the annual celebration with the return of the spring season. The pine tree is sacred to Attis, as he was either hanged on one in the shape of a "T"—called a *tau cross*—died under one, or after his death was made into one.

The Hanged Man is the representation of the dying god for the renewal of the earth. Numerologically, The Hanged Man is card number twelve, one plus two equals three, The Empress, a reference to the Great Mother Goddess in the myths. Knowing what we do now, how do we view The Hanged Man? We can let go of all the mythological "hoop da da" of dead gods. On the surface and for a more practical use, The Hanged Man represents letting go of what we cannot control and accepting what is given to us. It represents a pause in life, standing still. Sacrifice, however, still is relevant here, particularly self-sacrifice: giving something up, putting your needs on the back burner for the needs of others. It could also mean to take a new perspective on things. The man in the card is upside down. He is looking at the world in a completely different view. If something is wrong, go at it with a new approach.

Astrologically, The Hanged Man is associated with Neptune, the planet of mystery and illusion. It is a planet of mystic and spiritual qualities, of imagination and vision. This is in part because Neptune, being the god of the oceans, is connected with the enteral abyss before creation. These associations make The Hanged Man closely concerned with higher awareness and consciousness. However, the idealistic nature of Neptune may make you a martyr for causes that may be foolish or too ideal. Take a step back before you sacrifice something of yourself for another. Be sure it is for something more concrete and not for the sake of an inner ideal you wish to seek. The negative side of Neptune is the desire to escape, whether that is from a small matter or from a larger existential problem.

In a Reading

In readings, The Hanged Man appears to represent a need to suspend one's actions and to halt for a moment's time. Much like the Four of Swords, The Hanged Man shows us to rest, but unlike the Four of Swords, not to "sleep," but to seek higher awareness by indication of the halo. The passiveness of The Hanged Man urges us to let go. Do not hold on to what needs to be released. Go with the flow and the changes you may be experiencing. Release control and you will no longer have to struggle. The Hanged Man also represents sacrifices, things we give up in order to achieve something greater.

When ill dignified, The Hanged Man can represent foolish ideals and sacrifices to something unrealistic and unattainable. You may be forcing an issue too much and pushing against the natural flow and progress. Your own will is coming into confliction with the will of nature. You may be unable to release control and are untrusting of help. You may also have given up your pursuits. An ill-dignified Hanged Man can hide ulterior motives, plotting something while, to the public, it appears to be innocent.

Death

"As soon as one is born, one starts dying."

—Luigi Pirandello

Death is the great equalizer. Nobody, no matter who they are—peasant, priest, or king—can evade Death. The only thing for certain regarding all living things is that they will one day have an end. The Death card is a wonderful card despite the unwelcomed name it has. Death can be a blessing in disguise. This is because the card is not really about bodily death, but of a metaphorical death. Death in the Tarot is the great ending and transition card, for one thing comes to an end with the promise of something new.

Death is a part of history, culture, religion, and mythology so deeply that there is much symbolism and lore connection with it. In Greek mythology, Thanatos (death) is the twin brother to Hypnos (sleep). Thanatos is not a god, but a "daemon," which is a spirit between man and gods. While his sisters, the Keres, are associated with violent deaths, he is affiliated with a more peaceful passing. The companion to life, he was not seen as an evil entity. Thanatos has been depicted as a young man with wings and carrying a sword, unlike our modern depiction of the Grim Reaper.

Death has been portrayed since the medieval times as being a skeleton wielding a sickle. This is also the older depiction of the Death card in older decks. The reason Death is shown as a skeleton is because bones symbolize death. After someone dies and decays, only bones are left. Bones also symbolize the "eternal," because they can last for hundreds, even thousands, of years in the right conditions (and longer due to fossilization). Bones are also a symbol for what is at the core and "bare to the bones," the fundamental core of all people. Since skeletons look almost identical to one another, the skeleton is a universal symbol that represents all humans. The sickle is not present in the *Rider Waite* version, but it is in other decks. Just for reference, the sickle symbolizes the harvesting. In this case, it's death harvesting the souls of the living.

Death is riding a pale horse. This comes from the Book of Revelation as one of the four horsemen of the apocalypse.

"And I saw, and behold, a pale horse: and he that sat upon him, his name was Death" (Revelation 6:8).

The pale color of the horse is in reference to the sickly color of a corpse. This, however, is not entirely the case for symbolism in Tarot. Remember this card is not about real death. The image is borrowing Christian symbols and references, probably for the Christian audience that will be using the cards (at the time created). Death wears black armor. Together, the armor and white horse propose the balance of yin and yang. Life and death is a delicate balance.

Death is riding in slowly. He is not rushing into the scene and the people below him are aware of his presence. This gives the sense that when the death card shows up, you should already know of its influence. It should not be shock (unless in the future position). He holds a black banner with the mystic rose. The banner is a message that tells everyone of the pending news. This is a symbol of life. What odd concepts, you might be thinking, that a card named Death does not mean death and that he is holding a banner that signals life. To many religions, this is not an odd concept, but is fundamental to their faith. Death is not really the end. Life continues on after death. Death is only a transition.

In Kabbalah, when it is time for the soul to be separated from the body, the Angel of Death (Malach HaMavet) comes and separates them. It is taught and believed that the soul is reincarnated on the day of death. This is why the body must be buried within twenty-four hours or else the soul cannot move on to its next incarnation. Reincarnation is also central to Hinduism. In Christianity, it is believed that the soul either goes to heaven or hell after death. The same is true for Islam.

There are four other figures in the card. Death has crushed one already (a king—notice crown on the ground) and is supposedly dead; then we have someone who looks like the Pope, a child, and a maiden. This is telling us that all people are subject to death, be it king, pope, woman, or child. Another approach to viewing these people is that they represent how we react to change. That is, we can fight it (king), love it (child holding a flower), accept it as a blessing or praying for the best (pope) or being indifferent towards it (maiden). No matter how you react, the change comes. Just don't fight it (see dead king on the ground).

In the background, we see two pillars reminiscent of The Moon card with a rising or setting sun. The sun symbolizes the ending and new beginning theme of the card. The waterfalls, river, and boat in the background represent the unconscious mind and the travels we take through life, and the experiences of death. In mythology, many figures descend into the underworld and come back with a new awareness and understanding. This is what Joseph Campbell calls the stage of Apotheosis in the hero's journey.

Death is card number thirteen, a number that can mean change on different occasions. You become a teenager at thirteen, leaving childhood behind. Jewish boys have a bar Mitzvah at thirteen (and Jewish girls a bat Mitzvah), which is the start of adulthood. This all symbolizes a "death" and "rebirth," or simply a change. When thirteen is added together, one plus three equals four, we get The Emperor, who is the physical manifestation of the psychical world. He represents stability and security. Death, however, is in opposition to these things, as nothing remains stable and secure forever. No king or emperor can rule forever.

In our everyday lives, the Death card reminds us that life is about changes. Nothing stays the same. Without change, we cannot grow and develop. Death comes in many ways; things die in our lives all the time (metaphorically). Hobbies, interests, attitudes, beliefs, and relationships can all die. You might like chocolate ice cream as a child, but as an adult that preference dies and you want rocky road. You might be attached to a relationship that ends (dies) and you find someone else. Death, like I said before, can be a blessing, if you can look at the big picture.

Astrologically, Death is connected with Scorpio, the sign that deals with death and sex. Scorpio also corresponds with transformation, healing, and regeneration. Furthermore, Scorpio digs deep to reveal secrets. It probes the depths of everything. This makes Death appear more promising than it may appear at face value. Change and endings give us room for renewal to enter, which can bring healing, depending on the circumstances.

In a Reading

In readings, when the Death card appears, it clearly signals a change is coming, has happened, or is happening. It can be a welcome change if your question relates to issues about movement or problems, which trouble you as it signals their end and conclusion. If you ask about love, however, Death can be ambiguous. It could represent a "dying" relationship or simply a relationship going through transition.

Look at surrounding cards for clarification. Death urges you to get to the root of an issue, to the core of the underlying issue rather than superficial complaints.

When ill dignified, Death can manifest as denial and repression of emotions. For example, it can represent a person repressing grief. It can represent delays and stagnation. Most typically, it points to our active efforts to avoid the unavoidable or prolong something. You may be resisting change and endings. This resistance is rooted in fear of change and the unknown that is to come. Alternatively, you may be trying to rush the change or the process of whatever situation you are in.

Temperance

> "Disarm, disarm. The sword of murder is not the balance of justice. Blood does not wipe out dishonor, nor violence indicate possession."
> —Julia Ward Howe

This is the pinnacle card of "balance," the ultimate archetype of "just enough." This is one of the less ambiguous cards. It is easy to understand even if we are unable to fully embrace and embody its qualities and message. Temperance represents a middle road, moderation. We can understand these ideas, but in our modern lives, we often do not live in balance and harmony. For many people "balance" is juggling multiple jobs, running a family, etc., without going crazy. "Harmony" is the few moments in the day you get to sit on the toilet, and even that can get interrupted! So, in essence, if we don't have a true sense of balance and harmony, can we even truly understand what they are?

Along with this, we live in a world of extremism, people who are too far on one side. Extremism can manifest in the body through eating disorders. Some weigh so much due to compulsively eating, while others starve themselves. Both are unhealthy and threatening to the body. Political extremity is also propionate. It seems everyone is either too liberal or too conservative. Religious extremists are the most troubling and often create disfunction through violent acts.

Temperance is needed to keep things from falling into extremes. Without temperance, we cannot be open to other ideas. We become ignorant and closed-minded. Temperance is moderation. Moderation with food keeps you healthy. Moderation in politics keeps a stable government and moderation in religion lessens the likelihood of violence.

Balance symbolism is heavy in this card. Firstly, Temperance has one foot on land and the other in water. This balance teaches us how we balance the Major Arcana cards from The Magician to Strength. This can represent balance of reason or conscious (The Magician) and intuition or subconscious (The High Priestess). It can be a balance between qualities of the flexibility (The Empress) and structure (The Emperor). Temperance prevents you from becoming "holier than thou" by being able to live a material life (The Lovers) and still seeking the transcendent

(Hierophant). Being aggressive and assertive (The Chariot), but also showing mercy and holding back your aggression when needed (Strength). We can't live with one mindset or one way of doing things; we need a mix of both.

Temperance mixes water between two Cups. In some decks, it is the mixing of water and fire. This represents the mixing of two elements, finding the right balance of each. It is a common symbol for temperance found in European art. There is an exchange going on, which leads to another quality of Temperance communication.

On the chest, we have a triangle inside a square. The triangle is the sign of fire and the square is stabilization, containment. The fire is unable to overtake and run wild. It is moderated and used more effectively. On the forehead, we have a golden disk, which can be seen as the brow chakra (third eye), connecting the divine to the mundane. The clothing is loose and free moving; this denotes the flexibility. Unlike The Hanged Man who adapted because of a need to, Temperance adapts because he (or she) wants to.

When looking at the placement of Temperance (between Death and the Devil), it seems odd to see such a "good" card in between such "negative" cards. Traditionally, Temperance is seen as the guide of souls into the afterlife and judgment. Some say Temperance performs the judging. Because the sum of Temperance, one plus four equals five, is the Hierophant, who teaches us rules regarding how to live, Temperance judges how we use what we were taught. Taking this idea, it seems that Temperance can be a period of reflection of our deeds and actions. It could be a time of washing away sins, asking for forgiveness, and cleaning the soul. Much like a metaphorical baptism, we enter the pond and wash away our faults and mistakes and walk down the path to the left. We come across the golden crown in the sky. This is symbolic of the elevation of the ego, transcending the ego, and such ways of thinking or living. This is almost like a miniature judgment and rebirth.

Peace and serenity are brought to mind when looking at Temperance. The Angel is calm and composed. The rainbow in the back suggests this, as it is a reference to the covenant between God and man in Genesis. The rainbow represents the peace and mercy that God is showing to mankind:

> I do set my bow in the cloud, and it shall be for a token of a covenant between me and the earth. And it shall come to pass, when I bring a cloud over the earth, that the bow shall be seen in the cloud. And I will remember my covenant, which is between me and you and every living creature of all flesh; and the waters shall no more become a flood to destroy all flesh. And the bow shall be in the cloud; and I will look upon it, that I may remember the everlasting covenant between God and every living creature of all flesh that is upon the earth (Genesis 9:13-16).

Temperance is the second Angel we encounter and is often associated with the Archangel Michael. In the Bible, Michael is known to have defeated Lucifer before casting him out of heaven. In art, a common depiction of Michael shows him slaying a dragon (Lucifer). This is the triumph of light over dark. So, too, does Temperance overcome darkness with light by accepting the dark as an essential part to the light, keeping it in balance.

Astrologically, Temperance is associated with Sagittarius. Sagittarius understands, is open-minded, benevolent, and expresses freedom and exploration. This influences Temperance to be communicative and express cooperation between opposition. Temperance also is about mixing and matching, making combinations, all of which stem from Sagittarius's keen interest in knowledge and learning.

In a Reading

In a reading, Temperance appears to tell you to find the middle ground between two oppositions. There is a lot of wiggle room, because it is about trial and error, of playing with mixtures to see what works and what does not. Try not to worry about the end result. What matters is the journey, which is represented by the trail from the water to the rising sun in the background.

When ill dignified, Temperance becomes extremism, because we lose moderation and compromise. We find ourselves becoming fixed to one side of the issue. We can become off balance and out of harmony. This manifests as poor communication and the inability to adapt to changes. Excessiveness and impulsivity, Temperance often represents a drinking problem or other abuses. It can represent as mood swings as well.

The Devil

"Our demons are our own limitations, which shut us off from the realization of the ubiquity of the spirit...each of these demons is conquered in a vision quest."

—Joseph Campbell

Please don't run in horror reaching for the match and lighter fluid in the attempt to burn your deck because of this card. The Devil is one of those cards that people don't like to see (for obvious reasons) because they think it is bad. This is the one card that tends to make people fear the cards and think they are evil. Death, The Devil, and The Tower are the triple trifecta of "bad" cards, but in reality, they are not. This card, for example, does not represent Satan. Like all the cards, this card is symbolic.

The Devil follows after Temperance. As different as they may seem in imagery, they are not completely separate from one another in meaning. Temperance can be seen as guiding souls to the afterlife, being the place of transition from this life and to the next. The pond can be symbolic of washing away sins, creating balance, and overcoming evil or darkness. The Devil card can be seen as the testing ground. How do we react to temptation? Temperance teaches us moderation. Will we implement this teaching in The Devil card?

The Devil card depicts the hero's decent into underworld, a common motif in mythology. This is a stage in the hero's journey. There are many myths of people who, while alive, go down into the underworld to reclaim a lost loved one. In Greek mythology, Demeter goes into the underworld to get her daughter Persephone back from Hades, and Orpheus went to bring back his wife Eurydice. The most powerful story is the Sumerian myth of Inanna's descent into the underworld. As Inanna descends, she passed through seven gates and with each passing, she loses a part of her clothing. When she is finally naked, she is brought to the seven judges and her twin sister Ereshkigal. They all look at Inaana with the "look of death" and spoke to her with anger. Joseph Campbell viewed this as the journey we take into the unconscious mind to discover our strengths during a moment of helplessness. Campbell also viewed it as our coming to terms with our dark or negative self. The Devil card embodies these qualities. He asks us to look at our dark side, come to terms with it, and grow.

The Devil card depicts a dark scene. The only light is from a torch. This can be symbolic of the underworld or our unconscious mind. We are faced with our inner demons, our temptations, vices, addictions, and our deadly sins. This card is more about our inner processes, rather than some outside force (the Devil) causing havoc in our lives.

Another name for the Devil is Satan, and in Kabalistic teachings, Satan is a force inside each person, working against you. In psychological terms, this is the Ego. The Devil is the ego on steroids. You become focused on yourself, your needs, and desires, to a point that it becomes unhealthy, and you become codependent. Codependence is also a main theme for this card. It is mostly dependence on physical things, like drugs, money, sex, shopping, and people.

In the card, we see two figures that are loosely chained to the pedestal the "Devil" sits on. The Devil shown here is Baphomet. Baphomet is half-goat, half-man deity created by Eliphas Levi with a similar connection to the Greek god Pan. Pan represented sexual desire, lust, and wildness. Again, this refers back to the nature of The Devil card, which is temptation and lustful desires. The Devil card looks a lot like The Lovers card. The Devil is card fifteen, which, when added together and reduced, brings us to The Lovers. As an interesting fact, The Lovers was redrawn to look more like The Devil card. Traditionally, The Lovers had three people (one man and two women) with Cupid above. The Devil, as depicted in the Waite versions, stays close to traditional imagery. The Devil is the dark and perverted skew on The Lovers. In The Lovers, an angel blesses them and, in The Devil, Baphomet curses them. The loose chains around the necks of the man and woman can come off at any time by their will. This is not a permanent state. These figures either choose to be there or do not know they have the ability to leave. They don't look to be in physical pain. You could say they might actually enjoy this.

There is mocking going on in this card. If you look at the positions of the devil's hands, they are similar to The Magician's. One hand is raised above and the other is down. This is symbolic, again, of the "as above, so below" and of channeling energy. However, this is not a good channel. What is being channeled can be hinted by two symbols. On the right hand, we have the astrological symbol for Saturn, ruler of Capricorn. In the other hand, a torch is pointing down, burning the man.

Astrologically, The Devil is associated with Saturn. Saturn deals with boundaries and restrictions.

What does this all mean? It means that The Devil is channeling energy that is restrictive and limitative. This can be seen in ways of our thoughts. He is also channeling mental blindness—not being able to think clearly and objectively. The torch pointing down is symbolic of extinguishing inner light or knowledge. Relating the winter solstice to this, the Sun has reached its lowest point in the sky, which is symbolic to the death of the sun. Winter starts. In India, it is an ominous time. People do not have weddings during this period. That torch is the only light in the card. What would happen if it completely went out? Complete darkness, ignorance, fear, and uncertainty are what would happen. When you give in to your dark side, you become lost in it.

Above the head of the devil is an inverted pentagram. In normal conditions, the pentagram represents harmony between the elements. In the inverted depiction, it is the disharmony of the elements that are being expressed. When you become focused solely on the physical, you get out of sync with harmony.

In a Reading

In readings, The Devil refers to negative and deviant behaviors, addictions, dependence, and thinking in self-limiting ways leading to the restriction of your potential. It can also specify why and where you are blocked in regards to a question in a reading. The Devil also indicates that you may be depending on something or someone else and not on your own abilities. This card is about ignorance. You may not be aware of what's going on. Someone may be pulling strings in the background and you are oblivious. The great gift of this card is learning from and overcoming your "dark side." Limitations and boundaries are important to note. In readings, The Devil may represent how you limit yourself, your comfort zone (the space you keep yourself in to feel safe).

When ill dignified, The Devil represents much of the same as I have listed above. In addition, you may be actively projecting qualities of The Devil on to others. You see others as the source of your problems instead of looking at what you are doing to yourself or how you got into the situation you are in. You are looking for a scapegoat.

The Tower

"We should guard ourselves against pride because pride leads to downfall."

—Sam Veda

You may be asking yourself right about now "What is going on here?" First Death with that creepy skeleton, then The Devil and chained-up people, and now a Tower on fire with people falling to their demise! This is a normal thought process. Trust me. When I first picked up the cards, I thought that there was something freaky there. However, just as Death and The Devil seemed to be something "bad" on the surface, their deeper meanings really had something important to teach us. Each card builds on the previous card to reveal insights to our lives and the human experience.

The Tower builds upon The Devil. In The Devil, we entered the dark and journeyed into our subconscious to deal with our inner demons. We came face to face with temptation, the physical, and materialistic. Desire and lust consumed us as we focused on self-interests and ourselves. As we stayed in this darkness, we lost sight and became trapped in a mind game of self-limiting behaviors and ignorance. As we enter The Tower, we come to a breaking point of change and shaking up of what we have come to know and accept as the norm. The image here looks more troubling than that of other cards. This is a violent scene—lightning, a building on fire, and people falling. Everything is falling apart. Again, like in all the other cards, do not take this to be literal! It is metaphorical and has a deeper meaning.

One of the first things that came to my mind when viewing this card was the Tower of Babel from Genesis in the Bible. After Noah and the flood, people settled in the land of Shinar. Shinar is interpreted as Mesopotamia and, more specifically, Babylonia. The people said to themselves:

Come, let us make bricks and bake them thoroughly. [They had brick for stone, and they had asphalt for mortar.] (Gen. 11:3)

And they said:

Come, let us build ourselves a city, and a tower whose top is in the heavens; let us make a name for ourselves, lest we be scattered abroad over the face of the whole earth. (Gen. 11:4)

For this action, God scattered them and confused their language. As a result, they stopped building the tower. The reason for God's displeasure was one for debate. It is seen that the problem in building this large tower for the purpose of reaching God and His realm was wrong. It shows a strong amount of hubris, challenging God and His authority or, on another level, wanting to be God. In other passages in and outside the Old Testament, the people wanted to wage war with God. They wanted to strike the firmament (sky) with hatchets until it rained.

The interpretation and lesson from this story is that mankind should know its place in the world, not be ambitious to become like God or try to be better than God. In the Zohar, it is said that if the people came from a place of love and wanting to share the light of God with others, God would not have stopped them. But instead, their ambitions for glory got in the way.

How do you take the story of the Tower of Babel from Genesis and apply it to The Tower in Tarot? The main idea to take from that biblical story is the theme of misguided beliefs. The figures in the card had created themselves a building, a tall one, and sat themselves on top. They believed it to be safe and that they were powerful. They thought they were divine in nature. Their current conditions could never change. Things would stay static and unmoving. The Tower says otherwise. You are not safe, protected, all powerful, or divine. Things can change at any point and any moment without warning. You may be a king today, but tomorrow you can be a peasant. This is much like the lesson of The Wheel of Fortune, however, different in context.

This might seem bad, but really The Tower has many blessings to offer. The Tower is about shaking and waking us up to the reality of a given situation. This is the backhanded slap to your head from the universe. Think of it in this scenario. You spend more money than you have, maxing out your credit card, and "thinking" it is all right—you have 0% APR for one year and can pay it off. Meanwhile, you only make $1,000 a month. You won't be able to pay it off. So, when you conduct a reading asking about money and finances, what shows up? The Tower! It is yelling at you to wake up, stop spending, and change your mentality and behavior. It might just as well tell you that something big is going to occur soon regarding this, like missing a payment and that 0% is gone and now you have to pay 30% default APR. This is the embodiment of The Tower.

The lightning bolt is the main symbol in this card alluding to the fact that you need to pay attention— something is being pointed out to you. Lightning is seen as a force of destruction and creation. This represents that what is torn down allows for the rebuilding, but this time with a better foundation (understanding and knowledge). Going back to the credit card scenario: you got yourself into a bad problem, the problem was pointed out, you recognize it, and work to fix it.

The Tower of Babel still has more to offer us in understanding The Tower in Tarot. The passage of the Tower of Babel is an etiological myth, which explains why there are different languages and why God confused the builders so they could not communicate with one another. Confusion carries over and is applied to The Tower. The crown on top of the tower is Kether, the first Sephirot in the Tree of Life. The astrological association with Kether is Neptune, which is associated with confusion, idealism, and illusion. Prior to the striking of lightning, the crown was intact, serving as an indication that the people are in a state of illusion and idealism. After the strike, it breaks the crown off to release them from their idealistic and illusionary minds. At first it brings confusion and even chaos, because they don't understand what is happening, but that is temporary. Arthur Waite, in his *Pictorial Key to the Tarot*, states that The Tower, "signifies destruction on the intellectual side." This refers to the fact that this is a time when you don't need to overanalyze the details. The problem should be very obvious.

The lightning bolt is very important to the function and meaning of this card. It shows that things are moving in the right direction. The previous card, The Devil, was one of true darkness. With its lightning strike, The Tower is the first step back into the light. It is because of the lightning bolt that the couple in The Devil gets that wake-up call to get the chains off their necks. It can be a rough push in the right direction. From this point onward, the rest of the Major Arcana cards deal with a theme called the Progression of Enlightenment. Each step from The Tower onward reveals to us more light and thus more illumination of the soul, the reduction of the Ego, and awakening of the soul.

The Tower is card number sixteen. One plus six equals seven, The Chariot. One minus six equals five, The Hierophant. Hierophant and Chariot show that the status quo is uprooted and destroyed. It also shows what can happen when too much energy is not properly controlled.

Astrologically, The Tower is associated with the planet Mars, the planet of aggression, war, power, and action. Mars fits into The Tower because the explosiveness of the card reflects the nature of Mars as forceful. The unexpected change of The Tower is embodied in the influence of Mars as impulsiveness.

In a Reading

In readings, when The Tower appears, it represents an unexpected change in the situation. Things appear to be falling apart and are in ruins. However, The Towers allows you to rebuild new foundations for a stronger future. The card tells you that what you think and believe has many flaws. You are ignorant of things that you need liberation from. There is great opportunity for you to improve yourself at this moment. Give up old habits, old ways of thinking, and embrace the change.

When ill dignified, The Tower represents reluctance to change and clinging to what you believe makes you safe and secure. You ignore all the warning signs and think yourself to be invulnerable. This might also represent abandonment of hopes and dreams or to get out while you can and watch everybody else pay the price. Much like insider trading, you get a tip stocks will drop and you sell your shares and make money while the other shareholders lose.

The Star

"We need to find God, and he cannot be found in noise and restlessness. God is the friend of silence. See how nature—trees, flowers, grass—grows in silence; see the stars, the moon and the sun, how they move in silence... We need silence to be able to touch souls."

—Mother Teresa

Death came in on a white horse to bring endings and change to our lives. The Devil chained us to him, made us hold on to something that may give us comfort, and The Tower woke us up. These are some rough cards, but they are important cards. The challenging cards yield the best rewards. After this rumble and tumble, we find ourselves at The Star, that, in comparison to the previous three cards, is a welcomed sign of relief.

The most striking thing you might notice at first is the completely nude woman. We have nudity in The Lovers and The Devil, but with The Star, it is more in your face. This nakedness is very important to the understanding of this card. You see the woman wholly without anything to distract you, such as clothing or jewelry. What you see is what you get.

The Star is sister to Temperance as they share similar symbols. Like Temperance, who had two Cups and mixed water between them, The Star holds two jugs. She pours one into the lake and the other on land. It should also be noticed that, like Temperance, The Star has one foot in water and the other on land.

The major theme of this card is openness, sharing, and healing. After the great shaking of The Tower, we fall down from our false beliefs and notions. What we have built has been destroyed and we find ourselves "naked" by the experience, removed of all those things we held to be truth to start fresh and new. What does it mean to be naked? Being nude in these terms is not being ashamed as many people might think in our modern society. Does The Star look embarrassed that she is naked? No; nakedness here is freedom and innocence. We can relate this back to Adam and Eve when, after they ate from the Tree of Knowledge of good and evil, they become aware of themselves. They saw and understood their nakedness and covered themselves. The Star card is in the same state of innocence as Adam and Eve.

The Star represents a fresh start; the word star has star within it. The first step on this fresh start is reflecting. The Star looks pensively into the pond as she pours water from her jugs. This is reflection into her soul and mind. But why do we need reflection? The answer is simple: to learn from the errors we made in the past and the structures we built in our lives that were not strong, false, or incorrect. We take time in The Star to reflect on what it is we really want, what we believe in. Reflection allows us to modify these aspects of our lives.

The pouring of the two jugs is symbolic of being generous with what you have with others, but most importantly sharing what you have learned during your reflection with others. The pouring of water on land and in the pond is symbolic of even distribution and equality. This is expressed more by The Star's association with Aquarius, who distributes and shares equally. The pond could be seen as our subconscious and the land as our consciousness. The distribution of water is the nurturing of both sides. It is a balance between the two—between intuition and logic. For real reflection to occur, we need to use both intuition and logic to grow and learn. Water is also a symbol for cleansing and purification. The Star card represents a time when we clean, purify ourselves, and heal.

After having been off course for a while with The Devil and The Tower, The Star indicates that we are back on the right path. Before the invention of GPS and other technologies to help guide us, people used the stars. The Star navigates the soul and places us back on our path. Again, this is where reflection comes in handy. When we learn from reflection, we are put back on course.

A. E Waite, in his *Pictorial Key to The Tarot*, states that the mottoes of this card are "Waters of Life freely" and "Gifts of the Spirit." What is Waite speaking of when he mentioned the "Gifts of Spirit?" Looking at the card tells us that these gifts are from the seven rays/spirits of God. The card has eight stars shown in it. Seven smaller stars are indicative of the seven rays and the eighth is God himself.

The seven rays correspond with will, wisdom, love, purity, sciences, peace, and freedom. The first ray "Will," gives us power, the use of that power for good actions, and faith. "Wisdom" gives us understanding and knowledge. "Love" gives us creative energy, allows us to love, and to create beauty in the world. "Purity" gives us joy and teaches discipline. "Science" gives us truth. "Peace" gives us unity, friendship, and service to others. The seventh and final ray "Freedom" gives us freedom, free will, and the ability to choose justly. These seven rays can also be associated with the seven Chakras of Eastern Philosophy. Either way, the underlining meaning is balance of the mind, body and spirit. Again, it refers back to the healing aspect of this card.

The Star is the second card in the progression of enlightenment. The first was The Tower with its lightning bolt. The Tower was the start of light entering back into our consciousness. The Star is second, and light is increased a little more with starlight. If you ever get the chance to really see the night sky lit with stars, it gives an amazing feeling. You automatically feel small and also connected to the universe at large. It is this feeling that helps break the ego just a little bit. In the progression of enlightenment, The Star helps us move beyond Ego (The Devil) and to connect to something beyond ourselves. The starry night sky is a psychological symbol for flickering consciousness within the vast darkness of the unconscious.

The Star is card seventeen. One plus seven equals eight, Strength. Seven minus one equals six, The Lovers. The Star restores our innocence and purity, the state of grace before the Fall of Adam and Eve. We are cleansed. Our fortitude is also renewed. We are given new strength through hope.

Astrologically, The Star is associated with Aquarius through Aquarius's progressive nature. The Star moves forward, not backwards. It is hopeful and generous, which can be connected with Aquarius's altruistic nature.

In a Reading

When The Star appears in readings, it is a positive indication that there is still hope for whatever question is asked. It does not guarantee that you will have what you want, but it says not to give up hope and to keep trying. The Star suggests that you should be open, honest, and more willing to share certain aspects about yourself that you may have been hiding. For example, in a reading about a relationship, this card can mean that you need to tell your significant other that little secret you've been keeping. The Star indicates you need time to heal from something recent in your life. Also, The Star can indicate renewal and rejuvenation of your emotional and mental wellbeing. Waters are reflective like a mirror. The water in this card can imply that you may need to reflect on the situation being asked before making a decision. The Star pouring out her water shows a constant giving, which can represent generosity for others. You may need to consider others over yourself, depending on the question. Consider natural talents and skills, which you need to develop or utilize to help you.

When ill dignified, The Star can represent hopelessness, a sense of loss, and feeling of pessimism. Your hopes and dreams seem as if they will never manifest and come true. You have become disconnected with both your spiritual self, and your higher self, which can lead to lack of inspiration for creative projects. Physically, you may feel drained and tired.

The Moon

"Reality is wrong. Dreams are for real."

—Tupac Shakur

Leaving the serenity that is The Star, we come into contact with The Moon and are spellbound by its influence. Along with the stars, the Moon has captivated the imagination of mankind for millennia. When the moon is full, it glows bright, giving us a guiding light at night. Gazing into it can put you into a hypnotic state because of it beauty. The Moon is mysterious and is rich in mythology and symbolism.

The Moon card depicts a scene that is dark and mysterious. There are no humans, only animals. The full moon shines down on a dog and wolf that howl into the night. A lobster or crab is emerging from the water. A trail leads from the water and down into the foreground, passing two pillar structures similar to those we saw in the Death card.

The Moon is associated with the subconscious, emotion, intuition, and creativity. Because of shared similarities in regards to intuition, the subconscious, and psychic tendencies, The Moon is linked with the High Priestess. The water in the card represents our unconscious. This card is connected with right-brained activities, such as poetry, drawing, music, dramatic acting, and dance. Anything outside the realm of logic and order is in the realm of The Moon.

On the other hand, The Moon represents illusions and misinformation. Not everything is as it seems. The Moon does not actually produce its own light. It reflects the light from the Sun. The light from the Sun removes darkness and shows reality. Since the moon reflects only a part of the Sun's light, we only see some of the truth. We get part of the whole picture. The full moon lights the path in the card for us to walk, but we need to proceed with caution. We can't see far ahead and our eyes may play tricks on us. Was that a person or just a shadow? What is that sound? Is someone following me? There is a sense of paranoia here, doubt, and fear. Because we don't see the whole picture, we try to fill in the rest by what we perceive might be there. Our perceptions are subjective. Often our senses can fool us. It's all in the mind. The Moon is subjective, because of its nature of fluctuation. The Moon controls the tides on earth. The rising and lowering of the ocean represents the change in our emotions and fluctuation in mental perception.

The Moon is third in line of the stages of increasing enlightenment by the representation of increasing light. Remember, lightning from The Tower, starlight in The Star, and now moonlight. More is revealed to us via moonlight. However, it's not objective information. Things are not revealed by logic, but by intuition and the voice inside, especially by our dreams. Dreams are an important association to The Moon card. They reflect on the things we process during our waking conscious state. Dreams help us solve problems by offering solutions, allowing us to face our fears in a safe environment. They also can reveal future events and connect us with those who have passed on. Overall, The Moon advises you to pay attention to your dreams and intuition.

In classical mythology, the moon was personified as a female Goddess. In traditional esoteric thought, the energy of a female has been associated with intuition, the unconscious, and the unknown or mysterious side The Moon represents. Women are also associated with the moon because of the link between the moon's cycle and menstruation. The Triple Goddess is linked to the Moon because the phases of the moon reflects the maiden, mother, and crone. Hecate is an example of the Triple Goddess in the Greek tradition.

In Greek mythology, Selene, the Titan Goddess, is associated with the moon. This is pre-Olympian pantheon. When the Olympians took control, Artemis became the Goddess of the moon. Her twin, Apollo, became the God of the sun displacing the Titan Helios. She is the Goddess of the wilderness, wild animals, and hunting, among other roles. The wilderness and wild animals is an important one in association to The Moon card. This card features an open landscape set out in the wilderness. The dog and wolf represent our animal nature, one that is domesticated (dog) and the other, wild and free (wolf). Artemis had dogs as her companions during her hunts.

As mentioned previously, Hecate is associated with the moon. She is the Goddess of the crossroads and magic. Like Artemis, Hecate also had dogs in her company, as they were considered sacred. What is it about the dog that makes them so closely linked with the moon and the moon Goddess? Dogs have keener senses than that of humans; they can smell and hear things that we cannot. This ability makes the dog appear to have a sixth sense, and thus, makes them to appear as a psychic animal. Waite wrote that the dog and wolf are "the fears of the natural mind."

The crab emerging out of the water was seen by Waite as the manifesting of the animal nature. It can also be the manifestation of your intuition and the awakening of the unconscious. This is because the crab is a creature of the ocean. The emerging crab out of water onto dry land represents the rising unconscious into consciousness.

The Moon is card eighteen. One plus eight equals nine, The Hermit. The Hermit held a lantern into the darkness to bring illumination to the dark and to be a guiding light to others. While The Hermit is a guide for others, The Moon transcends this. The Moon is a guiding light in the darkness of night, calling people to be their own guides, to delve into the unconsciousness. Eight minus one equals seven, The Chariot. The Chariot and The Moon both depict two creatures. The Chariot has two sphinxes (black and white) and The Moon has a dog and wolf. The creatures in The Chariot are controlled. In The Moon, the creatures are free. This can represent the freedom of the imagination and the wildness of the self when it has no master (Logos/Logic), which is missing in The Moon.

Astrologically, The Moon is linked to Pisces and Neptune. The two fish swimming in opposite directions and linked by a think cord represent Pisces. The swimming in opposite directions can denote inability to make a decision. The Moon card is not a good card for making any actions or decisions, because, as we already understand, the facts are not all there. The picture is not complete, and all we have are our perceptions and subjective experiences of the situation. The direction of the fish can also be symbolic of being pulled in different directions, as is represented by the dog and wolf as two opposing forces. Neptune is the ruling planet here. It is associated with illusions, which reinforces the nature of The Moon.

In tradition, The Moon was seen as a negative card because of its female qualities. Of course a world ran by men would fear women, simply because they could not understand their nature. So cards like The Moon, which are heavily feminine in nature, would then be seen as negative. This is not the case, however. The Moon is not a negative card. It is just a mysterious card that is linked to the underworking of your unconscious. What can be so scary about that?

In a Reading

When The Moon appears in readings, it can indicate that you may need to be more conscious of the unconsciousness. That means you need to pay attention to the way you react to people and situations. The Moon is a card rooted in emotion and emotions can change at the drop of a hat. Pay attention to these shifts in moods and feelings. The Moon suggests that there may be influences at work in the situation, which remain unknown at the moment. There may be a person working in the shadows, influencing things, or there may be something at work internally that you are not aware of. For example, you may be jealous of someone, but you do not know this consciously. The Moon may suggest that things are changing and are not fixed at this time, so do not build houses on sand, so to speak. The concept of illusions is important, as The Moon may be telling you that things are not clear at the moment and you are only seeing illusions and filling in the missing parts with your mind. The Moon can also indicate lies and deceitful tactics, so be careful. Be more aware of what is happening around you.

When ill dignified, The Moon can represent deception, manipulation, and people trying to take advantage of you by tricking you. You may fall victim to your emotions. Repressed emotions, which you are not ready to handle at the moment, may bubble up. On the same token, you may be repressing a feeling that you are attempting to ignore. The Moon, when ill dignified, can also represent an escapist mentality in which you escape reality and attach yourself to a dream world. It is a card of denial.

The Sun

"Turn your face to the sun and the shadows fall behind you."
—Maori Proverb

Leaving the dimly lit mysterious wilderness that was The Moon, we come to find ourselves in a vastly different scene. We see the light, the bright sun in all of its warmth and glory. It is amazing and comforting to see The Sun after the last series of cards. The Sun is a major milestone in the progression of enlightenment after escaping the dark ignorance of The Devil. The Tower was the first card to shed light onto the darkness. With lightning, we were shocked and awoken to the darkness we were living. Falling out of this way of living, we found ourselves under the soft lights of the stars in The Star. The Star brought us comfort, reflection, and guidance. After reflection, we moved on and found The Moon, which is brighter than stars, but is only a reflection of the Sun's light. We faced our fears and issues from our unconscious, made it through the confusion, and found the real source of light we have wanted so much: The Sun. The Sun shines bright, removing any darkness that we experienced in the previous cards. We have reached a new level of enlightenment, a higher level of consciousness.

The Sun is the brightest card that we have come across so far. In the progress of enlightenment, The Sun stands as intellectual enlightenment. In Plato's *The Allegory of the Cave*, Plato explains the Theory of Forms, which is the idea that abstract "forms" or "ideas" have the highest and truest kinds of reality—that what we see in our world (which is corruptible and changes) is not true reality. The things in our world are imitations of their Form, the real reality of that object. For example, chairs come in all different shapes, sizes, colors, and styles. We understand and recognize a chair to be a chair, because we recognize the Form that makes it a chair. There is an essence of chairness, so to say. In *The Allegory of the Cave*, there are prisoners who have been kept in the cave since birth. They never move, their heads are fixed in place, and they look forward to the wall of the cave. Behind them is a large fire with a walkway, through which people walk, carrying wood cutouts of animals and the like. The prisoners watch the shadows that are cast on the wall and believe that the shadows are reality. One of the prisoners is unchained and is shown the real things that are causing the shadows. The prisoner does not recognize them and does not believe them to be the real thing. If the prisoner were to look at the fire, he would be blinded and turn away to look at the shadows. In the sunlight, he would be distraught and unable to see anything around him. After some time, he would adjust and see the Sun and the reality of the world.

How does this relate to The Sun in Tarot? In Plato's Cave, the sun is used as a metaphor for illumination. The fire inside the cave is a symbol for the sun in the sky, which we see. The sun outside of the cave is the sun's Form, which Plato called the Form of the Good, the ultimate object of knowledge. In essence, Plato's Cave states that we are the prisoners in the cave. The things we seen in the world are shadows of their true Forms. We seek true knowledge of things, and to understand these things, we must know their Forms. The Sun represents our ability to understand and see things clearly. We see reality based on the Form, not the shadows. I picked the quote "Turn your face to the sun and the shadows fall behind you" because it fits so elegantly with this philosophical theory.

The Sun can represent the intellectual enlightenment, in which Plato saw the Form of the Good to be. However, with The Sun, it does go deeper in spiritual meaning. In *The Pictorial Key to the Tarot*, Waite writes:

The card signifies, therefore, the transit from the manifest light of this world, represented by the glorious sun of earth, to the light of the world to come, which goes before aspiration and is typified by the heart of a child.

The heart of a child is the representation or a symbol of the light, which radiates from the sun. Waite makes two distinctions between the "manifest light of this world" and the "light of the world to come," which could relate to the Theory of the Form, and that the light from the sun has another outer worldly counterpart: its Form. In Jewish scriptures, *Olam Ha-Ba* means, "the world to come," which refers to the afterlife. Olam Ha-Ba also refers to the Messianic Age when the dead arise once more for Judgment. The Judgment card, in the next card, depicts the dead rising. Waite is making a comment that The Sun continues on into Judgment on a higher level. Again, I relate this back to the Theory of the Form.

The Sun depicts a scene of great joy, happiness, life, and vitality. The Sun spreads its light over everything. There is a naked child holding a banner and riding a white horse. A red feather sticks out of the child's head; flowers are in the child's hair. There is a stone wall with sunflowers growing up from behind. The child on the horse in front of the wall, to me, is a symbol of freedom from limitation or bondage. When compared to blackness of The Devil and the chained couple, The Sun represents the escape from this prison.

Like the woman in The Star, the child shown in the card is naked. Nudity, again, represents innocence and exposure to the world. Clothing serves as a way to hide our bodies. Being naked reveals ourselves. It is interesting to ponder why a child is riding the horse instead of an adult. An adult is depicted in The Star and then we jump to The Sun and we have a child. We can propose that the child is the same woman in The Star, only in child form. When enlightening yourself, you must revert back to a childlike state to be enlightened. This does not mean that children are more enlightened than adults. What the message here seems to be is that The Sun is closer to enlightenment and, as such, we must remove preconceived notions and most of the conditioning we are put through our whole lives. Why is it adults seem to be shocked by the things children say? Oftentimes, they say things adults would not think of saying because of what we conceive as proper or improper. Children often don't have the same kind of filter adults do. Children experience and perceive the world in an extremely different way than adults. Aristotle wrote of the idea that we are born a blank slate, that our minds contain no content, nor any programming for our behavior, and that we must learn everything. A child's slate is emptier than an adult, because adults are programmed how to behave, what to say, and what not to say. A child does not have all of these limitations and, because of that, is freer than adults. When we can remove the programming and conditioning and be more like a child, we make our first step to enlightenment. The child is also a symbol for joy, happiness, and life. The Sun is one of the best cards to have in a reading.

Because we can actually see The Sun, The Stars, and The Moon, these cards can be related to actual things in our lives. The other cards, on the other hand, are more abstract. We don't see Death trotting down the street on his horse. We do see The Stars, The Moon and The Sun in our everyday lives, so to understand these particular cards, we can look at how we understand these objects in our lives. When thinking of the sun, we see a bright disk illuminating the earth. We can't look at it directly, because it is so bright, it could blind us. We feel the warmth of its rays on our skin. It feels good. It makes us feel good (unless, of course, we're getting sunburned; then that's not fun at all!). We know that the sun is the reason why anything is alive on this planet and, if the Sun were not here, the Earth and other planets would not be here, either. Applying this to The Sun in Tarot, we can understand it to be a card of vitality and life. The Sun is a card of strong energy, giving you fuel to burn. It allows for growth and development particularly in the area of inspiration and creativity from the boost in desire and will.

The Sun is card nineteen. One plus nine equals ten, the Wheel of Fortune. Nine minus one equals eight, Strength. Strength is correlated with Leo as well. The Sun's connection to Strength could be expressing the positive outcomes that Strength yields in the end. The Wheel of Fortune can be also reduced to The Magician. The Magician expresses that The Sun is an example of what The Magician is manifesting, life. The connection with The Wheel of Fortune expresses The Sun to be a good sign of fortune. Remember that the wheel in the card looks like a sun.

Astrologically, the constellation Leo represents The Sun. In Astrology, the sun represents vitality, power, the ego, and the Self, the source of life, and willpower. Leo represents confidence, enthusiasm, love, and compassion. These traits can be found in The Sun card.

In Mythology, The Sun relates to the solar gods. As a general rule, the sun is a male energy and the moon is a female energy. Thus you will see, ninety-nine percent of the time, the moon associated with a goddess and the sun with a god. In Greek mythology, there are two gods: Helios and Apollo. Helios, whose name means "Sun," is a pre-Olympian titan associated with the sun. The Olympian god is Apollo, god of light. Originally, Apollo wasn't associated with the sun or anything solar in nature. However, when his cult formed, he became affiliated with the sun, thus replacing Helios.

In a Reading

When The Sun appears in readings, take it as a great sign. It pinpoints areas that are prospering, being enjoyed, and loved. It shows energy and focus in the question asked. The Sun removes ignorance and brings us new understandings. Things become clear to us. We see the truth in the matter. The Sun represents breakthroughs, that "eureka" moment, and the figurative light bulb above our heads. It can indicate strong energy, optimism, good health, happiness, and being in the position of a favorable outcome.

When ill dignified, The Sun can be very negative. Consider a star at the end of its life. It becomes volatile and dangerous. After that, it shrinks and becomes a white dwarf, also known as a dead star. The Sun, when ill dignified, can be seen as violent with too much energy being produced and no outlet for it, like hyperactive behavior. Alternatively, it can be seen as dead. Many times, when I conduct a reading on a relationship and the sun comes up in a negative position, such as "current influence" or "problem in the relationship," it most likely says that the relationship is "dead." There is no more fire, no more energy in the relationship. An ill dignified Sun represents depression, low energy, a lack of enthusiasm, and shortsightedness.

Judgment

"Life, death, and rebirth are inevitable."

—The Rig Veda

The Judgment card is a powerful card with its strong imagery. This impression is mainly because of its Christian theme of The Last Judgment. Because of this strong theme, when you look at this card, the first thing that may come to mind is the Book of Revelation, The Apocalypse, Judgment Day, etc. Because of this, some see this card as negative.

I once spoke to someone and asked him why he did not like this card. He said, "How can a card about Judgment day be a good thing?" Having a card with strong religious imagery can be good, but also can bring disadvantages. A bias can grow about what the card means based on the religious connotations. You can connect many of these cards, if not all of them, to something in the Bible or other religious texts. However, the cards have their own meanings. The relations to other sources add meaning, but do not define the card. Judgment can be related to Judgment Day, since the image in the card is similar to images in art about the subject. However, to define the card, we need to separate it from the religious doctrine. Waite said that those "who have inward eyes" will be able to understand the card's deeper meaning that is beyond the Last Judgment imagery.

The Judgment card has many borrowed elements from *Last Judgment* artwork, particularly the rising of the dead and blowing of the horns. There are, however, differences when comparing the art of the *Last Judgment* to the Judgment card. In the artwork, Jesus is always present. The actual act of Judgment and the destination of the soul to either Heaven or Hell is present in Christian art, but not in the Judgment card. In the card, we have the Archangel Gabriel, not Jesus, as the main figure. Most Last Judgment art is unnerving with devils eating people and the depictions of hell. In the Judgment card, however, we do not have any of that; the images and meanings are different. They do, however, share a commonality, which is a revelation.

The Book of Revelation is where we get most of our information about the Last Judgment. Revelation comes from the Greek word, *Apocalypse* (ἀποκάλυψις), which means the act of revealing or uncovering. It is a revelation and awakening, both of which are very important concepts for the Judgment card.

In the progression of enlightenment, Judgment represents a personal awakening to true self-understanding and purpose. Judgment comes after The Sun. As a recap, The Sun was about enlightenment and seeing the world clearly. However, The Sun is about enlightenment in an intellectual capacity. In contrast, revelation is a personal and spiritual enlightenment. So far, we have seen literal light increasing in the cards. We have had lightning, stars, moon, and sun. When looking at Judgment, it seems different because it does not appear to have any source of light. But there is. The Angel Gabriel is the source of divine light, which radiates within brighter than the sun, moon, and stars put together. The light from personal and spiritual revelation is much brighter, because this light allows you to understand much deeper things about who you are, your place, and purpose in life, or a particular issue you ask Tarot.

The Angel Gabriel is shown blowing a horn. The sound of the horn brings the dead back to life. The awaking of the dead in the card is symbolic of the revelation and the awakening one has. It is not a literal awakening of the dead; just of living to the higher consciousness. When you look around at people, does it not seem that we are living a life of mindlessness and minimal consciousness? We live our daily lives, waking, going to work, school, cooking, cleaning, and then off to bed to repeat the same thing the next day. This is a dead-like state.

When Judgment appears, however, it brings about a revelation, a divine alarm clock blaring to wake you up. We often lose sight of our purpose, goals, and path when we get caught up in our daily routines. We become out of touch with the divine. Judgment pokes, pinches, or blows a large horn to make you pay attention to what is important.

Readers typically associate Death with rebirth. Personally, I place rebirth in Judgment because of the dead being brought back to life. What could be a better sign for rebirth? The Angel Gabriel is associated with births. It was Gabriel who announced the births of Jesus and John the Baptist to their parents. Along with rebirth, Judgment is about rejuvenation and being healed. Up to now, we have been on a process of enlightenment, as well as healing. The Star was symbolic of the first step of healing. Judgment finishes it with being reborn and healed. Healing can be in the physical sense and the spiritual sense. Many people are spiritually sick, not knowing how to connect with the divine. Judgment is about being spiritually healed. Think about Born Again Christians. They call themselves "Born Again" because they feel they are reborn by coming to know Christ. Salvation in the Christian faith goes hand in hand with the concept of Healing, as the Greek word for salvation is the same as healing. Judgment could easily be looked at as a card of Salvation.

Even without the Christian association with this card, Judgment is about knowing the divine in whatever ways it may be. When you come to know the divine, you transform and change. The tombs in which the dead arise are symbolic of a cocoon. As the caterpillar changes into a butterfly, the human transforms spiritually. Interestingly, the ancient Greek word for butterfly is the same as soul.

Judgment is also known to be the card of eternal life, which is why it is associated with Temperance. Waite writes that Judgment is "card of eternal life, and for this reason it may be compared with that which passes under the name of Temperance." Temperance and Judgment have commonalties. Both deal with the cleansing of the soul. Temperance did this as perpetration for what was coming. Judgment is the final washing of sins and reward for making it through the progression of enlightenment.

Judgment has more practical meanings and ways to be interpreted. Often, we can look at the card's name itself. As with Justice, Temperance, or Death, the title of the card can give you an idea of what it means. Judgment deals with judgments and judging. It is closely interconnected with the Justice card, as it can also mean to use your judgment to determine what actions to take. However, they differ on a fundamental level. Justice is about equality and fair judgment based on a social context and a case-by-case perspective. Judgment has a higher role to play on a karmic level. Our actions create karma. Judgment can be seen as a signal for you to be conscious about what you are putting out into the universe and how it can affect you in the long run. Where Justice is specifically oriented, Judgment sees things as a part of a larger picture.

I once wrote a blog post about how we can use other languages to expand our understanding of concepts. For example, in Greek, the word for Judgment is the same as "crisis." What does this teach us? In the time of crisis, a judgment must be made. Action is needed. Judgment in Tarot can signify a time of personal crisis where we are faced with choices and must make a choice now.

Also, central to Judgment is forgiveness, which is very important. During a family discussion, we spoke about forgiving someone, and my sister asked, "Why is forgiveness so important?" When we forgive someone or forgive ourselves, we can finally move on from the issue that has caused us pain. When we forgive, we move on and feel healed. Forgiveness is an important teaching to all world religions. In Kabbalah, forgiveness is a part of spiritual growth by bringing inner balance with the world outside. When we forgive others and ourselves, we bring harmony to our lives. But when we do not forgive, we are holding on to something negative. It can create guilt, anger, hate, depression, and the like. Forgiveness removes all these and gives us freedom.

Another practical meaning to Judgment is hearing the calling. Angels are messengers. They would appear to humans with a message from God. In the practical life, this can be hearing an important message. Often the message is "the calling" or "hearing your call," such as knowing or not knowing the career you want. Then you have an experience where you become inspired to pursue a career related to said experience. Waite writes that the "summons is heard and answered from within," which means that the calling is a personal matter to be dealt within. The card itself in general is about inner spiritual work.

Astrologically, Judgment is associated with Pluto and Scorpio. Scorpio deals with death and resurrection, which is fitting for Judgment. Pluto is about regeneration, destruction, and transformation. Destruction may be a bit shocking for some, but how do we have transformation without something getting destroyed in the process? It does not have to be violent. That is why I see Judgment as releasing and letting go in order to transform.

Judgment is card twenty. Two plus zero equals two, The High Priestess. The number two is about duality and opposition. Judgment can be too strong of an influence for some people in that it can cause opposition within them. When someone hears "the calling," it may be too much for him or her and they are conflicted over it. The High Priestess holds hidden knowledge; this is the card where the "cat is let out of the bag." This could be reinforced with the image of the dead awaking in the middle of a sea. Water is associated with the unconscious and The High Priestess.

In a Reading

When Judgment appears in readings, it often signals that you need to pay close attention to the issue at hand. It can appear as a cosmic calling, where you are pulled to do something, go somewhere, or see someone. Also, it can be a calling to a new job or a place to live. Judgment may appear as a personal revelation, such as you finally understanding why you have been making poor choices in relationships. It may also denote that choices need to be made. It's time to act. Things fit together and make sense. You see the larger picture and your role in the situation. Lastly, Judgment may indicate feeling healed and rejuvenated, as though you have received a second life. If someone has a near death experience, Judgment can represent this experience and the aftermath of it.

When ill dignified, Judgment can represent an opposing force (resistance and or rejection)—too much of what Judgment stands for. It shows resistance to changes, making judgments, and choices. It may also show opposition to revelation and turning your back on what needs to be brought to attention. There may be delays in legal matters or decisions, like a promotion, at work. Judgment ill dignified can also represent regret, possibly from a missed opportunity. Doubt may arise, which keeps you from making any progress.

The World

"Force never moves in a straight line, but always in a curve vast as the universe, and therefore eventually returns whence it issued forth, but upon a higher arc, for the universe has progressed since it started."

—Kabbalah

When you listen to Judgment's call and have awoken, you will find yourself at The World. The last card of the Major Arcana is The World and represents completion, the end of our journey, accomplishment, and the ability to start a new cycle. Nothing ever really ends. In Tarot, the idea of cycles—life, death, and rebirth—is very common and constant. In the Major Arcana, we see it in The Wheel of Fortune, Death, Tower, The Moon, and Judgment. In the Minor Arcana, we see it as the Aces and Tens.

The reason for this is the philosophical idea of cyclical time versus linear time. Cyclical time is, by far, the most favored concept in Tarot. It is based on the idea that everything happens in patterns. The idea of birth, death, and rebirth is rooted in the idea of cyclical time. We see it all the time in our everyday lives, from the rising and setting of the sun to the phases of the moon. We also see it in the changing of the seasons. Life itself works on a cycle. As Tarot reflects life, it reflects those cycles and the World marks a completion of that cycle, an ending where you are whole and complete at the end.

When looking at The World, we come across familiar elements. From the Magician, we have the Wands in the hands of The World, only this time there are only two. The Wheel of Fortune gives us the four figures in each corner minus the books. We also get the Wheel's setting, as this card is also placed in the sky. From The Hanged Man, there is the placement of the legs. The main difference is that the figure is upright. Lastly, the woman in The World might be the same woman from The Star. All of these connections to the previous cards add meaning to The World, so let's break it down.

The Magician held a Wand in each hand, one pointing toward the heavens and the other toward the ground. This reflects the esoteric concept of "As above, so below," the channeling of the Divine energy to manifest and create life. In The World, the two Wands are now in the hand of the woman. It is fitting for The World to have an element of The Magician, since The Magician is the first card and The World is the last. Since it is the last card, it represents the completion of The Magician's work. However, The World is not The Magician. It only serves as a representation that his work is now complete. What was being manifested in The Magician went along the journey of the Major Arcana and has now reached The World. There is recognition and connection of the Divine. What was manifested knows where it came from. The Magician is a card of creation and of the Creator. The World brings the Creator back into focus when you recognize the Divine in you and become whole.

The Wheel of Fortune marked a turning point within the Major Arcana. As card ten, it is related to The Magician through the reduction of its number. The Wheel of Fortune was the first card to show a scene in the sky with no humans. There was a feeling that there is something special about this card, something that is above and beyond our control. Fate, destiny, the goddess Fortuna, whatever it may be—we know there is something amazing about this card. It is also the poster child for cycles and the idea of cyclical patterns. The wheel spins and, as someone loses wealth, another gains, just as one person is born and another dies. It is a cycle. You cannot control the cycle, only be subjected to it.

The World borrows from The Wheel of Fortune the four figures in the corners. These represent the fixed signs of the zodiac: Aquarius, Scorpio, Leo, and Taurus. What is missing are the blank books. The zodiac signs bring back into focus the universe, our world, and everything else in existence. The books are missing because their mysteries have been learned. What at one time seemed like random luck no longer matters. The World is reassurance that everything is fine. You're no longer subject to Fortune, thus restoring the four signs to their reliable nature.

There is an implicit philosophical connection between The Wheel of Fortune and The World that we can learn from Boethius, a Christian philosopher born in the sixth century of the Common Era. Boethius rose to high prestige and fame within government. Despite this, he was imprisoned on charges of treason. Distraught with this sudden change in his life (once high, now low), he wrote *The Consolation of Philosophy*, in which philosophy, personified as a woman (Lady Philosophy), appears to offer him comfort and reassure him that human affairs are governed by an all-encompassing providence. Boethius complains about his loss of good fortune to Lady Philosophy, and she responds that it is the nature of Fortune to be fickle. He accepted the fortune, which she brought in his life, and now he must also accept the reversals:

> Thou deemest Fortune to have changed towards thee; thou mistakest. Such ever were her ways, ever such her nature. Rather in her very mutability hath she preserved towards thee her true constancy. Such was she when she loaded thee with caresses, when she deluded thee with the allurements of a false happiness. (Book I—*The Consolation of Philosophy*)

Lady Philosophy then asserts that the goods of fortune are not true goods. Boethius is lamenting their loss, which does not bring true Happiness. Lady Philosophy tells Boethius that all humans strive for one thing. They seek this one thing in many paths and in different ways, but the goal is Happiness. When Happiness is attained, there are no desires left. Lady Philosophy says that people try to obtain Happiness through wealth, public office, kingship, celebrity, and pleasure. People think these paths will lead to happiness by self-sufficiency, respect, power, renown, and joy respectively.

Only an eternal and permanent Good can bring Happiness. God is the source of Good and Happiness. By this assertion, that God and happiness are the same, people become Happy by attaining divinity. The World represents this Happiness of the true Good and is the highest representation of the Divine that our minds can comprehend.

The Hanged Man is also seen in this card, particularly with the placement of the legs. In both cards, the legs are crossed. The Hanged Man has been turned right side up. Now remember that The Hanged Man was about a moment of pause, contemplation, looking at the world in a different perspective, surrendering to the will of a higher force, and sacrifice. In The World, all this has been lifted. No longer are we paused or suspended and waiting. We have reached the end and have completed what we desired. We have seen the world from a different perspective and now have a greater vision and knowledge of what the world is like. We are released from the will of that higher force. Our sacrifices have not gone in vain. The Hanged Man is often the traitor card. In The World, he has been deemed innocent. Along with the dying god mythology, The World possibly represents the idea of the second coming with peace on earth.

Finally, The World depicts The Star in the form of the half-naked woman. No one knows if they are the same woman, but that does not truly matter. It is all interpretation. The Star followed after The Tower, which was a card that woke us up to our ignorance, errors, and ego. The Star served as a card of hope and healing, navigating the soul to find meaning, and enlightenment. She is naked because the experience of The Tower was so shocking that it struck deep within us, making us naked metaphorically. The World shows a woman who is mostly naked, but is now wrapped with a long strip of cloth. This symbolizes the embracement of the Divine, infusion, and unity. We no longer have to hope and heal ourselves. What we have hoped for has been given. We are healed and completely whole.

Knowing how the previous cards relate to The World reveal great knowledge about its meaning. There is also great meaning to the card through its own unique symbolism. The center figures are what we notice first. We see a wreath surrounding the woman in the center. The woman is the *Anima Mundi*, the world soul. The idea of the world soul is found in the philosophy of Plato, who states that the world is a living being that has a soul and intelligence. The idea of the world soul can be also found in Hinduism as Brahman, the transcendent life force. The Anima Mundi is sealed with the wreath, which is an image rooted in Christian theology. That wreath is the Mandorla, which is depicted in religious imagery, mainly in the depiction of Christ in Majesty. In older decks, The World card depicted Christ at the center of the Mandorla and accompanied by the four evangelists on each corner. The Mandorla depicts a separate time and space, the Divine or transcendent time. This is separated from the outside world of human time and marked by the four signs of the zodiac, which represent our time and space. As time progressed, the image changed to remove its Christian influence but keeping the root of the meaning of the image intact. Christ was replaced by the Anima Mundi; however, they can be said to be the same, but with a different name.

Reflecting on the image of the Anima Mundi, surrounded by this wreath, I see something interesting: the human cell. The wreath is the nucleus and the Anima Mundi is our DNA. The cloth circling around the woman resembles a double helix. So, what does this mean for Tarot? It serves mainly as a reinforcement of already-established meanings of wholeness. Without our DNA, we would not exist.

The World is the highest card in the Major Arcana. It is the last card in our progression of enlightenment. It embodies the fulfillment of what Judgment introduced. When Judgment shows up, it brings with it a wake-up call both for action and an awakening. When we take the steps to accept the calling, take action, and understand our awakening, we transcend to The World. It is the highest form of enlightenment. Connection with the Divine light, nirvana, the oneness, God, or whatever it be—the light embraces us. In Kabbalah, it is taught that there is a division between our reality and the divine reality. They call our reality the one percent. The one percent makes up all the things that are physical in our world. On the other side of this division, we find the ninety-nine percent, where the Divine resides. I want to also point that the four zodiac signs can be symbolic of the one percent, while the Anima Mundi is the ninety-nine percent with the wreath serving as the divider between the two. The ninety-nine percent represents true reality. The source of everlasting fulfillment, joy, wisdom, and perfection; it is also the domain of the Light. The World represents this ninety-nine percent. You are enlightened, you will find yourself in the ninety-nine percent and bring happiness and fulfillment into your life. Adding everything up, from the Anima Mundi to DNA, the ninety-nine percent we see in The World represents the Divine and humanity—the complete package.

The World is card twenty-one. Two plus one equals three, The Empress. The Empress is the card of giving life and the Earth. She is the life force of the earth and The World is the Divine life force. They work together to make human and divine reality exist. Two minus one equals one, The Magician. Again, this represents the completion of manifestation. The World is the source in which The Magician is drawing his energy from.

Astrologically, The World is associated with Saturn, the planet that keeps the world intact through social order, establishing stability, and ensuring things work properly. Applying the social order aspect to The World, it fits into the meaning of wholeness. If there were no order in the world, our lives, or society, we could not be whole. Instead, we would find ourselves separated, our lives no longer complete.

In a Reading

In readings, when The World appears, it is an indication that things are finished. It is a sign that you will accomplish something and have success in your endeavor. You are rewarded for your work. The World card could represent the athlete who trained years for the Olympics and won the gold metal. The World indicates long-lasting success and fulfillment. The World is a sign that everything is going as you've planned. Things have fallen into place, as they should. You receive closure.

The World represents coming full circle—looking back at your journey, seeing how far you have come, and seeing how you can now pass on to someone else your experiences. It represents seeing the larger picture of what you are doing and the impact it can have on the world at large.

When ill dignified, The World can represent that things are not yet finished. Something may be blocking you reaching completion. You may lack closure on a subject, such as the case in relationships when things end without explanation. There may be an underlying feeling of emptiness that permeates within you, even in the face of success. You may have gotten that big promotion to the corner office at work, but for some reason it feels hollow and meaningless. You need to reevaluate your motivations and goals.

Final Thoughts

At the end of this journey, we now depart one another. It has been a privilege to be your guide as we've unlocked the Arcana together. I trust now that you have gained many insights about the seventy-eight cards. There is so much to learn.

Going forward as you continue your journey with the cards, I encourage you to work with them as much as possible. Get active with Tarot on social media. There are many Facebook groups devoted to Tarot. You can find readers on Instagram; follow them and snap a photo of your readings. Join me on YouTube and make some of your own videos. Start tweeting about Tarot on Twitter.

Get personal: find ways to connect to the Tarot community live. Look for a Tarot Meetup in your area or start one. Take workshops and classes. Attend one or many of the many Tarot conferences that are available. Never stop learning; never stop shuffling.

Bibliography

Amberstone, Wald, and Ruth Ann Amberstone. *The Secret Language of Tarot*. San Francisco, CA: Red Wheel/Weiser, 2008.

Banzhaf, Hajo. *Tarot and the Journey of the Hero*. York Beach, ME: Samuel Weiser, 2000.

Bloch, Douglas, and Demetra George. *Astrology for Yourself: How to Understand and Interpret Your Own Birth Chart: a Workbook for Personal Transformation.* Berwick, ME: Ibis, 2006.

Bunning, Joan. *Learning the Tarot: A Tarot Book for Beginners*. York Beach, ME: S. Weiser, 1998.

Cray, Philip. *Philosophy and Religion in the West*. Chantilly, VA: Teaching Co., 1999.

Fenton-Smith, Paul. *The Tarot Revealed: A Beginner's Guide*. Crows Nest, N.S.W.: Allen & Unwin, 2008.

Friedman, Richard Elliott. *Commentary on the Torah: with a new English translation.* San Francisco, CA: HarperSanFrancisco, 2001.

Gillentine, Julie. *Tarot & Dream Interpretation*. St. Paul, MN: Llewellyn, 2003.

Grudem, Wayne A. *The Gift of Prophecy in the New Testament and Today*. Westchester, IL: Crossway Books, 1988.

James, E. O. *The Ancient Gods: The History and Diffusion of Religion in the Ancient Near East and the Eastern Mediterranean*. New York: Putnam, 1960.

Johnston, Sarah Iles. *Ancient Greek Divination*. Malden, MA: Wiley-Blackwell, 2008.

Katz, Marcus. *Tarosophy: Tarot to Engage Life, Not Escape It*. Brisbane: Salamander and Sons, 2011.

Kenner, Corrine. *Tarot and Astrology: Enhance Your Readings with the Wisdom of the Zodiac*. Woodbury, MN: Llewellyn, 2011.

Kenny, Anthony. *Ancient Philosophy*. Oxford: Clarendon, 2004.

Louis, Anthony. *Tarot Plain and Simple*. St. Paul, MN: Llewellyn, 1996.

Nichols, Shaun. *Great Philosophical Debates Free Will and Determinism*. Chantilly, VA: Teaching Co., 2008.

Place, Robert Michael. *The Tarot: History, Symbolism, and Divination*. New York: Jeremy P. Tarcher/Penguin, 2005.

Robinson, Daniel N. *The Great Ideas of Psychology*. Chantilly, VA: Teaching Co., 2003.

Ronnberg, Ami, and Kathleen Martin. *The Book of Symbols*. Köln: Taschen, 2010.

Warwick-Smith, Kate. *The Tarot Court Cards: Archetypal Patterns of Relationship in the Minor Arcana*. Rochester, VT: Destiny Books, 2003.

Yale University. "INTRODUCTION OLD TESTAMENT." *YouTube*. n.d. www.youtube.com/playlist?list=PLV16HQsVJXeLGq3IE2XkPkee5WGka9wvS.

About the Author

Angelo Nasios, from Long Island, New York, was awarded the Tarot Professionals' "Tarosophist of the Year" for 2011. He has been studying Tarot for over a decade and has been sharing his passion for it through informative YouTube channel videos. Currently working towards his bachelor's degree in philosophy and religion, Angelo has a deeply rooted passion for history and understanding the human condition through different disciplines.

Find Angelo on Facebook and Twitter. Visit Angelo at www.AngeloNasios.com, www.ThatsTotallyTarot.com, and www.YouTube.com/user/AngeloNasios.